Introduction.. iv

Guide to cultural perspectives.................................... 2

Skills development activities

1.1 Searching for information................................... 4

1.2 Reading and recording....................................... 6

1.3 Setting up research.. 8

2.1 Identifying information...................................... 11

2.2 Understanding key issues 13

2.3 Identifying causes and consequences 15

2.4 Identifying and evaluating possible
    courses of action 17

2.5 Identifying different perspectives...................... 20

3.1 Questioning knowledge claims 22

3.2 Questioning the reliability of information 28

3.3 Evaluating causes and consequences 32

3.4 Questioning underlying beliefs 34

4 Developing a line of reasoning 35

5.1 Reflecting on issues and perspectives............... 38

5.2 Reflection on teamwork, outcomes and own
    performance... 40

5.3 Reflect on personal learning............................. 41

6.1 Planning a project.. 42

6.2 Teamwork and individual effort 46

7   Select evidence and present research............... 47

Team project

1 Conflict and peace... 49

2 Disease and health 54

3 Human rights 58

4 Language and communication 62

5 Poverty and inequality 66

6 Sport and recreation.. 70

7 Tradition, culture and identity 73

8 Water, food and agriculture 77

Individual report

1 Belief systems... 81

2 Biodiversity and ecosystem loss 85

3 Changing communities....................................... 88

4 Digital world.. 91

5 Family 93

6 Humans and other species 96

7 Sustainable living 98

8 Trade and aid 101

Written examination

1 Demographic change 105

2 Education 107

3 Employment... 110

4 Fuel and energy 114

5 Globalisation... 118

6 Law and criminality... 122

7 Migration... 125

8 Transport... 128

Additional worksheets 131

Answers to worksheets... 161

Introduction

A brief guide to teaching Global Perspectives

Teaching Global Perspectives is not the same as teaching other subjects in a traditional curriculum. To begin with, it isn't really a 'subject' with an agreed, traditional body of knowledge in which you, the teacher, have a degree and with which you are already very familiar.

The content of the Global Perspectives curriculum is the world we live in. Global Perspectives aims to help students to make this vast mass of subject matter manageable by teaching them to:

- find information about our world and about key issues in our world
- think and reflect critically and carefully about our world and the key issues in our world
- negotiate and understand their own place in our world
- act thoughtfully, realistically and purposefully to improve our world
- communicate information, ideas and reasoning to others in our world.

What does this mean for your teaching?

The nature of Global Perspectives has a number of consequences in terms of how it is taught:

- You will need to discuss the world, our place in it and key global issues with students.
- You will be concentrating on developing skills, not delivering content.
- You can follow the Global Perspectives Learning Process.
- You will mentor, guide and motivate students, and manage the environment rather than controlling students.
- You will develop strategies to respond to individual student needs.
- Resources will change frequently.

Discussing the world, our place in it and key global issues

You do *not* need to become an expert on world issues or learn everything there is to know about subjects such as global warming, climate change and the chemistry of fuel.

You *will*, however, find it helpful to do the following.

- Read newspapers regularly. This is invaluable preparation for teaching Global Perspectives.
- Read newspapers from different countries and cultures. Try http://www.world-newspapers.com/, a website that lists English language newspapers around the world. Although you will that find much of the same news is recycled around the world, you will also find genuinely different perspectives on global issues, especially in opinion pieces and blogs. Download news apps such as BBC News which make news accessible. Students may also find it useful to download news apps which they can check regularly.
- Encourage students to read local and international newspapers. Start with fun, accessible items and move on to more weighty analyses.
- Encourage students to find out about an issue and to explain it to you or to their peers. This is especially good for recent or current events, where you may not know the details or understand all the issues. Students will learn a lot by telling and explaining things to you and to one another.
- Run a weekly quiz, then discuss the ideas, issues and perspectives that arise from it.

  - Put fun news articles around the classroom and ask fun questions for students to answer. Try to include some explanation or opinion questions as well as facts and information. Once students are familiar with the format, they can develop their own questions, you can move on to conceptually more difficult questions, or you can broaden the field within which the answers can be found.

  - Run a 'cross-checking and verification' quiz, in which you or your students present information that includes mistakes and hoaxes, the task being to identify the correct information, mistakes and hoaxes using internet searches. In some cases, you could include a 'find the original source of this information' question.

  - If possible, show students excerpts from satirical news programmes. There are several of these in the UK, including *Have I Got News for You* and *Mock the Week*. Try to present a mixture of local and international excerpts so that students get different perspectives on current affairs. Students might like to produce one of these shows themselves.

Remember that you only have to be able to guide your students to IGCSE level. They are not working on a PhD!

- Develop your questioning techniques. These will help you to encourage students to want to research, discuss, debate, reflect, and reason about world issues.

Question	Comment
What is infrastructure? When was the UN formed?	✗ These questions are asking for information. This will not prompt debate, and instead put the emphasis on acquisition of facts. Encourage the students *themselves* to ask these questions, and to answer them through research. Ask: What do you need to know to answer this question? How can you find out what infrastructure is? Who can find out the fastest (and most accurately) when the UN was formed?'
Do you understand?	✗ We all ask this but it is problematic. Firstly, you can't trust the answer. 'Yes, I understand' could mean, for example, 'No, not a clue, but I'm not admitting it' or 'Yes, it's obvious, but I'm missing three layers of deeper meaning.' 'No, I don't understand' might mean 'No, I haven't a clue,' 'No, I haven't even thought about it,' or 'I have a deep conceptual question that's bothering me but that's way beyond IGCSE level.' Secondly, this question creates a mental construct in which you either do understand or you don't understand, and this limits the possibility for increasing understanding or making the effort to move from 'don't understand' to 'do understand.' Try 'Tell me how much you understand…', 'Explain what you are having trouble with…' or 'Can you just explain what I've asked you all to do?'

Question	Comment
How will you find out?	✓ This question will aid research skills and independence, although it might not stimulate immediate debate. It assumes both that the student *can* find out and that they *will*, so it creates an expectation and a sense of capability in students' minds. This is an important transition from waiting to be told.
What do you think of / about…?	✓ This question is open-ended, so allows the student to develop their *own* thinking rather than trying to guess what you are thinking. This is important because we want students to know that their own opinions and actions are important, and that their relationship with the world is important.
Why?	✓ This is one of the most important questions you can use. It requires students to think to the next level and to justify their opinions, assertions and values, so it's excellent for encouraging debate and discussion. It can elicit evidence, explanation and argument. It is also very useful when you aren't an expert in an area that interests a student or group of students.
You're thinking very much from your personal perspective. What you say is interesting. Do you think the national perspective is the same as your personal perspective? Why might it be different?'	✓ This line of questioning recognises the value of the student's personal perspective, but encourages them to think beyond it and to take the debate further.

Developing skills, not delivering content

The most important consequence of the difference between traditional subjects and Global Perspectives is that you don't need to concentrate on transmitting content or knowledge. This does not mean that the course is meaningless or free of content, however. Students will learn about important issues, but they will not all learn the same information about the same issues. This is a major shift in attitude to our teaching.

With Global Perspectives, it is more important that a student is able to *find out about* and *think about* an important issue than it is for them to have detailed content knowledge about any specific area. It is more important that students find their own place in the world than that they are directed to a specific place.

It is worth noting that the information given in this resource is intended to guide teachers. It is sometimes beyond the level expected of students in order to provide help and background for teachers who may be new to this kind of examination of cultural perspectives. Equally, the information is not comprehensive – you may well find that you notice things which have not been mentioned. That's good!

Freedom

The Global Perspectives course gives both you and your students a wonderful freedom to explore interesting world issues and to respond to students' own interests. It is possible (and sometimes even desirable) to have different students researching and debating different issues.

- Kalia and Sabiha could research traditional animistic religious practices in African tribes and their consequences in modern state of Liberia. This could lead to an Individual Report on Belief Systems or a Team Project on Tradition, Culture and Identity.

- Anna and Tom could start researching chocolate. They could look at its environmental impact, its human impact (for example, child slavery, poverty, and health issues), and the various belief systems and traditions around chocolate. This could fit into a number of different topics. For example, it could lead to a Team Project on Poverty and Inequality, Human Rights, or Tradition, Culture and Identity; or it could lead to an Individual Report on Trade and Aid. Alternatively, Anna and Tom could put together a collection of resources on globalisation in the chocolate trade, which could form the basis for a practice examination paper.

- Nkosi and Fran could investigate fashion. They might consider fashion as an aspect of Tradition, Culture and Identity, with a focus on the male and female aspects of fashion, which might lead to a Team Project. Alternatively, they might consider the environmental and human impacts of fashion and complete Individual Reports on this, within the topic of Sustainable Living.

- Miguel and Katrina might look at football. The obvious starting point would be a Team Project on Sport and Recreation, but they might also look at the traditional and cultural roles of football, and the belief systems that people build up around the game, the teams, and the players. They might consider the technological and employment aspects of the sport or explore the consequences for a city in terms of transport and infrastructure if it were to host a major international football tournament. This would lead to interesting and unique Individual Reports or Team Projects. Alternatively, Miguel and Katrina could put together a collection of resources on aspects of football that fall under topics such as Transport Systems, Law and Criminality, Globalisation, or Fuel and Energy, which could be used as the basis for practice examination papers.

For assessment purposes, all students will need to put their ideas into an appropriate context and format, considering and analysing issues, causes, consequences, perspectives, and possible solutions. However, Global Perspectives allows students to follow an interest that the rest of the class might not share; and, as it is possible to take almost any area of interest and find aspects that fit into one or more of the Global Perspectives topics, it should be possible to find something to excite and motivate every student.

Note that the *Student Book* is organised around the more standard topics, but there are opportunities for you and your students to move beyond what is suggested.

How to develop skills

You can develop students' skills in a number of ways.

- Keeping your focus and your students' focus on skills rather than content. Ask questions like these:

  - How can you find out?

  - What else do you need to know?

  - Is that a reliable source?

  - Do you agree with that opinion? Is it well supported?

  - Does that author predict realistic consequences?

  - You've read four different articles. What do you think are the *main* causes of the problem? Can you think of a solution?

  - What about the global perspective?

- Planning carefully so that you can encourage students to find, question and use information themselves, rather than doing it for them. Try strategies like these:

  - Using the time you used to spend talking to the whole class to discuss progress with individual students.

  - Asking, 'Kalia, if you make a map of the personal, national and global perspectives, do you think you'll see where the gaps in your thinking are?'

  - Asking, 'Miguel, I can see that you've researched lots of causes and thought about them carefully. What is the main cause? What do you think the consequences might be? How can you find out?'

- Planning carefully so that, rather than telling students what to do, you encourage them to tell you what they are doing within a framework you have set. For example:

  - 'I'll be walking round talking to you all about your plans while you carry on with your work. Is there anyone who needs to ask me questions sooner rather than later?'

- Using questions, comments and feedback to encourage skills development. Develop open questions where there are a number of answers or room for reflection.

Anna, today you need to find out about child slaves in chocolate farms. Look on the UN website.	✗	This puts the onus on you to decide what needs to be researched and where to find the information. It takes the power away from Anna and means that she doesn't need to develop her own skills.
Anna, what have you planned for today? You made a note at the end of last lesson on what you were planning for today, didn't you? Have you given any more thought to your sources from last week?	✓	This puts the onus on Anna to plan her own work, to decide what needs to be researched, and to keep a log of her progress. The question at the end reminds Anna to question information as well as finding it, motivates her and allows either for an interesting discussion about Anna's sources, her progress and her thinking or can act as a prompt to Anna to address something she has not yet done.

Anna, that's very good. Well done.	✗	This gives Anna her reward and suggests that she doesn't need to do anything else. This kind of praise puts an end to thinking, effort and skills development. It also puts the power of decision about Anna's place (in the class, in the world) in your hands, rather than in Anna's. We do, of course, need to praise our students, but we have to be careful about *how* we do it if we want them to develop skills and independence. It can be hard to avoid this limiting kind of praise, but it's worth making the effort.
Anna, you've been working really hard on this research. Are you pleased with your progress? Can you explain to me why you think that issues of child labour in Fairtrade chocolate still need to be addressed?	✓	This rewards the effort rather than the product, so encourages Anna to keep working. It puts the onus on Anna to evaluate her progress (note, *progress* not product), so she is using her thinking skills to consider how she can improve her work further. The question about the issues shows an interest and engages Anna in real discussion that uses her skills. This might be a way of opening a discussion about an unreliable source, the unintended consequences of the Fairtrade intervention, or how the Fairtrade system could be improved.

Following the Global Perspectives Learning Process

You will need to ensure that each group is following the Global Perspectives Learning Process:

- Researching information, ideas and arguments
- Questioning information, ideas and arguments
- Reflecting and planning
- Presenting and acting.

This can be achieved through the following:

- Regular, focused skills activities.

- Regular, short routes through the Learning Process; for example, a short research activity, followed by questioning, reflection and a short, one- or two-sentence talk.

- Regular reminders that students should use their skills during longer research and project work. For example:

  - Reminders to the class.

  - Specific questions to individuals and groups focused on particular skills.

  - Visual prompts in the classroom that serve as reminders of the Learning Process and about specific skills, produced by the students themselves.

- Modelling, by you, of the steps in the Learning Process.

- Emphasis placed, by you, on the *skills* in the Learning Process rather than on the knowledge and information acquired during it.

- Open discussions about the value of the knowledge gained, issues explored and skills developed during the Learning Process.

Mentoring, guiding and motivating students, and managing the environment

In the *Student Book*, the course is designed to allow for a gradual transition from students who are dependent on you, as the teacher, to students who are independent in many ways and who can relate to you as a mentor and guide.

This requires you to have a different relationship with your students than you might in a traditional classroom. Students will gradually start to decide for themselves what they are doing and will then need you to focus on the following.

- Ensuring that the necessary facilities and equipment are available.

- Ensuring that there is a productive working atmosphere in the classroom. For example, that:

  - it is not too noisy

  - students are well-behaved and not proving a distraction to others, that consistent expectations about behaviour are set, and that behaviour is well-managed

- students are interested and motivated

- feedback is regular and constructive.

- Ensuring that you are present, available and interested. Your attention should be evenly shared. This should actually be easier if students' attention is on their own projects than if it is solely on you.

Think about what you would want from an effective mentor and guide, and aim to provide these things for your students. For example:

- Show an interest in the students and their work.

- Give clear guidelines and explanations.

- Be consistent in your expectations.

- Offer suggestions and questions aimed at helping each student to develop one step further.

- Be willing to negotiate with the students to meet their interests and to help them move beyond their initial perspectives.

- Make time to listen.

- Offer support, deadline reminders and constructive feedback.

- Maintain a healthy sense of humour.

Developing strategies to respond to individual student needs

There are several strategies you could use to respond to the needs of individual students.

- Walk around the classroom, checking on progress (through observation and questioning) as groups and individuals work. This will help you to notice individual needs.

- Keep a professional log or journal with space for notes about individual needs.

- Encourage students to identify their own needs and to come to you when they need your help (though do encourage them to try to find their own solutions as much as possible).

- During longer-term research activities and project planning, schedule meetings with individuals or groups to discuss progress. In these meetings, you might:

  - discuss and set research questions

  - discuss sources

  - discuss issues, causes and consequences, different perspectives, and possible solutions

  - discuss and set active outcomes for projects

  - discuss how to plan activities

- discuss evidence of active project
- discuss individual needs, such as help with research, focused skills activities, what else the student needs to know, how the student can use their research to answer a question, or how well the student is meeting assessment requirements
- discuss group needs, such as budgeting for materials, help with motivating a team member, organising technical support for a concert, or organising cross-cultural collaboration.

Resources that change frequently

Global Perspectives is about the world, topical issues and current affairs. As a result, the resources that are relevant to the course will change regularly. Don't try to build up a library of definitive resources; instead, try the following.

- Teach students how to find their own resources. After all, this is a key aim of the course! Students will get more out of searching for and finding their own resources than from reading material that you have put together. Each student will be better able to meet their own needs and interests if they can search for and find the relevant information themselves.
- Use local, national and international newspapers and magazines, television and radio to cover current events.
- Use http://www.world-newspapers.com/ to build up a collection of online newspapers and magazines that you know you can rely on to provide particular perspectives. *China Daily*, for example, is an English language paper with a very Chinese perspective; it's also quite good at explaining its perspective in a reasonable way. This can help non-Chinese students to engage with the different perspectives offered and help Chinese students to articulate their perspectives in English, and to bridge the gap with other materials in English.
- Encourage students to find and bring in interesting resources.
- Be flexible. Respond to the memes that students are aware of on the internet and encourage students to develop them in order to respond to Global Perspectives issues.

Language

Encourage students to learn and practise using technical terms. In the *Student Book,* each topic chapter includes some language activities and many of these focus on technical terms. Further language activities can be found in the additional worksheets at the end of this *Teacher Guide.*

Try to encourage students to begin using academic English: to use complete, formal sentences; to try to sound objective; and to avoid slang, spoken English, textspeak or strong statements.

If your students speak English as a second (or third or fourth) language, suggest they keep lists of key vocabulary and language structures that they come across. If you do this work for them and create a Global Perspectives glossary, the benefit to the students will be reduced; the real learning comes in categorising and using new language.

Key language structures

Most of the Global Perspectives course can be accessed via fairly simple English language structures.

- Simple statements in the present, past or future. For example:
  - The main issue is habitat loss.
  - The cause was habitat loss.
  - A new airport will solve the problem.
- Questions. For example:
  - How can we solve this problem?
  - What do other people think?

Simple language structures like this should be adequate, and the use of more simple language can help students to summarise issues and to analyse causes, effects and perspectives to their essentials.

Clearly, however, students who can master more complex language structures will be able to express more nuanced ideas. For example, students will certainly benefit from mastering language structures that relate to the prediction of consequences.

- If + present → (then) + future; for example, If we build an airport, (then) we will cause habitat loss.
- If + past → (then) + conditional; for example, If we built an airport, (then) we would cause habitat loss.

Some of the topic chapters in the *Student Book* include activities that focus on these structures, and more can be found in this *Teacher Guide.*

Guide to cultural perspectives

The new Cambridge syllabus for IGCSE® Global Perspectives requires students to research and discuss different cultural perspectives as part of their Team Project.

What is a cultural perspective?

A cultural perspective is a way of looking at the world shared by groups of people, which is based in shared beliefs and values. These beliefs and values can be affected by education, socio-economic status, religion, politics, and by key thinkers of an age. Many of these beliefs and values are deep rooted and grounded in long standing ways of thinking. They are also somewhat resistant to evidence, capable of contradictory overlap and extremely complex. Dangerously, we tend to believe that our perspectives are the way things are, rather than recognising them as perspectives.

Encourage students to approach cultural perspectives by asking questions such as:

- What beliefs do people in this group share?
- What does this cultural perspective value most highly?
- Where do their beliefs come from?
- How do people in this group see the world?
- How do people in this group understand their place in the world?

Cultural beliefs are often unconscious or subconscious, and can often conflict with our conscious, personal perspectives. For example, a woman can be a feminist who believes in gender equality and equal partnership between male and female, and yet still feel guilty for not doing enough housework, or looking after her partner.

Another example would be a person who is, rationally speaking, not a racist, and who genuinely believes that all people are equal, but is inclined to give business favours to others of the same ethnic group (whether this is majority or minority). An interesting example of this is the short story 'Batik' by Romesh Gunesekera, found in *Monkfish Moon*. In this story we see a mixed marriage; beliefs from subconscious cultural perspectives are brought into conflict with conscious choices and chosen beliefs when fighting breaks out in the couple's distant homeland.

Another, slightly different example could be a Global Perspectives writer or teacher, who recognises that human rights are seen as a Western imposition by some, and who recognises that it is not always right for the powerful, wealthy West to impose its views on other countries. And yet this Global Perspectives professional cannot get beyond their own ingrained perspective that everyone does indeed have human rights, by virtue of being human, whether or not their government recognises them.

Who has cultural perspectives?

We all have cultural perspectives – in fact each of us probably has several.

We might have one or more cultural perspectives associated with our religion. There are fundamental beliefs in each religion which can – but does not necessarily – shape almost everything else we believe, and shape our entire view of the world. For example, Christians firmly believe that Jesus gave his life for mankind – ideas about redemption, second chances, salvation through love penetrate Christian cultures, even in apparently secular areas of life. Muslims belief that fasting will help them to attain piety, gain self-control over weak bodies and weak wills, and come closer to Allah. This can affect beliefs in other areas of Muslims' lives. Clearly, there isn't a single Christian, Muslim, Sikh, Hindu or other religious perspective. In each religion there are many, but in each religion there are also a few guiding beliefs which affect other aspects of life.

People who are born poor might always see the world through the lens of poverty, hunger and the need to strive – this could make them desire fairness and justice, or it could drive them to selfish, individual gain, but the beliefs formed in early life and poverty would continue to shape their world. Conversely, people who are born wealthy, into powerful ruling families tend to believe that it is their right to rule, even if circumstances change.

To take a historical example, the colonial British elite was formed of wealthy nobles and county families with long family histories of rule. They believed in their right to rule and their superiority over those who had been born into 'inferior' families. The boys were sent to boarding schools at a very young age, and their natural affections were attached to institutions – so they tended to value the school, the nobility and the country, and to prioritise these institutions over personal considerations. These young people were brought up to want to do the right thing – but the right thing was defined as right for the country and the ruling class. It wouldn't have occurred to many of these individuals that exploiting the poor was wrong. Even when it did occur, the poor were always seen as a separate group, never as fully human.

How deep does students' understanding of cultural perspectives need to be?

Students are required to:

- research different cultural perspectives.

- use their research findings to inform or support their project.
- explain what they have learned about different cultural perspectives.

This means that they need more than a merely superficial, descriptive knowledge, and that they must make use of their findings.

So, let's say that a team wishes to make a short video about the causes of civil war in Syria.

A description of the five pillars of Islam and a report about Islamic festivals.	✗ This would be inadequate in terms of research, and it does not consider the perspectives based on Islamic beliefs.
A list of some different types of Islamic belief and who is on the different sides.	– This is getting there, but is in danger of being a simple description and list. It would need to move towards understanding the perspectives of people who adhere to each type of belief.
A discussion of the roles that Sunni, Alawite, Wahhabi, and Christianity play in this conflict, and how each of these groups has their own perspective on the conflict – and on each other.	✓ This has potential to be done well. It considers different perspectives and uses them to look at the causes of the conflict.
A discussion of political, economic and religious perspectives, showing how each contributes to the conflict. Looking at the importance of oil, water and other economic resources in the conflict. Looking at the importance of Syria as a political battleground – where Russia, Saudi, the USA and Europe are all trying to have influence. Deciding whether religion is more or less important than these other factors.	✓ This has potential to be done well. It considers different perspectives and uses them to look at the causes of the conflict.
How Enlightenment Philosophy underpinning Western democratic liberal perspectives conflicts with Salafi Jihadist 'End of History' perspectives, fuelling war.	If you have a student who can think at this level, please don't hold them back! However, this level of depth and underpinning of the perspectives is not necessary.

Alternatively, candidates might produce a web page evaluating the effects of a major sporting event on the local community.

Listing local sporting clubs which were able to watch the event.	✗ This does not look at different perspectives.
Contrasting the effect on elite competitive sport with the effect on ordinary people engaging in sport.	✗ This doesn't mention perspectives – but it could involve research into the cultural perspectives of people training for elite sport and people who have started doing more exercise for fun. Then it would be more promising.
An investigation into the cultural perspectives of a wealthy part of the community and a deprived part of the community, and how they feel the event affected them.	✓ This considers different cultural perspectives, and uses them to answer the question about whether the sporting event was beneficial.

Searching for information

Guide to the skill

Today there is an overwhelming mass of information available, mostly on the internet. Navigating this data is a life skill and searching for a precise piece of information, or specific, relevant ideas and arguments is one of the key skills that young people need to develop.

We tend to think that young people are 'digital natives' and that they know instinctively how to navigate the internet. However, evidence indicates that, while young people are good at social networking and using specific apps, they are not good at searching for particular information. Even able students are inclined to use vague search terms, find something on Wikipedia, and print it out without even reading it. Equally, they might find something in their native language and use a dubious internet translation tool to convert it into the desired language. The exercises in this section will help them to understand why they need to improve their skills in searching for information, and how to achieve this.

In this chapter, we will look at:

- the types of information needed to answer different questions
- using precise and targeted search terms
- skimming titles and first paragraphs to judge whether a result is relevant
- changing search terms if necessary
- searching within sites belonging to specific organisations, such as NGOs
- using advanced searches provided by search engines
- comparing results from different search engines.

Suggested answers: Level 1

These activities are introductory. Students may struggle to understand that they need to think about *types of information* rather than trying to give answers. Students may also need to discuss the specific answers to maintain their engagement. This is fine, as long as all students understand that different kinds of questions require different types of answers, and that this understanding can help them to improve their research skills.

Activity 1

1. **(a)** Definition

   (b) Fact

   (c) Definition is the superficial answer. However, opinions and value judgements play a part in forming that definition. It is possible to argue about the definition of education. Is it (only) the preparation of a workforce for the future? Is it the development of a love of learning? Is it about the development of free spirits? Is it transmission of knowledge, or of culture? Is the definition of education fundamentally altered by the *purpose* of education?

      Some classes will respond to this kind of discussion with enthusiasm. Allow students to debate and engage, but bring them back to the type of information that is needed to answer the question. Help them to recognise that, in this case, debate is helpful as there is no simple, easy answer.

   (d) Opinion/value judgement

   (e) Fact

   (f) Opinion/value judgement

   (g) Opinion/value judgement

   (h) Fact

   (i) Value judgement

   (j) Fact, value judgement and prediction.

Allow students to discuss which question is most interesting. It will aid in their understanding.

Suggested answers: Level 2

These activities build on Activity 1 in Level 1. It may be possible to move straight from Level 1 to Level 2; alternatively, there may be value in taking a more cyclical approach and coming back to Level 2 after some introductory work in other skills.

Remind students not to read a page or site if it doesn't look useful.

Activity 2

1. Discuss findings with students. Broadly speaking, it is likely that:

   (a) A search for 'family' will lead to sites such as Wikipedia, local news bulletins reporting on family-related events, family records sites, childcare, and family film sites. This search is not likely to be very helpful in answering questions.

   (b) A search for 'family values' will lead to sites such as Wikipedia, sites belong to religious groups, and sensationalist articles in national newspapers deploring the loss of family values. This search may be useful in understanding local or national opinions about family values, but the search results may be too deeply rooted in a particular set of values (often polemical) to help answer questions in a thoughtful way.

   (c) A search for 'effect divorce family values' will lead to academic articles, or sites belonging to support or legal groups. These sites might be quite hard for students to follow, but they are likely to provide thoughtful answers to some of the questions.

2. Discuss students' findings. Expect them to explain their findings and to talk about the different kinds of site and different kinds of information they found for each search.

3. Discuss students' ideas. Encourage them to try out their ideas and to compare the different results they get with different search terms. For example, to answer the question 'What effect is globalisation having on Pakistan?' they could compare the results they get by searching for 'globalisation Pakistan' and 'effect globalisation Pakistan'.

Suggested answers: Level 3

These activities are intended as extension to help students once they have already begun the process of research and have some practical experience of trial and error.

Activity 3

1. **(c)** http://www.amnesty.org

   (d) http://www.unesco.org

   (e) http://www.un.org

Amnesty International is focused on fighting human rights abuses. UNESCO's remit includes the right to education and freedom of expression as essential to a peaceful world. The UN deals with many issues, but it is here that the Universal Declaration of Human Rights can be found.

2. Discuss the ideas, information and perspectives that students find.

   (a) It is likely that results from http://www.oxfam.org will focus on girls' education and the alleviation of poverty through education.

   (b) It is likely that results from http://www.oecd.org will focus on the financial and aid aspects of education, with more scholarly and technical findings.

   (c) A general search engine is likely to bring up information sites such as Wikipedia, some information from NGOs, and opinion pieces from reputable, broadsheet newspapers. It should also give the option to select scholarly articles. Encourage students to articulate what the differences are themselves.

3. Encourage students to think individually, to discuss their ideas in groups, and to feed back through questioning.

Katja, why do you think that http://www.amnesty.org will help you to discuss conflict and peace?	✓ Asked with real interest, this will help Katja to think about what exactly she hopes to gain from the website. It will help you to establish whether she has really thought about the ways in which human rights abuses are linked to conflict, whether she is simply writing down a website to keep you happy, or whether she has misunderstood the task.

Activity 4

1. Encourage students to try out the advanced search to see how it takes them to what they want more quickly and precisely.

2. to **4.** Encourage students to discuss and compare their results using different search engines, and to use this approach in their own research, especially if they need different perspectives.

Reflection

Encourage students to reflect carefully on their own performance and to take this activity seriously.

1.2 Reading and recording

Guide to the skill

Reading is one of the most important ways of gaining information, but navigating dense blocks of text can be a challenge.

Once students learn to move around a text freely rather than reading every word, they will find it easier to locate and retrieve relevant information. Many students naturally skim read online, looking for posts that interest them, or that are written by people they care about. Ask them to think about the skills they use when they use the internet in this way.

Students need to learn specific reading skills to help them with their research and studies:

Identify key words that will help to locate relevant information

↓

Skim read to locate key words

↓

Read for relevance

↓

Read for detail

They need to learn to ask themselves:

- Is this passage on the right topic?
- Is it about the right *aspect* of the topic?
- Will it help to answer my specific question?

Recording information effectively is also essential to remembering it and to being able to find it again at a later stage of the research process.

Skim reading for key words

Skim reading for key words is much like doing word search puzzles or looking for a small image hiding in a busy picture. For some learners it may be useful to start with activities like these to help them to move away from the preconception that they need to look at and understand each word in turn. Another game that can help to prepare for skim reading is Snap, which trains the brain to respond to key stimuli. Looking for two identical cards is similar to looking for specific words and reacting when you see them. Snap could be adapted to use word cards; students could make their own snap games.

When skim reading, encourage students to do the following.

- Loosen their eyes and let them move around the text.
- Avoid focusing on every word.
- Skip.
- Ignore words they do not understand.
- Briefly to check the first paragraph of an article. Is it on the right topic?
- Briefly to check the content of each paragraph. Is it relevant?
- Use their knowledge and understanding of how texts are structured. Is this a chronological list, or is it alphabetic? Is it a journalistic article or an academic paper? Each of these types of text has a structure that can help students to navigate the content.

Reading for relevance

Once students have located key words, they should read some of the material around those key words to see if the content is relevant. At this point, it is still unnecessary to read every word in detail, but students need to look for other words that will help them to use or to discount a passage. For example, if students are thinking about the question 'Are single-parent families a recent change to family structures?', looking for words relating to time or to change will be useful. Words that relate to moral values will be a clue to stop reading as the passage is on the wrong aspect of the topic.

Reading for detail

Reading for detail is a completely different skill to skim reading. Students should do the following.

- Slow down!
- Minimise distractions.
- Make sure they are relaxed and focused.
- Think about the *meaning* of what they read.
- Look up important words they do not understand.
- Think about *what* they are reading. Does the text contain facts, opinions, predictions or value judgements?
- Think about *how* the content will answer the question. Is the argument for, against, or neutral?
- Make notes, organising ideas as they do so.
- Practise their skills.

While skim reading works well when reading on screen, research suggests that reading for detail and meaning is best done on paper, so students should print out specific paragraphs that they think will be useful to them.

Recording information

Help students to be selective and thoughtful about what they record. The following are essential:

- Key ideas
- Sources and references.

One of the most useful things that students can do to ensure they record information effectively is to process and use the information and ideas. This will help them to understand and remember what they read. For example, rather than simply copying information, students should get into the habit of using tables, diagrams and mind maps to record what they find, or of organising their notes into 'for' and 'against' to help them retain the focus of the question they need to answer.

Suggested answers: Level 1

These are introductory activities.

Key words

Activity 1

1. Encourage students to think about which words are key (in bold below), how many of them they really need, and how many they can hold in their minds while they skim read. Students should also think about synonyms. The words in brackets below could be added later, when they read for relevance.

   (a) Are **single-parent families** a recent change to (**family structures**)? Consider 'single mother' and 'single father' as synonyms.

   (b) Is it possible to have a truly (**fair**) **sports competition** between (**nations**)?

   (c) How can we (**prevent**) **species extinction**?

   (d) How can we (**combat**) **international crime**? Consider the synonym 'fight crime'.

   (e) Is investing in the (**future**) more important than **preserving traditions**? Consider 'keeping traditions alive' as a synonym.

Skim read

Activity 2

1. Passage 1 – question 1 b   Passage 4 – question 1 a
   Passage 2 – no   Passage 5 – no
   Passage 3 – question 1 c

Suggested answers: Level 2

These activities build on those in Level 1. It may be possible to move straight from Level 1 to Level 2; alternatively, there may be value in taking a more cyclical approach and coming back to Level 2 after some introductory work on other skills.

Making notes

Try an experiment. Give half of the students a text to remember, telling them there will be questions to test their memory; give the other half an activity in which they have to organise and process the information and ideas from the same text. Give both sets of students questions on the text to see who remembers more.

Activity 3

Encourage students to become more organised and independent in applying their skills.

Suggested answers: Level 3

These activities are intended as extension to help students once they have already begun the process of research.

It does not matter which referencing system students use, as long as they consistently reference their sources. Examiners can recognise when students are using someone else's work without referencing, and plagiarism is taken very seriously by exam boards.

References

Activity 4

1. **(a)** Not properly referenced. It is impossible to tell where this information comes from.

   (b) Adequately referenced (although an academic reference would need more detail). It is possible to find the document.

   (c) Not properly referenced. http://www.amnesty .org is a huge site and a precise URL is needed in order to find the information again.

2. Encourage students to reference properly and to go back and do it again if they have not.

3. Encourage thorough referencing.

Reflection

Reflection is an important part of the course. Allow students sufficient time to reflect.

1.3 Setting up research

Guide to the skill

Setting up research is a key skill for students to develop in order to become independent of the teacher. Students who are able to set up their own lines of enquiry are likely to:

- respond effectively to questions about setting up a line of enquiry in the written examination
- score more highly in the Individual Report
- score more highly in the Team Project.

What is involved in setting up research?

In order to set up their research – their lines of enquiry – effectively, students need to know the purpose or goal of the research. For example, is the purpose or goal to:

- gather information (In Global Perspectives this is not enough!)
- use ideas and information to answer a question
- use information to inform a project outcome
- evaluate different local, national, global and/or cultural perspectives?

Setting up research includes the following skills:

- Getting started
  - Asking questions
  - Doing quick searches to investigate key issues that are worth researching further
- Setting global questions that can be answered from different perspectives
- Planning
  - Thinking about different kinds of information
  - Thinking about different sources of information
  - Time management: What is the time limit or deadline? What needs to be done by the deadline and how long will it take?
- Organising
  - Notes and references
  - Ideas: For and against, causes, consequences and solutions, different perspectives, own opinions
- Questioning the information found
- Reflecting on the information found

- Reviewing
  - Are there any gaps that need to be filled with new research?
  - Are there any problems that need to be solved?
  - Does the research meet the aims?
- Writing. By this stage, most of the work should be done, but students should take care not to underestimate the time that writing takes.

Suggested answers: Level 1

These activities are introductory.

In the first instance, it will probably be necessary to present students with some ideas and information to use as stimulus and to help them get started. However, the ability to find out what the key issues are and to find relevant sources is of paramount importance. Even at this early stage it is vital to start asking students to think about how to find things out for themselves:

- What do you need to know to answer that question?
- What sort of information do you need to answer that question?
- How do you think you could find out?

Encourage students to use targeted internet searches to find out what the issues are and to raise questions. For example, searches such as 'key issues migration' or 'key issues migration Australia' or 'why migrants matter' can lead students to a range of questions.

Asking questions

Activity 1

1. **(a)** Encourage students to think of their own rules.

   (b) Encourage students to work together to think of questions, and ask students to write their ideas on the board, using mind mapping techniques.

   (c) Encourage discussion and debate. This question must be answered with predictions and inferences from data, whereas the question in part (b) can be answered with facts.

2. Remind students that they are thinking about questions they can ask to set up research; they are not yet answering the questions. Encourage students to refer back to the discussion on families. Some of the question structures might be the same'; for example, 'How do migration patterns differ between two different countries?' Many students will have opinions that can be used to generate questions. For example, the opinion, 'migrants take our jobs', can be used to generate questions such as these: 'What different types of migrants are there?', 'What sort of jobs do migrants do?', 'Do local people really want these jobs?', 'Are local people qualified to do these jobs?', 'What laws are there in my country relating to migrants and work?', 'What do you mean by 'our' jobs?', 'Do local people have a right to the jobs in their area if other people would do the jobs better?'.

More specific questions

Activity 2

The skill here is still that of planning research: thinking about what information is needed and how to find it. Having the debate is less important. However, some students may find it useful to engage in debate and to think about what they need to know as they continue to work. What facts do they need to back up their opinions? What questions should they be asking in order to justify their opinions?

1. Students can start by thinking about questions. They can think about what sort of facts, opinions, predictions and values they need in order to answer the question they have chosen. Using diagrams and tables is an excellent way to structure and plan research.

Encourage students to become more independent and to apply their skills.

Suggested answers: Level 2

These activities build on those in Level 1. It may be possible to move straight from Level 1 to Level 2; alternatively, there may be value in taking a more cyclical approach, coming back to Level 2 after some introductory work on other skills.

Asking lots of questions

Activity 3

1. Accept any reasonable answers. For example:

   (a) Fact: What problems does my region have?
   Prediction: What happens if food prices rise?
   Opinion / value judgement: How do we prevent this happening?

(b) to (d) Encourage students to apply and develop their skills.

(e) Encourage students to ask questions and to think about where these will lead in terms of research.

Activity 4

Encourage students to think for themselves and to help each other.

Suggested answers: Level 3

These activities are intended as extension to help students once they have already undertaken research activities, and are getting closer to engaging in assessed research.

Planning a line of enquiry

Activity 5

Encourage students to apply their skills.

Setting a question

The focus of these questions is the Individual Report, but a similar process can be used to make sure that students are asking appropriate questions to set up their Team Projects.

Activity 6

What are the key issues in poverty and inequality?	× This is a weak question. It is a simple question asking for a list of issues.
Should we build a new airport in my area?	− This question does raise an issue; it is possible to look at causes, consequences and perspectives. However, it would need to be linked to a specific local plan: there would not be much to research if there is no plan to build an airport in your area. The student would also need to make sure they link this question to one of the eight topics for the Individual Report; it could be linked to Sustainable Living, Biodiversity or Changing Communities, but all their research would need to focus on the topic of their choice. A basic pros and cons essay would not meet assessment requirements: it would fall into the category of transport.

Question		Comment
What is the quality of life like in Delhi, Mexico, Hanoi, or Dubai?	✗	This does not raise an issue. It asks for a simple investigation of facts.
What are the effects of urbanisation on people's quality of life? How can we deal with these effects?	✓	These questions relate directly to Changing Communities, and raise an issue as well as the need for a solution. It can be addressed with a range of perspectives.
How can we ensure that all children are vaccinated against serious diseases?	✗	The question itself is good, but it falls within the topic 'Disease and Health', which is not suitable for an Individual Report.
How can we create more jobs in my region?	–	The question is good, but it would need to be carefully linked to one of the eight topics. For example, this wording should be more effective: 'How can we sustainably create more jobs in my region?' Alternatively, the focus could be more clearly on the roles of Trade and Aid in creating jobs in the region. It would also be necessary to make sure that global perspectives can be included.
What were the causes of the economic crisis in 2008?	✗	This requires only a list of causes. It does not meet the criteria.
Should people in developed countries give their old computers to people in developing countries?	✓	This question explores a global issue within one of the eight topics for the Individual Report. It is possible to talk about causes, consequences, different perspectives and to argue for or against a specific solution.
What is the best way to help struggling communities (in my region / in developing countries)?	✓	This question explores a global issue within one of the eight topics for the Individual Report. It is possible to talk about causes, consequences and different perspectives, and to argue for or against a specific solution.
Should we punish criminals?	✗	This asks a philosophical question that is not well suited to a Global Perspectives report. An exceptional candidate might be able to make a related question fit into the topic of Belief Systems, but the more obvious topic here is Law and Criminality, which is not an Individual Report topic.
What are the best ways to deal with international crimes such as smuggling?	–	The question meets the criteria, but this falls into the topic of Law and Criminality, which is not an Individual Report topic.
The benefits of trade and aid.	✗	This question is very general, does not deal with an issue and is unlikely to generate a discussion of causes, consequences and perspectives.
In times of economic recession, should governments reduce the amount of aid they give to foreign countries?	✓	This question has a current focus and meets the criteria.
What sorts of aid are there?	✗	This question asks only for a list of types of aid. It will not generate a strong response.

2.1 Identifying information and trends

Guide to the skill

Identifying information and trends is about being able to extract, understand and interpret information from written and graphic material.

Identifying different kinds of information is important during the research process. Different kinds of question call for different kinds of information. In turn, these different kinds of information require different thinking processes, and these skills are dealt with in later chapters. Here, students learn how to recognise different kinds of information:

- Factual information can be verified or falsifed. It needs to be verified and cross-checked to ensure that it is accurate. It is also possible to consider the reliability of the source of factual information as a guide to whether or not to accept it, but this should never be a replacement for proper checking with other sources.

- Statistical information needs to be interpreted carefully and correctly, including reading the information that accompanies it, such as labels on axes. This kind of information should be verified as far as possible, but it is not always possible to adequately verify statistical information gathered by government agencies, for example: this kind of information gathering is beyond the individual. However, individuals can look for inconsistencies and misinterpretations. During research, students should ensure that they interpret statistical information correctly, and think about whether it comes from a reliable source.

- Opinions cannot be verified, but they can be discussed and debated. They can be supported by facts, statistics and reasoning. During research, students will need to consider whether or not the opinions they find are well supported.

- Predictions can be identified because they talk about what may happen in the future. They cannot be verified, but they can be supported with thoughts about causes, consequences and what is likely. During research, students should consider whether or not the predictions they come across are well supported and plausible. They may well come across extreme and unlikely predictions during internet searches.

- Like opinions, value judgements cannot be verified. They are a type of opinion that relates to ideas about good, bad and what should be the case, and they are closely related to moral values. The new syllabus does not require students to be able to identify value judgements in isolation. However, the assumptions that underlie different perspectives are often related to value judgements, and understanding different perspectives is on the syllabus, so it is useful for students to be able to recognise and evaluate value judgements.

It is important that students understand the difference between a wrong or inaccurate piece of factual information and an opinion. For example, if someone says 'The moon is made of cheese', this is clearly something that can be checked and demonstrated to be incorrect. This means that it is not an opinion, which is a kind of belief that cannot be demonstrated to be right or wrong.

There is one further kind of information that needs to be identified: 'information that I need to know but do not yet know'. This kind of information is important for two reasons:

- It can help students to guide their research. In order to undertake efficient research, students need to know what information to look for, so identifying what they need to know is a crucial step.

- It can help students to evaluate reasoning by recognising missing steps; information that is needed but not given can be very important. Has someone simply assumed too much? Has someone deliberately suppressed necessary information because it contradicts their point of view?

Suggested answers: Level 1

These are introductory activities.

Facts, opinions, predictions and judgements

Activity 1

(a) Fact, as it can be verified and cross-checked. It is not a matter for dispute or discussion.

(b) Opinion based on value judgements. It cannot be verified and can be disputed. Anything that relates to what is 'good' is likely to involve a value judgement somewhere in the justification process, although this may often be assumed and unstated.

(c) Opinion based on value judgement. This cannot be verified; anything relating to fairness is likely to involve a value judgement.

(d) Fact, as it can be cross-checked and verified.

(e) Opinion, as it cannot be verified, and it might be possible to argue that humans destroy habitats for selfless reasons.

(f) Opinion, as it cannot be verified. It would be easy to argue against this idea.

(g) Opinion, as it cannot be verified. It is possible to argue both for and against this point; for example, you could support it with reasons about the value of education to a child's future, or oppose it with arguments relating to the superior value of love.

(h) Prediction. This says what will happen in the future.

Activity 2

1. This is a prediction. It is talking about what will happen to the unemployment rate in the future.

2. Encourage students to think about what is likely. Suggested answers: growing youth population, slow world economy.

3. Facts (if true): 'I have been looking for a job for over a year now', 'I have good qualifications'. It is debatable whether the statement 'there are no jobs' is factual or whether it is only Saira's perception. There may be jobs that she isn't getting, isn't hearing about, or isn't qualified or experienced enough to do. On the other hand, it may be a simple fact that there are no (or few) jobs.

4. Opinions: 'If young people wanted to work, they would find jobs', 'Their lives are too easy'. Encourage students to separate @Hungry Fox's tweet into two separate opinions in this way.

Suggested answers: Level 2

These activities build on those in Level 1.

Information from charts and graphs

Activity 3

1. (a) Around the end of 2009 and beginning of 2010.

   (b) Unemployment was low and gradually falling until 2007. In 2008, it then rose rapidly from about 4.5% to about 10% by the end of 2009, stayed high into 2010 and slowly declined to about 5.5% by 2015.

(c) This is probably true, but we cannot be certain about this. The graph shows the unemployment rate as a percentage of the population. So if the population has shrunk, there might be fewer unemployed people in 2015, even though there is a slightly higher rate of unemployment. The actual population figures would need to be checked; students might find it useful to do this.

2. (a) This is not true. Figure 2 shows youth unemployment rates in different parts of the world. It is arranged from the region with the lowest youth unemployment rate to the region with the highest.

   (b) Encourage students to think and to research. Suggested answers: large youth population, economies dominated by oil with little other development, cultural attitudes.

   (c) Encourage students to think and to research to support their ideas. Consequences are likely to include: civil unrest, poor social and economic development for individuals and the region, possible efforts to improve education in the region.

   (d) Encourage students to apply their research skills, thinking about the precise search terms they need to use, as well as how to skim for the information they need.

Suggested answers: Level 3

These are intended as extension activities.

Activity 4

Passage 1: We need to know what other reasons the green movement may have for opposing GE crops. We need to know what other consequences and side effects GE can have. For example, does it lead to harmful effects on humans? What does it do to the environment? In order to stop opposing something, you would need to know that your reasons for opposing something had been nullified or outweighed.

Passage 2: In order to decide whether or not to invest, we need to be able to predict with reasonable certainly that we will get some money back from our investment. So we need to know a lot more about John, Jasvinder and their product, as well as about the potential market. Are John and Jasvinder competent? Do they have good business sense? Have they done their market research? Who are their competitors? Is there a market for their products? Are they charging the right amount of money for their products?

Activity 5

Encourage students to apply their skills.

2.2 Understanding key issues

Guide to the skill

The first skill developed in this chapter is that of discriminating between facts and issues, which are problems that need to be discussed or debated. The second is the skill of discriminating between key issues and less important issues. These are both important research skills, and will help students to choose research questions that allow for rich responses.

In order to discriminate between key issues and less important issues, students are guided to consider the following aspects of a problem: consequences, urgency, severity and perspectives. There are, of course, other methods, and you are free to introduce them.

The method used here recognises that key issues will vary from region to region and according to the value systems of a particular region. For example, climate change is recognised as a much more urgent – and therefore more important – issue in countries already suffering its severe consequences than in countries it has yet to affect. In part, this may be explained by an emotional imperative: in Europe we *know* that climate change is important, but in the Maldives, which may soon be flooded, the people *feel* the importance of the change as well as knowing it. This *feeling*, arguably, makes people more likely to act and make changes.

Value systems can also affect perspectives, which can in turn affect judgements about what constitutes a key issue. Nationalist politicians and their supporters tend to adhere to a value system that prioritises the wellbeing of people native to a particular country, and they tend to perceive migrants as a threat to this wellbeing; for these politicians, a key issue is 'How can we prevent migrants from entering our country?' Other groups of people tend to adhere to a value system that prioritises charity for those in need; for these people, the key issue is 'How can we help people who have lost their homes and their countries?' Yet others adhere to a value system that prioritises economic benefits; in this case, the key issue is 'What measures do we need to put in place to ensure that these migrants become economically productive as soon as possible?'

Suggested answers: Level 1

These activities are introductory.

Issues

Activity 1

1. **(a)** This does not raise an issue. There are simple factual answers to this question, and it is likely to generate a list rather than a debate.

    (b) This does raise issues. There is an underlying debate about whether migrants should integrate at all. There is also a debate about the best way to achieve this.

    (c) This raises issues of importance and values, which need to be discussed and debated.

    (d) This raises issues that can be debated. Food security is a real problem in a world with a growing population and with climate change that is threatening traditional food production. There is also considerable debate about whether genetic engineering is safe or whether it will have more negative consequences than positive, whether it genuinely can improve crop yields or whether it is merely a tool for big companies to gain dominance in the agricultural marketplace.

    (e) This does not raise an issue. There is a fairly simple scientific answer to this question, which is that hydroelectricity is one of the more efficient ways of producing electricity.

    (f) This does raise issues because the focus is on values and opinions that can be debated.

    (g) This does not raise issues for debate, as there is a simple, factual answer: yes, we could use rainforest plants for medicines, indeed we already do. There is potential for scientific research into *which* plants could be used for medicines, but in terms of a piece of work for Global Perspectives, this question would simply generate a list.

Suggested answers: Level 2

These activities build on those in Level 1. It may be possible to move straight from Level 1 to Level 2; alternatively, there may be value in taking a more cyclical approach, coming back to Level 2 after some introductory work on other skills.

Going beyond facts to issues

Activity 2

1. There is a very wide range of possible answers here. Encourage students to think carefully and to use quick internet searches to help them if necessary. Encourage them to take different directions as appropriate. Retain a focus on key issues rather than less important issues by reminding students to consider the criteria for a key issue.

Suggested answers: Level 3

These activities are intended as extension.

Key issues

Activity 3

1. As with Activity 2, there is a very wide range of possible answers here, and these will be informed by students' local and national perspectives. Students in countries near Syria will have a very different perspective on the Syrian civil war than students in Argentina or Hong Kong, for example. Encourage students to think deeply and to discuss their different views.

2. and 3. Encourage debate and discussion.

4. Encourage students to apply this skill thoughtfully to their own research.

5. Encourage students to explore how their own perspectives are affected by where they live.

6. Encourage students to explore how different national perspectives can lead to conflict. Introduce different national perspectives from newspaper extracts written in different countries if necessary.

Reflection

Reflection is an important part of the course. Allow students sufficient time to reflect.

2.3 Identifying causes and consequences

Guide to the skill

This chapter focuses on the identification of causes and consequences, first in simple sentences and contexts, then building up to more complex passages. The evaluation of possible courses of action is addressed in Chapter 2.4.

Students sometimes need help with the concept of cause and consequence and how it is different from a sequence of events (first one thing and then another). To understand the concept, they need to focus on the idea that one thing makes another thing happen. This could be illustrated with small balls on a surface:

- Roll one ball towards another ball so that the first ball causes the second ball to move. This is an example of cause and consequence.

- Roll one ball across the surface. Then roll the second ball across the surface, making sure that it does not touch the first ball. This is an example of a sequence of events, rather than cause and consequences.

Suggested answers: Level 1

These activities are introductory.

Causes and consequences

Activity 1

1. **(a)** I. Cause: Dmitri stole $1 million.
       Consequence: Dmitri went to jail.

   II. Cause: Rich nations can afford to find, develop, and train elite athletes.
       Consequence: Rich nations do better in international sporting events than poor nations.

   III. Cause: People are no longer having as many children as they used to.
       Consequence: The nation's population is ageing.

   IV. Cause: There is 50% unemployment amongst young men.
       Consequence: There have been protests and riots.

   V. This is a chain of causes and consequences. Each consequence becomes a cause for the next consequence in the chain.
       Cause: Frank got a bad mark in his maths exam.
       Consequence: He believed he was bad at maths.
       Further consequence: He stopped trying.
       Further consequence: He became bad at maths.
       Further consequence: When Frank opened his own business, he made a mess of the accounts.
       Further consequence: His business failed.

   VI. This is another chain, in which each consequence becomes a cause for the next consequence.
       Cause: Ilke got a bad mark in her maths exam.
       Consequence: She worked hard for her next maths exam.
       Further consequence: She got a better mark.
       Further consequence: She realized that hard work could lead to success.

   VII. Cause 1: People are living longer lives than they used to.
       Cause 2: People are also having fewer children.
       Consequence: A small number of adults are providing for a large number of older people.

   (b) I. therefore

       II. because

       III. therefore

       IV. because

       V. because

Possible consequences

Activity 2

Encourage students to think about the possibilities. It may be useful to think broadly and creatively before refining the possibilities to give likely consequences.

Suggested answers: Level 2

These activities build on those in Level 1. It may be possible to move straight from Level 1 to Level 2; alternatively, there may be value in taking a more cyclical approach, coming back to Level 2 after some introductory work on other skills.

Complex causes and consequences

Activity 3

1.

> Passage 1: (1) Ari and Harjanti Budiman are poor but have high hopes for their children, Ridwan and Liana. (2) Ari is offered a government contract logging in the rainforest. (3) He thinks that cutting down ancient trees is wrong, but (4) the money allows him to send Ridwan and Liana to school. (5) Ridwan and Liana do well at school, and (6) eventually get good jobs with good money. (7) However, logging in the rainforest has caused habitat loss and species extinction.

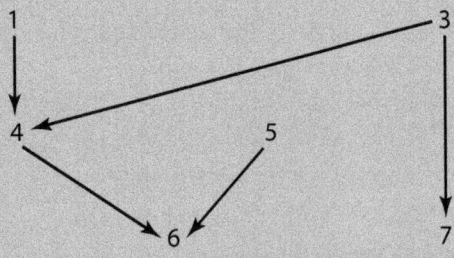

Note that (2) is not shown in the diagram because Ari's belief does not lead to any consequences. Different interpretations of the passage are possible; for instance, you could show a chain of causes:

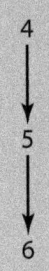

> Passage 2: (1) Deforestation, farming, overgrazing and development all result in (2) irreversible changes such as soil compaction, erosion, desertification, or the alteration of local climatic conditions. (3) Such land-use practices lead to habitat loss.

1 ⟶ 2 ⟶ 3

Suggested answers: Level 3

These activities are intended as extension.

Possible causes

Activity 4

1. **(a)** Encourage students to think of reasonable and likely causes. For example, Khalila is more likely to have been given a detention because she didn't do her homework than because she set off fireworks in class. Setting off fireworks in class is a much less normal thing to do, and it is a dangerous and extreme act that would probably lead to a more serious punishment than a detention. However, cultural norms will affect what is likely in different countries; in some schools, for example, wearing nail varnish or make-up might lead to a detention, whereas in other schools this would be normal.

    (b) Encourage students to think of ways that are specific to each event. For example, asking Khalila, her teacher and her classmates what happened would be ways of getting and checking information about Khalila's detention.

Recognising causes and consequences in more complex texts

Activity 5

1. Cause: Anti-vaccination scaremongering.
    Consequence: Parents are afraid to have their children vaccinated.
    Further consequence: Parents are rejecting the triple MMR vaccine for their children.
    Further consequence: Loss of 'herd immunity'.
    Further consequence: Measles is exploding.
    Further consequence: Education about vaccines is needed.

Activity 6

Encourage students to apply their skills. The focus of the task is to find out about and identify causes and consequences, but students will need to use their other skills too.

Reflection

Reflection is an important part of the course. Allow students sufficient time to reflect.

2.4 Identifying and evaluating possible courses of action

This chapter focuses on the skills needed to identify and evaluate possible courses of action. In Level 1, the focus is on identifying courses of action and deciding which course of action is most appropriate for different people, groups and institutions. In Levels 2 and 3, the focus is on evaluating possible courses of action by predicting and assessing consequences in order to decide on the best course of action to take.

There are very few 'right' answers in this section. It is more important for students to develop a way of thinking that allows them to make effective decisions, and to support these decisions with evidence and with reasoning. This can be as simple as asking questions such as:

- What are the consequences?
- Which individuals, groups or institutions are affected by these consequences?
- Are these consequences short-term or long-term?
- Are these consequences likely?
- Are these consequences serious?
- Are these consequences mainly positive or negative?
- Are the negative consequences more serious than the positive consequences?
- How do the consequences of *this* action compare with the consequences of *that* action?

Suggested answers: Level 1

These activities are introductory.

Who can take action?

Activity 1

Encourage students to think about who can realistically take which actions. There are many possible answers; accept any answer that is reasonable.

1. Suggested answers:

   (a) Tidy the school, get involved in behaviour improvement measures, possibly help with painting.

   (b) Enforce behaviour codes, encourage students to keep the school tidy.

   (c) Set and enforce policies that will lead to improvement in behaviour and cleanliness, try to find money to improve the school, work with parents.

   (d) Teach children the merits of good behaviour and cleanliness, support the school's behaviour policies.

   (e) If this is a government/state-run school, and if there is money available, the government could provide money to modernise the school's buildings.

   (f) No realistic actions.

2. Encourage students to think carefully about what each group of people could reasonably be expected to do.

3. Encourage students to think carefully about who could do what in each case.

4. Encourage students to think carefully about who could do what. Suggested answers:

a) Who can take action?	b) What should those actions be?
Individuals	Use public transport or walk, rather than travelling by car; reduce heating / air conditioning; buy local food.
Community groups	Set up car sharing schemes; work together to grow local food.
Businesses	Provide incentives to encourage workers to walk, cycle or use public transport to get to work, rather than drive; reduce the company's energy consumption by controlling heating and lighting.

a) Who can take action?	b) What should those actions be?
Local and national governments	Provide tax incentives to businesses to switch to environmentally friendly and energy efficient practices; provide incentives to encourage people to use public transport rather than driving; provide efficient and affordable public transport in local areas and nationally.

Suggested answers: Level 2

These activities build on those in Level 1. It may be possible to move straight from Level 1 to Level 2; alternatively, there may be value in taking a more cyclical approach, coming back to Level 2 after some introductory work on other skills.

Possible consequences of future actions

Activity 2

1. Encourage students to think through the possible consequences and to consider which are most likely. They could discuss which of these courses of action are most appropriate and most likely to lead to positive change.

    (a) Johann is likely to miss some experiences that he would have enjoyed. His decision is unlikely to have consequences for FIFA unless he persuades many other people to protest with him, or unless many other people choose to act in a similar way. If enough other people do act, then FIFA might decide to make changes to avoid financial loses.

    (b) This is unlikely to have consequences for FIFA on its own. If everyone acts like Karim, FIFA is unlikely to feel the effects and they will make no changes.

    (c) If Tomas and Justina are organised and funded well, and get a lot of press attention, they may manage to attract a lot of people to join their cause; this may exert pressure on FIFA's governing body, which could lead to changes. If Tomas and Justina are not well organised, this would have little effect.

(d) This could lead to less corruption in FIFA; national governments may not have jurisdiction over international sporting organisations like FIFA, but they can have influence. At the very least, one possible consequence is that some individuals within FIFA might be arrested for crimes and corruption committed in that country. Another possible consequence is that the country might invest resources in a review of FIFA's decisions, rather than spending the money in another area where it is badly needed.

(e) This is likely to have significant consequences for FIFA because sporting broadcasts are a major source of revenue for the organisation.

2. Encourage students to think carefully, and to discuss what is likely.

3. Encourage students to review their work thoughtfully and to make appropriate alterations. This gives students the opportunity to practise the vital skills of editing and amending, as well as to demonstrate their growing understanding of possible courses of action and their likely consequences.

Suggested answers: Level 3

These activities are intended as extension.

Weighing up possible consequences

Activity 3

1. Encourage students to think carefully. Suggested answers:

    (a) Driving, positive: He will keep warm and should arrive on time (assuming the roads are clear).
    Driving, negative: It is likely to contribute to traffic congestion and air pollution.
    Walking, positive: Walking regularly is good for fitness and good for the environment.
    Walking, negative: It can look unprofessional if you arrive at work wet or sweaty. It is unpleasant and unhealthy to sit in damp clothes at work.
    Overall, the short-term consequences of driving are positive, while those of walking are negative. However, the overall long-term consequences of walking are positive, while those of driving are negative.

    (b) Not very likely, as colds are transmitted by viruses. However, being cold can suppress the immune system, so it may somewhat increase his chance of getting a cold, especially if he is already a little unwell.

(c) Not very serious for most people.

(d) Certain: even electric cars contribute to air pollution.

(e) Extremely likely.

(f) Very small. However, the problem is that lots of very small contributions together create a big contribution.

(g) In the short-term, getting a cold is more annoying for Zaki, and may have consequences at work. Looking at the bigger picture, contributing to air pollution and climate change is more serious.

(h) Encourage students to discuss this value. We may not express it in this way, but many of us will take actions to protect our own immediate health rather than to address bigger, more remote problems.

(i) to **(l)** Encourage students to think through and discuss these hypothetical questions, thinking about the different value judgements, and the different decisions we might make in different circumstances.

2. Encourage individuals or small groups to work through this activity thoughtfully, applying their skills.

3. Encourage students to think carefully and to come up with relevant examples. This activity is an important part of evaluation: too many students are inclined to think that a greater number of bad consequences must be worse than a single very bad consequence.

4. Encourage students to think carefully. This activity should help them to see courses of action from different perspectives, and to understand that there isn't always one 'right' answer or course of action.

5. Encourage students to review their work carefully, to bring their skills together to make a decision, and to write a case to support that decision.

6. Encourage students to apply their skills.

Reflection

Reflection is an important part of the course. Allow students sufficient time to reflect.

2.5 Identifying different perspectives

Guide to the skill

What is a perspective? It is a standpoint, a viewpoint, a way of seeing the world and the issues in the world. A perspective can include opinions and arguments, but is not limited to a single opinion or argument. Most importantly, perspectives tend to be based on underlying beliefs and assumptions, which are often value judgements.

Understanding different perspectives is an important part of developing an international outlook and an ability to work in teams, especially international teams.

The first stage in understanding different perspectives is to recognise that other people *have* different perspectives, even if we cannot understand them. It is then important to recognise that these other perspectives might be as reasonable as our own.

We can go beyond this stage, however. We can identify different types of perspective:

- Personal perspectives – our own and those of others
- Local perspectives – our own and those of others
- National perspectives – our own and those of others
- Global perspectives – our own and those of others

We can begin to understand how these perspectives are formed, including the value judgements, underlying beliefs and assumptions that shape them.

It is also important to understand that these perspectives are complex and interdependent. My personal perspective is influenced by my national perspective: my way of seeing the world is affected by my (geopolitical) position in the world, as well as by my feelings for my country. However, any given national perspective includes conflicting opinions on particular issues, and different strands. The nationalist British perspective is very different from the internationalist British perspective, for example.

My personal perspective is also influenced by a range of global perspectives, which may themselves overlap and conflict, and which may be partly linked to national perspectives. Global perspectives are linked to religious beliefs, socio-economic status, levels of education, shared interests and beliefs about what is important: knowledge, the environment, power, human endeavour, human dignity and so on.

This chapter provides practice in identifying and exploring these different perspectives.

Note that different kinds of perspectives are assessed in different parts of the Global Perspectives qualification, but that this skills chapter focuses on the skills of identifying and thinking about perspectives in general.

Any kind of perspective can be assessed in the written examination. The Individual Report requires candidates to consider issues from local, national and global perspectives, and then to write about the development of the candidate's personal perspective on the issue. The Team Project requires candidates to research and consider different cultural perspectives relating to their chosen area of research and action.

Suggested answers: Level 1

These activities are introductory.

Local, national and global perspectives

Activity 1

1. There are no 'right' answers here. Encourage students to think, and to ask questions such as 'Is it really of national importance?' Allow students to recognise that some questions have greater personal perspectives than international, for example. Here is an example:

c) Is it acceptable to eat meat from animals that have been kept in poor conditions?		
Personal	**National**	**Global**
I don't want to eat meat from animals that have been kept in poor conditions. It's cruel and disgusting.	Keeping animals intensively can make meat cheap enough for everyone to be able to afford it, which is good for the health of the population → less sickness → better economy?	Making meat cheap in Europe means that Europeans only eat the best cuts, such as chicken breast fillets. The rest of the meat is sent to Africa and offloaded → African chicken farming industry suffers → Africa more dependent on Europe.

2. **(a)** This is a personal expression of a national perspective. There is some consideration of global issues, but from this national perspective.

(b) This is a personal expression of a national perspective. It focuses on a global issue, but exclusively from the perspective of the consequences it will have on the person's own country.

(c) This is a personal – and possibly rather self-centred – perspective.

(d) This is a global perspective, with consideration of local perspectives.

Suggested answers: Level 2

These activities build on those in Level 1. It may be possible to move straight from Level 1 to Level 2; alternatively, there may be value in taking a more cyclical approach, coming back to Level 2 after some introductory work on other skills.

Local, national and global perspectives

Activity 2

1. A, personal
B, local/national
C, global

2. **(a)** G

(b) D

(c) F

(d) E

Different cultural perspectives

Activity 3

1. Encourage students to say what they think initially, and then to discuss and research, Does their research change anything?

2. Encourage students to think about the different cultural perspectives and the attitudes and values that underlie them. Accept any reason answers. Some suggested answers are as follows:

(a) Educated and well travelled, exposed to a variety of different perspectives. Compassionate and wanting to help – there is an underlying belief that the speaker is in a position of power ('those of use who have opportunities') and should use it to benefit others.

(b) Less well educated and less well travelled than (a). In less of a position of power ('Life's already hard for us'). Committed to one familiar way of life and afraid of change. Sees migrants as an economic and existential threat.

(c) This is the perspective of someone from a dominant society, based on beliefs that their ways of doing things are the best, are universal, and that they have the right and the duty to impose their ways on others. There is a belief that their dominance gives them the right to intervene/interfere in others' affairs.

Suggested answers: Level 3

These activities are intended as extension.

Complex perspectives

Activity 4

Encourage students to apply their skills, and to bring different skills together.

Reflection

Reflection is an important part of the course. Allow students sufficient time to reflect.

Questioning knowledge claims

Guide to the skill

This chapter looks at the skills of questioning knowledge claims and evaluating the reasoning used to support claims.

What is a knowledge claim? The term 'knowledge claim' as it is used in the Global Perspectives syllabus is quite a broad one. It covers all the different kinds of claim made by people in articles, blogs and in speech. Questioning a knowledge claim has two parts:

- Thinking about what kind of claim it is: fact, opinion, prediction or value judgement. Students could consider the difference between speculation and prediction of reasonable, likely consequences. We can also think about whether these kinds of claim can be really *known*, or only believed.

- Considering whether the claim is supported by strong reasoning, so that it seems to be reasonable knowledge.

The Student Book suggests techniques that can be used to check whether the reasoning is strong, including thinking about emotive language, whether a passage is logical, whether predicted consequences are likely and whether they accept the value sunderlying a passage. The Student Book also provides guidance on common ways of being illogical in reasoning, such as generalisation, poor use of facts, contradiction and inconsistency, not answering someone's argument, attacking the arguer rather than the argument, and restricting the options. It is not necessary for them to know these terms, but a familiarity with these weak, illogical patterns of reasoning can help students to recognise weak arguments.

Much more important than knowing the terms to describe weak patterns of argument is the ability to explain and justify what is wrong with an argument. Why is this passage illogical? What is wrong with the consequences predicted and why? What effect does the emotive language have?

Suggested answers: Level 1

These activities are introductory.

Activity 1

1. Encourage students to remember and revise this basic understanding independently.

2. Here, it is worth having a brief discussion about what it means to *know* something, in a way that is appropriate to your class. For example:

   - What is the difference between believing something and knowing it?

   - Is 'I am sure' the same as 'I know'?

   - What is the difference between knowing something, knowing someone and knowing how to do something?

   - Are facts the only things that we can know?

   - Do facts have to be true for us to know them?

   - Does it make more sense to know a fact than to know an opinion?

   - What about value judgements? These are a subset of opinion, but people often claim to *know* what is right, or fair, or wrong.

There are no fixed answers; the following are suggestions to aid discussion.

(a) This is an opinion that can be disagreed with. Can we really know something if someone else could reasonably disagree? If someone else said that the Karakoram Highway that runs from China to Pakistan was a better place for beautiful scenery, could they also be said to know this?

(b) This is a fact that can be known, according to the traditional definitions of knowledge, which include justified true belief.

(c) Is this a fact that can be known? Is it an opinion that can only be believed? 'Beautiful' is a value judgement and others could disagree. Does general opinion about beauty turn a statement like this into something that can be known? If I see pictures of buildings that I think are beautiful in the United Arab Emirates, can I say that I know that there are beautiful buildings there, or only that I *believe* that some of the buildings there are beautiful.

(d) This is a prediction and we cannot know what it going to happen in the future. We can, however, discuss how *likely* this prediction is. If a prediction is very likely, can we speak of knowing what will happen? For example, can we say that we know that the sun will come up tomorrow?

(e) This is a proposal for action and it can be disagreed with, so it is an opinion. It is not knowledge according to the traditional definitions of knowledge.

Quality of reasoning in source materials

Activity 2

1. Encourage students to think things through as far as they can, always pushing for one more step in the reasoning. The sample answers given below are quite sophisticated, but many young people have the ability to arrive at similar thoughts, especially if they are helped in keeping a focus on whether the reasoning works well. Without this focus, students are generally inclined simply either to agree or disagree.

They do need to use oil to develop the economy because poverty will kill them before global warming does.	✗ This student has simply repeated a part of the reasoning; it is possible they are expressing agreement but it also possible that they are just copying the argument. Encourage the student to express their agreement giving additional reasons for it, and using more of their own words. Ask them to consider whether the people are so poor that poverty is killing them, and whether there are alternative solutions to developing an oil-based economy.
This is really good. Why shouldn't they use their oil to develop their economy? They deserve to get richer.	− This student has started to think about the issue and to react to it. However, at the moment they are simply agreeing with the opinions in the argument and stating an additional opinion. The student has not looked at how good the reasoning in the argument is. Encourage the student to use the questions on page 54 of the Student Book, or help them to tease out the emotions that are bound up in the issues of fairness here.
It's irrelevant that people in developed countries are rich. Global warming is happening anyway.	✓ This student has thought of an important point, but has not used it to show how the reasoning is weak. Encourage this student by asking them if they can explain how this point makes the reasoning in the argument weak.
This is emotional reasoning, and uses a loaded, rhetorical question to make the reader feel upset and as though the West is being unfair to them. But if you think about trying to answer the question, it's obvious: they should use less oil because it will harm them as well as the West, and harm places like the Maldives too, which aren't even rich. So it's not logical.	✓✓ This student has really thought through what is wrong with the argument, and explained it in terms of emotional and logical reasoning. It will be an unusual student who thinks this clearly and deeply at this stage of the course, but if they do, encourage them to progress by asking further questions. So, is it all bad? Is there anything that's reasonable here? Is there anything else that makes the argument weak? Overall, how good is this reasoning?'

Indicative content:

Passage 1: There is some logic in this reasoning, but some emotion is also used to make the reader agree. 'Poverty will kill our people faster than global warming' could be a reason to use oil to develop the economy, but it is a not well-structured argument or very logically connected. It is almost as though two different thoughts are coming together here, and the point might also be too extreme. The question in the middle of the reasoning is using emotions, presenting developed countries only as selfish, and presenting climate change as a problem that only rich countries are worried about. This isn't good logic: just one example could show that some less developed countries have real concerns. There is a real concern in this passage, which could be argued better.

Passage 2: The use of evidence to make a prediction in the first part of this reasoning is strong. We can check the statistic (that 80% of the Maldives are less than a metre above sea level) and if this is verified, then permanent flooding in the Maldives *will* be likely with even a small rise in sea levels. The phrase 'it's destroying my home' is emotional, seems quite extreme and there are gaps in the information – other things we also need to know. Encourage students to suggest some of these. For example, the reasoning requires that we accept that burning oil is causing the rise of sea levels, but we can accept this point because there is good scientific evidence for it (through global warming). However, if a significant proportion of the Maldives is flooded, then this person's home will have been destroyed, so the point is reasonable. The point about people in the West 'burning oil to make their lives more convenient' is more emotional than logical. It trivialises the reasons for using oil and is likely to upset people in the West rather than triggering a logical response. Here, again, we have a reasonable point, presented with some logic, but where the way it is presented is generally too emotional.

Passage 3: From a purely personal (and rather selfish) point of view, there is a logic to this: one holiday option has been eliminated, so another must be used. However, this is not constructed as a logical argument; it does not give any reasons or evidence. The main problem with this argument is the offensive narrowness of the perspective and the lack of empathy for people living in the Maldives.

Passage 4: This is an argument to support the proposal that the UN has to (must) 'work with national governments to reduce ecosystem destruction around the world'. It gives logical reasons, examples and evidence as to why these ecosystems provide global benefits; it is very objective and is not emotional. However, it is a limited argument, with gaps in the reasoning. For example, we do not know whether or to what extent it is possible to reduce ecosystem destruction. We do not know whether the cost of preventing ecosystem destruction will be worth the benefits it brings. We do not know why the UN should be involved. What can they do that national governments cannot?

Suggested answers: Level 2

These activities build on those in Level 1. It may be possible to move straight from Level 1 to Level 2; alternatively, there may be value in taking a more cyclical approach, coming back to Level 2 after some introductory work on other skills.

Activity 3

1. Encourage students to think beyond the obvious, to question their initial responses and to consider different circumstances carefully. Some sample answers are given below.

Some people don't deserve to be helped. They just don't.	✗ This student is not fully engaging with the activity, or thinking through their opinions. Encourage them to think of circumstances in which people should or should not be helped, and *why* some people should not be helped. Is this linked to their circumstances, their actions or their characters? What about students who struggle at school and fail to do their homework? Should they be helped?
I think everybody deserves to be helped. We are all human. But people who take advantage of those who help them shouldn't be helped any more. They should be punished.	– This student has thought of one circumstance in which people should not be helped, and has some good ideas, however, the student needs to be encouraged to explore their ideas further, and to justify them. What do they mean by 'take advantage'? Why does 'We are all human' mean that we deserve to be helped?

Everybody deserves help at least once but they also have to learn to help themselves. For example, if someone has lost their job and is struggling in life, someone helping might mean that they can find another job and sort their life out. We hear a lot about people who eat too much or smoke, and harm themselves. People say they don't deserve help. But I think that they should get help: help to stop overeating, or to stop smoking. It's not always easy to make good choices.	✓ This student has thought quite hard about the different circumstances in which we might give or withhold help. They could be prompted to talk further about their comment 'they also have to learn to help themselves', and to think about what exactly the limits on our help are.

Activity 4

1. Encourage students to think for themselves, and to justify their responses with reference to the text and using their skills. Some sample answers are given below.

This passage makes a bad argument to support trade not aid.	✗ This response says that the argument is bad but does not say why. Encourage this student to say *why* the argument is bad.
This argument predicts extreme consequences and makes a false dilemma.	− This response makes two reasonable points, but needs to explain and justify them. Ask the student which consequences are extreme, and why. Ask the student to explain how and why the passage makes a false dilemma, and what is wrong with it.

This argument makes a false dilemma by suggesting that we can either choose trade or aid. In fact, we may be able to use a combination of both to get the best result. So it is a weak argument.	✓ This is only one of many points that could be made, but it is explained well and related to the strength of the reasoning. Ask this student to now think about the predicted consequences in the argument.

Indicative content:

The passage asserts without support that aid leads to a number of negative consequences, without allowing for any possible positive consequences. The predicted negative consequences are too extreme and do not apply in all circumstances. For example, someone who is starving may well value food given freely and may well value opportunities for education to improve their circumstances. The passage also asserts that trade can lead to positive consequences and, again, the examples given are all too extreme. The argument does not consider, for example, the possibility of exploitation in trade, which is a significant negative consequence. It does not consider that some aid might be necessary to enable people to engage in trade, either at all or on fair terms. No reasons or evidence are provided to support these predictions or consequences, and it is therefore illogical to say that we should 'promote trade not aid'. This is also a false dilemma: some circumstances may require both trade and aid.

Activity 5

1. Encourage students to think for themselves, and to justify their responses with reference to the text and using their skills. Some sample answers are given below.

Using statistical information shows this argument is strong.	✗ Although you do often need statistical information to support a conclusion, it is not enough. It has to be good information and well used. Encourage this student to look at whether the statistical information demonstrates the point it is supposed to support.

The statistical information comes from a reliable source: the OECD is unlikely to invent statistics about aid.	– This student has made a reasonable point about the reliability of the source information. However, they have missed the significant point that the interpretation of this information is deeply flawed. Ask this student to think about whether a drop in aid really means that aid is no longer needed.
The author's conclusion is illogical. Just because aid has fallen doesn't mean it isn't needed. I might give less to charity, but that doesn't mean that charity isn't needed. It only means I haven't got any money, or that I am being selfish. So countries might not have any money, or they might be selfish.	✓ This student has identified the key weakness in this short argument and explained it, using a personal analogy and giving other reasons why aid might have fallen.

Indicative content:

Passage 1: The statistical information is likely to be accurate, and is from a reliable, relevant source. However, the conclusion drawn from this statistical information is not logical. There are many reasons why development aid might have fallen; for example, global recession leading to countries feeling poor, and prioritising spending at home rather than abroad.

Passage 2: This passage is emotional and uses emotive language, making huge assumptions and leaps of logic. The language paints aid in a very negative light; not all aid is 'pouring billions of dollars into the pockets of foreign dictators who don't respect human rights'. There are a number of values underlying this argument and we may wish to address the xenophobia reflected in the passage. There is a real issue with corruption and aid being diverted, but this does not happen to all aid. There is also an argument to suggest that it is precisely those countries that have poor records on human rights that need aid in order to promote human rights. The phrase 'slashing the budgets' is emotive, but it could represent a real cut in budgets. There is some logic in

this passage if you strip away the emotive language, but it still relies on us accepting reasons that have not been stated. For example, if we accept that corruption makes aid ineffective, and that we need to develop our own country, then it is clear that we might need to spend our money differently. This is the first unstated part of the argument. We also need to accept that using aid to 'get our national companies investing in infrastructure in developing countries' will achieve our aims: that it will help those who need help whilst also providing opportunities for young people at home. This seems reasonable, but we would really need to see arguments and evidence to show how this would work. On the other hand, this author is also making the false dilemma of 'trade or aid', assuming that we can only have one or the other. There is an alternative that is not explored in the argument: that we should choose aid projects more carefully and spend less money, whilst also encouraging investment abroad.

Passage 3: This passage also uses emotive language. It is more a statement of personal desperation than an argument. It does, however, draw on a personal experience that shows that new technology does not always create employment.

Suggested answers: Level 3

These activities are intended as extension.

Activity 6

Encourage students to recap and revise what they already know, and to think about what they need to improve on and how. This form of reflection on learning is an important part of becoming an independent learner: students should begin to develop the ability to identify their own learning needs and to consider how to address them.

More ways of being illogical

Activity 7

Encourage students to think for themselves and to justify their answers. For example:

1. A predicts some fairly unlikely consequences: all being rich and all economic problems solved is a big jump from making Hollywood-style blockbusters. It is not impossible that this kind of film-making could put Localia on the map and generate revenue but, as C suggests, there are plausible alternatives. That they would all become rich is impossible, and is wishful thinking that is unsupported by evidence or reasoning. So the argument here is not effective.

2. B answers the points made by A and D very badly. The first response to A 'That's utter rubbish' is rude, and doesn't give us a reason why it's rubbish. 'We need to spend less time dreaming about beautiful American actresses' is somewhat irrelevant, because A is suggesting that there should be beautiful Localian actresses for people to dream about. On a kind reading, B has a relevant point (made badly) that escapist blockbuster films don't help people to get to grips with reality. The response to D does little more than disagree and object. In fact, the support for American values and the concern about 'going on about ancient Localian traditions' is inconsistent with B's response to A, which advocates a greater focus on Localian culture. It is inconsistent and illogical to say that focusing on Localia is being 'stuck in the past', and B fails to answer D's point about young people recognising the importance of Localia.

3. C's reasoning is quite effective. It is both plausible and likely that copying Hollywood would lead to a poor imitation and that something new and different might be needed to attract audiences. C's second comment engages with what D says, and shows how a new compromise could be reached, giving reasons rather than using emotions. The idea that as a place develops, values and traditions develop and should develop is very interesting, but needs some support.

4. D engages with what C has said, answering the point, explaining how they disagree and giving reasons why they don't need something new. The argument is reasoned, not emotional. However, it doesn't justify why Localians need their own traditions rather that American ones; this point could do with more support. It assumes that young people will pay enough attention to traditional films, and that they will take from them the message that Localia is important (rather than, for example, a traditional, old-fashioned backwater. This assumption needs more support. Encourage students to create a list of the key vocabulary used in these example answers, for example, 'illogical', 'emotive', 'weak'. Then ask the students to rank these words in terms of their strength to ensure they can understand when to use them.

Reflection

Reflection is an important part of the course. Allow students sufficient time to reflect.

Questioning the reliability of information

3.2

Guide to the skill

The purpose of considering the reliability of information is to help us to decide what to believe, and to what extent we should believe it. Students are all too likely to believe what they read on the internet and in the newspapers. They are also likely either to *believe* something fully, or to *disbelieve* it fully. In reality, we need to suspend our belief while we check a claim we have read, and then place that claim on a scale from very reliable and probably true to highly unreliable and probably untrue.

There are a number of checks that we can undertake. We can think about the claim itself:

- Is this an accurate claim?
- Can I verify this claim as a fact?
- Is this claim plausible? Is it something that could be true?
- Can I cross-check this claim using a number of sources?

We can think about the source of the information:

- Is this a reliable source?
- Is this source an expert (individual or institution)?
- Does this source support opinions with evidence?
- Does this source have a reason to lie? Is the source biased? Does the source have a vested interest?
- Does this source have relevant information?

Suggested answers: Level 1

These activities are introductory.

What sort of information can be reliable?

Activity 1

1. **(a)** This is incorrect but factual in nature. According to the Pew Research Centre in 2015, 71% of people were living on less than $10 a day in 2011.

    (b) An opinion, not a fact, as it cannot be verified.

    (c) This is a value judgement (opinion).

    (d) An opinion, not a fact; not every statistic is used in a factual way.

    (e) This is a prediction about the future, not a fact.

Activity 2

1. **(a)**

    - Sophie Maclean lacks expertise as she is only a high school student. She does not live in Pakistan, or take part in reputable scientific studies, so her access to information is limited. A high school student's blog could be of variable quality, and is certainly not recommended as a source of information about scientific information relating to another country.

    - Dr. A. Hamid does live in a mountainous part of Pakistan. He is in a position to observe actual changes and, as he records conditions, he should have relevant information. As a medical doctor, he has scientific training, which is not the same as meteorological training but does put him in a good position to make accurate recordings. He can also talk about the quality of life and how it is changing in response to climate change. However, here he can only give one point of view. So overall, he is quite reliable, but not as good as a meteorologist with access to much more data would be.

    - This is an irrelevant source of information: bridal customs are unlikely to tell us about the effects of climate change.

    - A report from the Pakistani Ministry of Climate ought to be a reliable source of information. There should be no reason for them to produce false data, or to misinterpret it, and they should have access to large quantities of reliable data.

    (b)

    - This is likely to be reasonably reliable. The Migration Policy Institute is an independent, American institute, aiming to promote research and intelligent, humanitarian migration policies. It has underlying American values, but seems to aim to be objective in its research. They have no apparent reason to misrepresent what is happening or to lie.

    - This seems likely to be reasonably reliable. The Australian government is likely to have access to high calibre scientists and good data. They have no obvious reason to lie. Their report will have Australian values underlying it, and may be influenced by Australian political aims, but a research group is likely to try to be scientific and objective.

- This is useful first-hand information, giving insight into the experiences of someone who is living through a change of community. However, the boy may exaggerate or even lie online for effect. In addition, he certainly only sees one part of the bigger picture, and he may not be fully aware of how communities around him are changing as he may be too busy dealing with the changes in terms of how they affect him. So this may be insightful, but is overall only somewhat reliable.

- This depends on whether your grandmother is Vietnamese, and whether she has lived through changing communities in Vietnam. If she is Vietnamese, she may have experienced a great deal of change in local communities – due to climate change on the coast, or due to changing cities and modernisation. She will be able to give a valuable first-hand account of the changes that she has seen, but not a full picture, and her account may be exaggerated, affected by limitations of human memory, and possibly biased by her beliefs. So, like the migrant boy's diary, this may be insightful and valuable, but only somewhat reliable.

(c)

- UK laws mean that facts printed in UK newspapers must be accurate, but some daily tabloid newspapers tend to omit facts they do not like, and to use questions and implications to make people believe certain things. Daily papers like this often have a biased viewpoint and reputation sensationalism, so are not very reliable.

- Wikipedia can be a useful place to start finding information. Although the content on the site is checked, it is possible for anyone to edit the information, and so could become inaccurate. So this is neither very reliable nor very unreliable, but everything from this site should be cross-checked.

- This is likely to be unreliable and biased, and may consist mainly of rants. There are reliable blogs written by well-informed people about football, but the name of this blogger is typical of the more sensationalist kind of blog. (The blogger's name is fictional, intended to provoke this kind of response.)

- Forbes is a reputable financial online magazine that specialises in financial issues, so it is likely to have access to journalists who are expert at unpicking financial wrongdoing and finding the truth. It is likely to make some effort to be objective.

Fakes, hoxes, misunderstandings and mistakes

Activity 3

1. **(a)** The purpose of this activity is to encourage students to be on their guard for hoaxes and false information on the internet, and to counter their tendency to believe everything they read. It is possible to make this into a game: students could bring in two or three reports each, featuring at least one hoax, and then work in teams to spot the hoaxes. Another option would to create a display of internet hoaxes.

   (b) The idea of catching an asteroid in a bag seems like a hoax, but reliable sources indicate that it is a real plan. Whether or not the plan is realistic is another matter.

Suggested answers: Level 2

These activities build on those in Level 1. It may be possible to move straight from Level 1 to Level 2; alternatively, there may be value in taking a more cyclical approach, coming back to Level 2 after some introductory work on other skills.

Cross-checking facts

Activity 4

1. As ever, encourage students to think things through and to justify their views. Encourage them to focus on whether the facts have been sufficiently checked rather than on whether the facts are correct. It is important that students arrive at their understanding independently, but it is also important to ensure they understand that facts need to be checked sufficiently and why.

   The answers below are suggestions only. Encourage students who think through other relevant ideas.

   (a) This has not been sufficiently checked. It is plausible, but the source is unreliable. You could check a reliable health care site, or a reputable scientific journal or magazine. You can ask what evidence there is; some people who have used mobile phones may have brain cancer, but would they have got brain cancer anyway? How many millions, even billions, of people use mobile phones without getting brain cancer? Did the people with brain cancer use their phones a lot more than those without cancer? Had they been using phones over a longer period of time? Have mobile phones been around for long enough for this to be a fact rather than a hypothesis?

(b) This has not been sufficiently checked. If you live in a country like the UK, where in winter there is sometimes enough snow to close schools but not enough for local government to invest in snow ploughs to clear the roads, then this is plausible. It is not plausible if it is summertime or if you live, for example, in Singapore. Your friends are more likely to be reliable about this than about mobile phones causing cancer. However, it's also plausible that someone might start this as a hoax, and for others to believe it and share it without checking. You could check the school's website, telephone the school or listen to local radio. You could also check whether the weather forecast has predicted heavy snow, and whether the school usually closes or stays open in these circumstances.

(c) This has (in the end) been sufficiently checked. There seems to be a clear error in the social networking report, which may have arisen from a misunderstanding of several newspaper reports.

(d) This has not been sufficiently checked. It needs to be checked against other sources, for example other newspapers, or preferably an original source such as a UN agency. In fact, this is inaccurate; it is quite common that a typographical error in one source is accepted without checking and then becomes commonly accepted.

(e) This has been thoroughly checked.

2. Encourage students to apply their skills to check these facts.

Checking facts, evaluating opinions, predictions and value judgements

Activity 5

1. There are no fixed answers here. Encourage students to think carefully, and to go beyond the simplistic response. This can involve weighing up reputation and reason to lie, for example, or thinking about access to accurate data and how that data might be collected.

    (a) These organisations collect data and try to be accurate about it. However, they are limited by weaknesses in the data collection systems in the countries they work with, which tend to be run by influential members of MEDCs. This type of source is fairly reliable but may only give a part of the picture.

    (b) This depends on the government. In MEDCs, the governments tend to have high-quality data collection systems, and laws to ensure that they publish accurate and true data. However, they are able to choose which data to collect and publish, so they can distort public perception or they can change the way that data is collected to obscure issues. In LEDCs, there can be problems collecting any data at all. In some countries, governments allegedly publish what they want the public to hear, regardless of whether or not it is true.

    (c) These large charities have access to sophisticated data collection systems, and fund their own data collection and research. They tend be truthful in their presentation of data. As above, however, they are limited by the data collection systems in some countries. Their agendas as charities also affect the questions they ask. This type of source is fairly reliable but may only give a part of the picture. Data from this source could usefully be combined with government and supranational agency information to give a bigger picture.

    (d) Small charities have much less access to sophisticated data collection systems, and may be much more swayed by their desire to help a cause or to portray the data in a particular light. These are generally less reliable as a source than large charities, but are not completely unreliable. (Note, however, that there tends to be great variability between small charities.) Here, it is best to check that the charity exists, and to cross-check facts as far as possible.

    (e) Anyone can post on social media pages and some people enjoy deception, so anything written on social media pages should be treated as unreliable (although, clearly some of it is true). Here, it is important to check that the cause actually exists and to cross-check carefully.

    (f) Data and statistics are likely to be accurate as far as they go: multinational corporations have teams of experts writing website content, and they have access to experts and lawyers who will make sure that they are not infringing laws. However, they are likely to be highly selective in support of their own interests and tend to favour interpretations that suit them. This type of source has some reliability, but it is important to look for other possibilities and the evidence that they have omitted.

(g) Small local companies may write their websites themselves without access to data collection, experts or lawyers. These may be excellent, or they may contain mistakes and opinions presented as facts. Like small charities, this type of source should be cross-checked very carefully.

(h) Blogs can be written by anyone. Check who the author is. If the author is a leading expert, and if you can find references to them elsewhere, then their facts are likely to be accurate, although they may be selected to support the author's own views. If the blog is written by someone without expertise and who is simply expressing their own opinion, without access to data, then the source should be treated as unreliable.

(i) Serious newspapers in most countries will present and analyse facts as accurately as possible. They should employ investigative journalists and experts in their field to find the most accurate information. The facts they choose and the way they interpret them will vary according to the general political stance of the paper. It is always worth cross-checking, as mistakes can be made, but serious newspapers are fairly reliable.

(j) Cross-check everything you find in a sensationalist newspaper. Their facts ought to be accurate, but sensationalist newspapers are very good at making suggestion and inferences, and at using questions and other strategies to make you believe things that are unsupported by facts.

Suggested answers: Level 3

These activities are intended as extension.

Can I trust this information?

Activity 6

1. Encourage students to think carefully about the following.
   - Plausibility, types of claim and possible reasons for the source to be untruthful.
   - Perspectives, agendas and bias. Too often, students dismiss a source as 'biased' because they disagree with its particular perspective or agenda, yet they accept a source they agree with, ignoring (or not even noticing) that this, too, may have its own agenda or perspective. Encourage students to think through the difference between a bias that might make you lie and an opinion, agenda or perspective.

2. Encourage students to be thorough and realistic. Almost every source has an opinion, agenda or perspective, so it is not possible to assume that

their knowledge claims are inaccurate for this reason; however, if a source is completely biased and makes no attempt to be objective, then this is cause to be wary. If a source has expertise but may have a reason to lie, does this mean the source will *definitely* lie and that their knowledge claims are all inaccurate? Should this source and its knowledge claims be discarded or just cross-checked carefully?

Encourage students to also think through the implications of what they say about knowledge claims. If they identify a knowledge claim as unreliable, are they still going to use it? If they identify a knowledge claim as an opinion rather than a fact, what does this mean for how they use it?

Some sample answers are given below:

The knowledge claims in Document 1 come from a reliable source: a serious, politically independent British newspaper. The claims in Document 3 come from a charity, which is biased because it wants to take your money, so it might lie.	✗ This candidate is looking at the source rather than at the knowledge claims. Ask whether a reliable newspaper might make a mistake. What questions need to be asked about the research? Is the charity 'just' trying to take your money, or does it have other aims? What does it want the money for? Is the charity really likely to lie? Is there an important difference between lying, being mistaken and seeing a different side of the truth?
Document 2 is giving opinions as if they were facts. They are plausible opinions, but I'd need more information to support them, such as an example of an 'aspirational but impractical' policy, or evidence that millions of dollars have been wasted on 'ill-conceived' projects. At present, it would be difficult to cross-check, because it's just opinion.	✓ This student has noticed that the knowledge claims here are not actually facts, which is good. They have also thought about plausibility and cross-checking. Discuss with this student how they could find examples and evidence to support or oppose this opinion.

3.3 Evaluating causes and consequences

Guide to the skill

Evaluating causes and consequences mainly involves consideration of these questions:

- Is this really likely?
- Are there alternative possible causes?
- Are there alternative possible consequences?

Three specific problems with predicted causes are:

- Exaggeration
- Oversimplification
- Ignoring other possibilities.

Suggested answers: Level 1

These activities are introductory.

Activity 1

1. Encourage students to think of a range of possible causes, before narrowing them down to the most likely few. The following are suggestions only.

   (a) Toby failed his English exam because: he didn't work hard enough; the exam was too hard; he had problems at home; he was unwell.

   (b) Most old people in homes are there because: their families cannot care for their complex needs; they are no longer able to care for themselves; people are living longer but not staying healthy; their families have to work.

   (c) There is a shortage of housing because: not enough new houses are being built; there are more single-person households; the population is growing.

   (d) The main cause of disagreements about water use in the Nile basin is: old agreements about who could use the water, which were not necessarily fair; increasing water consumption per person.

   (e) The main cause of destruction of natural ecosystems is: human development; capitalism; pollution; climate change.

Activity 2

1. Encourage students to think carefully about what is likely and to justify their answers thoughtfully.

2. Encourage students to apply their skills while enjoying the game.

Activity 3

1. Encourage students to think widely about possible consequences, before narrowing them down to the most likely few. The following are suggestions only.

   (a) We will all feel homesick; China will cease to develop; my children will resent me for making them leave their friends.

   (b) He will not be able to get a job; he will not develop the skills he needs to succeed; he will earn less money during his lifetime.

   (c) There could be significant consequences for the environment and for climate change; we might simply use more fossil fuels.

   (d) Local residents might complain about the wind farm.

Suggested answers: Level 2

These activities build on those in Level 1. It may be possible to move straight from Level 1 to Level 2; alternatively, there may be value in taking a more cyclical approach, coming back to Level 2 after some introductory work on other skills.

Activity 4

1. (a) This is possible, but probably over-optimistic. Building new roads may well attract more business, but more business is likely to attract more traffic, so the traffic will not be much better.

   (b) This is possible, but an alternative possibility is that the investment will not work and you will find yourself in debt.

   (c) Evidence indicates that most regional development agencies do not stop people from migrating to the cities. An alternative possibility is that people will go to the cities anyway because they are prosperous and exciting, and that the government's money will be wasted.

(d) An alternative is that at least some people will use mosquito nets to protect their children and that these children will not get malaria. It may be that the money also allows for education initiatives to help people understand the value of mosquito nets.

(e) An alternative possibility is that people will ignore the law, or resent being made to act in the same way as their grandparents. Simply making a law cannot change people's attitudes.

Suggested answers: Level 3

These activities are intended as extension.

What about the causes and consequences?

Activity 5

Encourage students to think carefully about what might happen and to justify their answers with evidence, applying the skills they have developed.

Passage 1: This depends on the context. In a very high economic development country, getting broadband to the last few people is unlikely to have a significant effect because those people who do not already have it are likely not to be economically active, such as the elderly. In this case, the returns on getting broadband to the last few people will not be significant. In a very low economic development country, it is possible that broadband access will not help to improve the economy because there are insufficient computers, or because people are too busy trying to survive to set up businesses. However, in most circumstances, it is likely that if we can get broadband internet access to everyone, or at least to most people, that the economy will improve significantly. Broadband alone may not be sufficient, but these days it is probably necessary.

Passage 2: This passage suggests quite extreme consequences and implies that they are relevant to all circumstances. Aid might sometimes lead to 'dependency, corruption and waste', but thoughtful, relevant aid that focuses on human development and engages local people in projects might lead to improvements in many areas, such as education, human rights and self-government. It may be true that people who are given free things do not always value them, yet a person who is given free food when they might otherwise starve to death will certainly value it. It might be quite likely that some forms of aid lead to people's

belief that they cannot achieve for themselves, but other forms of aid can counter this, especially where local people are involved in making decisions. The consequences described here are not consequences of all aid, but only of some types of aid. Trade can also lead to exploitation of people in low economic development countries, and to a prioritisation of Western economic aims. Unequal trade can lead to a loss of independence as multinationals take over.

Passage 3: This argument is more moderate in its prediction of consequences and does try to look for middle ground. It is probably optimistic to say that using aid to provide loans will 'combine the advantages of aid and trade' but without any of their disadvantages. There are always disadvantages. For example, some people are likely to be unable to repay their loans – possibly because of a lack of education, or because of poor personal and financial skills – and these people will find themselves in a difficult financial situation.

Activity 6

Encourage students to apply their skills.

Reflection

Reflection is an important part of the course. Allow students sufficient time to reflect.

3.4 Questioning underlying beliefs

Guide to the skill

Understanding other perspectives is difficult because we are generally very firmly rooted in our own perspectives. Understanding that our fundamental beliefs are a *way* of seeing – a perspective – rather than an absolute part of the way the world is, is both challenging and essential to being able to understand others.

Different perspectives are complex, and stem from different interpretations of the world that are based on different beliefs and different values. Unpicking these different beliefs and values will help to understand the perspectives. To do this, we can use conscious, intellectual skills, and these are practised in the main activities that follow. We can also use subconscious, empathetic skills to aid understanding. What does it feel like to be in this situation? What might I believe and feel if I were there?

Suggested answers: Level 1

Unspoken beliefs

Activity 1

1. **(a)** C, D

    (b) B (G is possible, but not necessary; the statement may not refer to a neighbouring country and there are other reasons why going to war could be seen as the only option)

    (c) F, H

    (d) A, E

2. Encourage students to understand that it would help Mia and Amon to see one another's point of view and to understand one another's beliefs. Their conflict is founded on mistaken beliefs.

3. Encourage students to think carefully about the beliefs underlying these statements. Suggested answers:

    (a) Poor neighbourhoods are more likely to produce killers than richer neighbourhoods.

    (b) Swimming pools waste water; we need to save water; water should be saved for drinking and growing crops. The lady also believes that she has a right to tell her neighbour how to use water.

    (c) Amira either dislikes shopping malls or does not like the person she is talking to enough to spend a whole day with them. There may be other concerns underlying this; for example, Amira may be busy with work or projects that interest her more than shopping.

Suggested answers: Level 2

Beliefs underpinning perspectives

Activity 2

1. Encourage students to think carefully about these values in their own society. Encourage them to research what other societies believe. Generally speaking, Western countries are individualistic, with a focus on individual rights and equality, whereas Eastern countries prioritise families and social groups, with an emphasis on social stability.

Suggested answers: Level 3

Activity 3

1. Encourage students to think through the beliefs and values underlying a current conflict.

2. Encourage students to think this through. Suggested answers:

    (a) The main value underlying this comment is the belief that to be rich and famous, and to have an important place in the world, is of the greatest significance. Additional beliefs and values include: energetic young producers are more likely to achieve the aims than older ones; Hollywood-style action movies are more likely to achieve the aims than any other kind.

    (b) The main value underlying this comment is the belief that the Localian's own traditions are important, and that they should value their country for what it is rather than trying to copy another country. Additional beliefs and values include: it is bad that Localian traditions and language are being swept away by American traditions and language (*not* that American traditions and language are bad in themselves).

Activity 4

Encourage students to think these situations through with care, and to take their thinking a step deeper.

Developing a line of reasoning

4

Guide to the skill

The skill of developing a line of reasoning involves logic, structure and the organisation of ideas. Many students are inclined to write down what they know with little thought to organisation. A line of reasoning, however, is deliberate and well thought through, and involves the following.

- Considering the ultimate purpose of the writing. What *exactly* am I trying to argue for or against?

- Considering how to support the purpose of the writing. What reasons, examples and mini conclusions will help me to support my purpose?

- Considering the overall structure. How can I organise my ideas logically?

- Considering logical and linguistic flow. How can I link my ideas together?

- Considering other perspectives and counterarguments.

- Showing that you have reflected on the issues.

Suggested answers: Level 1

These activities are introductory.

Giving reasons for your opinions

Activity 1

1. **(a)** It is important to give reasons, here, and not merely to agree or disagree. Some students tend to state their opinions and think that this is enough, but all opinions can in some way be supported with reasons or countered with opposing opinions and reasons. Some sample answers are given below.

Sport isn't boring; it's exciting.	✗ This is disagreement without giving a reason. Simply stating the opposite of a claim is not a reason to disagree with it. Encourage them to say what makes sport exciting, and help them to understand that this provides a reason for their opinion.

Watching sport is boring but playing sport is exciting. This is because you don't get to join in when you are watching, but you do get to join in when you are playing.	✓ This student has made a relevant distinction and given reasons for their opinion. Encourage them to give reasons why joining in makes playing sport more exciting.

(b) By working with someone who disagrees with them, students should be able to extend their ability to give reasons and to answer counterarguments. Encourage students to engage fully, rather than simply disagreeing.

Activity 2

1. **(a)** Ari should take the job *because* it will allow him to educate his children and *because* education for his children is the most important thing. *In addition*, if work is hard to find, you take what you can get.

   (Alternative: Education for his children is the most important thing, *so* Ari should take the job *because* it will allow him to educate his children. *In addition*, if work is hard to find, you take what you can get.)

   (b) International sports competitions put different nations in opposition to each other, *so* it is like a mini war. You are happy when the other country loses *because* you believe that your country winning is the most important aspect. *For example*, during the Olympics, I really wanted the competitor from my country to win, even though the other competitor was better. *Therefore*, international sports competitions actually make us less peaceful.

   (Alternative: It is like a mini war *because* you are happy when the other country loses and *because* you believe that your country winning is the most important aspect. *For example*, during the Olympics, I really wanted the competitor from my country to win, even though the other competitor was better. *So* international sports competitions put different nations in opposition to each other and *therefore* international sports competitions actually make us less peaceful.)

2. Encourage students to think about what really counts as a reason. Some sample answers are given below.

Some children are better off working than in school because school is boring.	✗ This student has attempted to give a reason, but school being boring is not really a reason why some children are better off working than in school. School is beneficial for children even if they don't find it interesting. Encourage them to think about how working would make a child *better off*. This could relate to their financial situation, how they learn, what kind of skills they have, or what kind of career they want.
Some children are better off working than in school because they want careers in areas that are better learned on the job than in the classroom. For example, building or farming.	✓ This student has given relevant, focused reasons and examples. You can argue against this opinion, as you can point out that there is a lot that builders and farmers can learn in a classroom, but the reasons given support the conclusion. Encourage this student to think about what builders and farmers can learn in the classroom; for example, how can science help farmers become more productive.

Suggested answers: Level 2

These activities build on those in Level 1. It may be possible to move straight from Level 1 to Level 2; alternatively, there may be value in taking a more cyclical approach, coming back to Level 2 after some introductory work on other skills.

Developing a line of reasoning

Activity 3

1. Explanation. This is telling us how and why the coral reef is declining; it is not persuading us to believe that it is declining.
2. Argument. This is using logic to persuade us to accept the conclusion that we should work together as a community to reduce our consumption and recycle our waste.

Activity 4

Encourage students to think about what really counts as a reason, and what makes a genuinely good example. Some sample answers are given below.

The government should increase funding for eco-friendly buses to help the environment.	✗ This student has given the ultimate aim of providing funding, but has not really given a reason for *increasing* funding. There are also no examples given.
The government should increase funding for eco-friendly buses because air pollution in the city is very bad, and normal buses contribute significantly to air pollution. For example, electric buses produce less carbon monoxide than diesel buses.	✓ This student has given two relevant, focused reasons and a reasonable example. This student could be encouraged to research and find out more about eco-friendly buses to improve their argument.

Activity 5

1. Encourage friendly discussion about circumstances when punishment is or is not appropriate for selfish behaviour. Expect students to remember their own rules for class or group discussion. If students are ready, ask them to think about different kinds of punishment as well, and to consider the difference between punishment and discipline.
2. Encourage students to think carefully, to use their own language, and to focus on what would be good reasons. Ask questions such as 'Why is that a reason for us to turn the lights off?' Some sample answers are given below.

We need to reduce consumption of water. We are using too much water. We need to use less.	✗ This student is not focusing on how water consumption can be achieved. Encourage them to make a specific suggestion about how the school could reduce water use. Also, the reasons here restate the problem, rather than supporting an opinion or proposal.

One way for the school to reduce energy use is to put solar panels on the roof. We live in a hot, sunny country. Making our own electricity would mean that we don't need to buy so much.	– This student has made a specific proposal, and given two reasons, but makes little connection between the points. Encourage them to explain why living in a hot sunny country means that solar panels are a good idea, and to use connecting words such as *because, therefore* and *so*. Ask the student why making electricity would reduce energy use. Encourage them also to persuade the head teacher that solar panels would be a good idea – not just one option.
The best option for our school to reduce our energy use would be to put solar panels on the roof and to have a meter in each classroom showing how we are using the energy. This is because we live in a hot sunny country, so we could generate a lot of electricity with solar panels, which are cleaner than burning oil. If we could also measure exactly how much energy we were using, this would make us more aware, and help us to use less.	✓ This is a thoughtful and ✓ focused argument that is logically structured using mini conclusions. The student has considered how the proposal would reduce energy use. Encourage them to explain why generating solar energy will help to reduce use. Ask them why being more aware of our energy use can help to reduce it. This would take the argument to the next level. Most students will not be at this level at this stage of the course but if they are, push them to develop and improve.

Activity 6

Encourage students to apply the skills they learned in chapter 2.3 (Identifying causes and consequences). Encourage them to use *because, so, this results in* and other connecting words in their explanations. Some sample answers are given below.

Climate change is the way the climate is changing. We burn fossil fuels and the weather changes.	✗ This is a weak, tautological definition of climate change, with one cause and one consequence, which are linked with *and*. It is not at all clear that the student understands the causes and consequences.
The causes of climate change include burning fossil fuels, clearing rainforests and grazing large herds of cows for meat. Burning fossil fuels causes a layer of greenhouse gases to collect in the upper atmosphere. These gases trap heat on Earth, which affects weather patterns. Mostly, this additional heat makes the planet warmer, leading to more drought, which is leading to crop failure. As a consequence, people do not have enough food.	✓ This student has made a good start. This is an explanation that names three causes, one of which is explained in more detail, with reference to how it works. A chain of consequences is identified. They have also used connecting words such as 'causes,' 'affects' and 'leading to'. Encourage them to provide more detail on the other two causes they mention.

Suggested answers: Level 3

These activities are intended as extension.

Reflection in your reasoning

Activity 7

No specific answers. Encourage students to apply their skills and to remain logical.

Activity 8

Use the most recent Cambridge mark schemes.

5.1 Reflecting on issues and perspectives

Guide to the skill

Reflection is an important part of the Global Perspectives course, so it is worth giving it class time. It is also an intensely personal process, and one that is usually quiet and internal. It can be perplexing for students who are used to constant stimuli to stop and turn inwards to consider issues, perspectives and the links between them. We can help students by:

- providing a quiet space for reflection
- helping them to develop strategies for reflection
- providing interesting material and dilemmas that promote reflection; in other words, material where there is no single, easy answer.

Try these strategies to promote reflection:

- Set students a dilemma, and give them a creative or practical task to do quietly before they discuss it. For example, students could work on a display, draw a picture, or write a story or poem.
- Have a regular, quiet 'reflection time' as part of the course.
- Include regular, short riddles, puzzles and dilemmas to break up lessons. Where there are specific answers to these activities, withhold them between lessons so that students have time to think about them. You may find these resources useful:

  - http://www.philosophyexperiments.com/
  - http://www.friesian.com/valley/dilemmas.htm
  - http://ww3.haverford.edu/psychology/ddavis/p109g/kohlberg.dilemmas.html
  - Gilbert, Ian, *The Little Book of Thunks* (Crown House Publishing, 2007)

Suggested answers: Level 1

These activities are introductory.

What is reflection?

Activity 1

No specific answers. Encourage students to take this quiz seriously.

It is worth revisiting this quiz later in the course to see how students' attitudes have changed.

Activity 2

Encourage real reflection, and debate and discussion as appropriate. Encourage students always to take their thinking one step further. This might involve unpicking the values beneath their own perspectives. It is crucial that students realise that this is about more than simply defending their initial opinion: it is about developing opinions and perspectives.

Reflection

Encourage real reflection.

Suggested answers: Level 2

These activities build on those in Level 1. It may be possible to move straight from Level 1 to Level 2; alternatively, there may be value in taking a more cyclical approach, coming back to Level 2 after some introductory work on other skills.

Activity 3

1. For example: diagrams, mind maps, stories, poems, pictures. Encourage students to find the strategies that work best for them.

2. Come back to these questions every so often. Break them down so that students only have to think about small parts of them at any one time; for example, 'How important is honesty to you?' or 'Do you want to live in a world of constant surveillance?'.

Activity 4

1. Encourage reflection. The outline answers below are suggestions only; there are many other possibilities.

   (a) If the rule of law is strong, then people are less likely to turn to crime. If there are good employment options, then people are less likely to turn to crime. If there is a lot of crime in an area, this will negatively affect legal employment, possibly driving legal employers into different areas and making it more likely that young people from that area will turn to crime.

(b) Demographic change can drive migration, transport systems make migration possible (although desperate people will try any type of transport and do not rely on existing networks), and migration, in turn, causes demographic change.

(c) Globalisation requires people around the world to gain a higher level of education in order to compete in the world economy; it also requires a different sort of education, one that prepares people to be flexible and to work with others who are different from themselves. This drives demographic change, as educated people move around the world.

(d) Globalisation includes international transport systems, especially container shipping and air traffic; container ships and air transport are extremely high users of fossil fuels, which drives climate change.

(e) Encourage students to draw their own links.

2. Encourage students to reflect and apply their skills.

Suggested answers: Level 3

These activities are intended as extension.

At this stage, you may wish students to repeat the quiz from Activity 1 (Student Book, page 66), to consider any changes in their thinking.

Activity 5

Encourage students to imagine themselves in this position as clearly as they can, and to respond as if they were experiencing the scenario in their own lives. Creative writing and drawing should help students to empathise here.

Activity 6

As students work through this activity, keep asking questions. Suggest possible problems or pitfalls and ask students how they will deal with them.

Things to note:

• No one knows which 25% of the settlers will catch the local disease; if students decide they will be one of the volunteers, they will have to consider the idea that they may be one of those who falls ill.

• For part b), the questions about government, resources, employment and economy, health care/aid, and crime are all based on an empty world. What changes if there are intelligent beings already living on the planet? Students need to think about values here. They also need to think about possible consequences. Do they need to plan for defence? It might be useful to reverse the thought experiment and consider how we would react if a group of beings from another planet came to colonise Earth.

Reflection on teamwork, outcomes and own performance

Guide to the skill

Reflecting on teamwork, on outcomes and on their own performance requires students to think about how they and their teams are working, and whether they are achieving their aims.

Suggested answers: Level 1

These activities are introductory.

Reflecting on teamwork

Activity 1

In this activity, students look at how other teams work as a stepping stone towards reflecting on their own teamwork. Encourage students to come up with their own ideas about what the problem is in each case and how to solve it. Talk them through how they can apply this process to their own teamwork.
Suggested answers:

(a) Establish why Carita and Kamal are doing all the work and why the others are doing none. Is this because Carita and Kamal have taken over and prefer not to involve other - perhaps weaker or shyer – team members? Are Carita and Kamal afraid of poor grades if the work is not all done to their usual high standards? If so, how can Carita and Kamal be persuaded to work as part of a bigger team? Alternatively, are Carita and Kamal doing all the work because the others are not interested? How can they be encouraged to take an interest? Would it help to assign roles with clear responsibilities?

(b) This team needs to plan and organise their work so that they avoid doubling up. It would make sense for each team member to research a different area of fuel and energy.

(c) This team needs to assign clear responsibilities. It needs a single leader. The members need to listen to one another and be prepared to cooperate.

Reflecting on outcomes

Activity 2

Encourage students to work with Cambridge's assessment requirements to see if the outcomes here would fit the requirements. Encourage them to judge whether the outcomes are as intended.

Team	
A	Not fully successful, as the aim was to raise awareness of a charity and to donate money. The success of the concert is good, but the concert was supposed to be the means of raising awareness, not an aim in itself, and the charity poster went unnoticed.
B	Unsuccessful. Both the aim and outcome are unspecific and neither is in line with assessment requirements. There is no value at all in copying and pasting information, especially if you do so without reading it.
C	Successful, as far as we can tell. There is no information on the quality of the plan or on how realistic it was, so we cannot judge this aspect. However, this team have done what they set out to do, and it is possible the head teacher will approve the plan.
D	Unsuccessful. The aim and outcome both need to be developed in line with assessment requirements, to allow for actions, for an issue to be resolved and for examination of cultural perspectives. The actual outcome is very limited, showing lack of effort.

Activity 3

Reflection on their own performance and on their teamwork needs to be an ongoing process for students. It is also part of the assessment, so it is important that students get into the habit of asking themselves these questions, and thinking about how to change what they do in the light of their reflection.

Suggested answers: Level 2

Activity 4

Encourage students to apply their skills. This activity can be done multiple times as a way of helping students to reflect and improve.

Suggested answers: Level 3

Reflection

This activity involves reflecting on reflection on teamwork. Some students may need help differentiating between reflection on their teamwork and reflecting on that reflection.

5.3 Reflect on personal learning

Guide to the skill

Reflecting on their own learning is a new skill for many students. It involves thinking about what kinds of learning they are engaging in, what learning strategies they are using, which of these strategies are effective for them, how they feel about their learning, what is stopping them from learning more effectively, and how they can improve their learning.

Many students will be inclined simply to describe their lessons and what they have learned. Encourage them to move on to thinking about:

- how they have learned
- how they can learn better
- why what they have learned matters.

As with other forms of reflection, the skill needs to be practised often, and it is important to encourage students gradually to deepen their reflection, providing justifications. Keeping a learning log, in which students write down their reflections and you respond, can be very useful. Avoid responses that judge; instead, ask further questions and expect responses. Useful questions can include:

- Why was this difficult for you?
- Why do you feel like this?
- What *exactly* do you think you can do to improve here?

Suggested answers: Level 1

These activities are introductory.

Activity 1

Give students class time to work on their learning log. Try to use the log to engage them in a dialogue about their learning. Avoid 'marking' the work, or judging it, as students are unlikely to open up and reflect honestly if you do. Instead, respond to their thoughts, guiding them to find their own solutions.

It is likely that a learning log will include reflection on perspectives and issues as well as reflection on personal learning. This is acceptable, as it is an important way in which students can develop their personal perspectives. However, it is important that students also reflect on *how* they are learning, as this is one of the most important tools for improving performance.

Suggested answers: Level 2

These activities build on those in Level 1. It may be possible to move straight from Level 1 to Level 2; alternatively, there may be value in taking a more cyclical approach, coming back to Level 2 after some introductory work on other skills.

Activity 2

This activity is intended to come later in the course rather than directly after Activity 1. It is intended to prompt ongoing reflective learning as well as a review of progress.

Encourage the student first to find their own solutions using available resources, or to work with friends to find a solution. When a student identifies an area with which they really need your help, try to respond individually. This may involve providing an exercise to help them practise a skill they struggle with, or finding time to talk to them individually while other students are engaged in research.

Suggested answers: Level 3

These activities are intended as extension.

Activity 3

This activity is intended to come later in the course rather than directly after Activity 2. It raises the level of demand, preparing students for the kinds of thinking that will help them to score highly in the assessment. This will be useful for students developing their personal perspectives in the Individual Report. Together with the skills they have developed in Section 5.2 (Reflection on teamwork, outcomes and own performance), this will help students with their individual reflection for the Team Project.

Reflection

This activity involves reflecting on reflection on personal learning. Just like any other skill, reflection can be improved by thinking about it. Some students may need help differentiating between reflection on personal learning, and reflection on that reflection.

6.1 Planning a project

Guide to the skill

The key to this skill is to focus on the planning rather than on the content of the project. The content of the project is also important, of course, but the skill of planning involves:

- setting an appropriate aim and identifying an outcome
- identifying tasks that need to be done
- scheduling tasks
- reviewing progress
- amending schedules
- carrying out tasks
- evaluating the project.

Note that planning a project is very different from planning the content of an essay or presentation.

Suggested answers: Level 1

These activities are introductory.

Activity 1

1. Encourage students to think for themselves and to justify their views. Note that this activity does not ask students to think about whether these projects meet assessment requirements, but ultimately they will have to consider this too.

Outcome	Specific	Measurable	Achievable	Realistic	Time Bound	Can this be improved to be SMART?
(a)	N	N	N	N	N	N
(b)	Y	Y (You can measure whether a video is produced)	Y	Y	N	Y (Set a deadline)
(c)	N	N	N	N	N	N
(d)	Y	Y (You can measure whether a song is written)	Y (For musical, creative students)	Y	Y (The school event provides a deadline)	—
(e)	Y	Y	Y	Y	Y (Once a week)	—

2. Encourage students to think of a range of possibilities and to use grids to evaluate them against the SMART criteria.

Activity 2

1. Encourage students to work more independently.

Outcome	Specific	Measurable	Achievable	Realistic	Time Bound	Can this be improved to be SMART?
(a)	N	N	N	N	N	N
(b)	Y	Y (You can measure sending the letter, but not its effects)	Y	Y	N	Y (Set a deadline)
(c)	Y	Y	Y	Y	Y (For a month)	—
(d)	N	Y	Y	Y	N	Y (Specify the topic, set a deadline)
(e)	Y	Y	Y	Y	N	Y (Set a deadline)

Mini project plan

Activity 3

1. It is useful for students to complete a trial project management activity to help them focus on the planning processes without the pressure of assessment. Encourage students to work as independently as possible, to think about who is doing what and when, and in what order.

2. Encourage students to be independent.

3. Encourage students to give careful thought to how the event went. Students are sometimes inclined to be excessively positive or excessively negative; generally speaking, they will need to evaluate both positive and negative aspects. They will also need to use their criticisms to feed into and improve the next project they organise.

Reflection

Reflection is an important part of the course. Allow students sufficient time to reflect.

When students are doing assessed projects, they often make comments such as 'I was waiting for another student to complete their tasks before I could do mine. This was frustrating'. With this in mind, it is useful for students to think in advance about which tasks depend on others having been completed. Students can then make sure that everyone is aware of where their tasks sit in the overall project, and that their scheduling takes these dependencies into consideration.

For example, it would be unwise to buy food and drink for a party before you have sent the invitations and received responses, as you would not know how much to buy. It would also be rash to concentrate on the kind of music you will play and leave money-raising activities to the last minute.

Suggested answers: Level 2

These activities build on those in Level 1. It may be possible to move straight from Level 1 to Level 2; alternatively, there may be value in taking a more cyclical approach, coming back to Level 2 after some introductory work on other skills.

Choosing an action/outcome

Activity 4

1. Some outline answers are suggested below. Students should, of course, come up with and be rewarded for their own ideas. Note that, although students should submit a project plan, this is not evidence that a project has been carried out.

Cleaning a local river, together with members of the community	**(a)** This does involve an issue, assuming that the river does in fact need to be cleaned. It is an action rather than an essay. Dirty rivers and the question of who is (or should be) responsible for cleaning them do raise issues that could be explored in background research. It is likely that there will be different cultural perspectives within the community on issues such as whose responsibility it is to keep the rivers clean. **(b)** Research might include the causes of dirty rivers, such as individuals throwing rubbish away, commercial waste and sewage, and so on. It could include the consequences of dirty rivers, such as ugly neighbourhoods, dirty drinking water and health

issues. The action could be physically cleaning rubbish from a part of the river, campaigning with a community group to get companies to stop polluting it or to get local government to take action.

(c) Evidence could include photographs or videos of students joining in with physical cleaning, photographs of students and community members meeting local business leaders or local government members, or copies of emails or letters sent.

Organising a project to vaccinate children in a village in Malawi	This is probably not realistic for a group of students (unless, possibly, the students are organizing the project in their own village, which changes the challenge by making it much less remote).
Raising funds to support a charity that vaccinates children in Malawi	**(a)** This deals with an issue or problem, involves action, requires background research and there are different cultural perspectives. **(b)** Research might include the causes of disease, the uses and costs of vaccines, the benefits and consequences of vaccination, the barriers to vaccination, and the issues underlying this kind of charity work. The action would be undertaken in order to raise funds. **(c)** Evidence could include photographs of students engaging in fund raising activities, financial records, comments from donors, or a letter or email from the charity in thanks for the donation.

▶

Make a poster about poverty	This is too vague and is a task that would simply involve writing what you know about a topic. The topic needs to be narrowed down, an issue chosen, and an action decided upon.
Produce a video campaigning for or against a local hospital project	**(a)** This is specific, involves issues and actions, and has a decision that needs to be made. There are likely to be different cultural perspectives. **(b)** Background research could include the perceived need for the project and its causes, the reasons why people oppose or support it, and its possible consequences. **(c)** Evidence would include the video itself and could also include photographs of the video being shot, as well as emails and correspondence with various interested parties.
Make a poster to publicise a local sporting event	This does not deal with an issue or require background research, and different cultural perspectives are likely to be limited (unless the sporting event is something like a bullfight, in which case making a poster to publicise it is a rather limited action to take). Making a poster is not really a sufficient action. Whilst designing a poster on a suitable software package and organizing for it to be printed and distributed requires some planning skills, a hand drawn poster does not.
Write a research report on urbanisation	This is not appropriate. It involves writing an essay/report rather than taking action, there is no issue or problem to resolve, and the topic is far too general.

Project planning process

Activity 5

There are no specific answers; encourage groups to think of their own. Suggestions include:

(a) It could be themed. The publicity could draw attention to the issue.

(b) Publicity material such as posters could refer to the issue with large type and images; posters could be displayed both at the entrance and inside the concert venue. A DJ or presenter could mention the issue between musical items. There could be one or more short videos relating to the issue between musical items. People who are affected by the issue could talk between musical items. There could be people on the doors and inside the venue collecting money to support the issue.

(c) Use questions to prompt students to think of things they have forgotten.

(d) Use questions to prompt students to think of tasks they have forgotten.

(e) Encourage students to think about necessary sequences of events and encourage them to use Gantt charts (http://www.gantt.com/).

Suggested answers: Level 3

These activities are intended as extension.

Planning and evaluating project work

Activity 6

1. Encourage students to remember this acronym, with which they should now be familiar: Specific, Measurable, Achievable, Realistic, Time Bound.

2. Encourage students to remember as much as possible before they check. The more familiar students are with these stages, the more likely they are to organise a strong project.

3. This activity should help students to think about what sort of evidence they will need to keep when they are managing their assessed project. It will also help to refocus them on the need to keep records of the project management process as well as of the project itself.

   (a) For example: a project plan, including a list of tasks; a schedule; a Gantt chart; minutes of meetings and discussions; a record of amendments to the original plan.

(b) For example: the playscript; photos of the performance; copies of publicity materials; financial records; correspondence with the centre; photos of students at the centre handing the donation over.

Activity 7

1. Encourage students to apply the skills they have learned to their own project, and to use the resources and guidelines in the student book to help them.

Activity 8

1. Encourage students to think carefully about how to improve. Some suggestions for answers to part d) are given below.

Make a film about the traditions of an immigrant group in your country.	This could end up being descriptive rather than dealing with an issue or a problem that needs to be resolved. However, it could be improved to deal with an issue; for example, the need for different immigrant groups to understand each other in order to avoid conflict. A film is a large-scale undertaking; a short video would be more appropriate.
Learn a language.	This is too broad, too vague and is not related to an issue or problem that needs to be resolved.
Work with a group of students from another country to investigate how language, culture and identity are linked, by learning a bit of each other's languages and considering important aspects of culture and identity.	This is rather vague and has no active outcome. There would need to be a video or some similar active outcome. However, the general plan has potential.

Visit a refugee camp and report back to other students and parents.	This depends on where you live. If you are near a refugee camp, and it is safe to enter, this could be the beginning of a very interesting project. At the moment, it is too vague and there is no real aim or outcome. It would be necessary to define a much more focused purpose.

Reflection

Reflection is an important part of the course. Allow students sufficient time to reflect.

6.2 Teamwork and individual effort

Guide to the skill

Teamwork is one of the skills that employers value the most in young people. It includes the following skills:

- Listening to others
- Trusting others in the team
- Communicating in a range of ways
- Negotiating and compromising
- Encouraging, motivating and inspiring others
- Advising others tactfully
- Influencing and leading
- Knowing when not to lead.

Becoming aware of these skills, and knowing that they are assessed on how well they work together, can help students to improve.

Practice is also important. There are a range of active teamwork games available online, such as here: http://wilderdom.com/games/InitiativeGames.html. Games like these need to be used with focus, though, and in conjunction with reflective activities to ensure that the right lessons are learned from them and that these lessons can be applied to future teamwork.

Suggested answers: Level 1

Activity 1

Encourage students to come to their own conclusions about teamwork, planning and leadership based on these activities. Discourage personal comments or discussion about the tasks per se.

Suggested answers: Level 2

Activity 2

1. Encourage students to work as a team to answer the questions.

Suggested answers: Level 3

Activity 3

1. Encourage students to come up with a variety of possible solutions and to negotiate the best possible solution. Try to feed back on their teamwork rather than on their answers; it may be necessary to prompt them with questions. The answers below are suggestions only.

(a) Talk to Bik. Point out that the Team Project is assessed and also an important part of Bik's course. The team leader will need to consider when to involve the teacher, but ideally the team will find their own solution.

(b) Keep calm! Suggest that Cara looks in the library and phones the bus company. Check if anyone has recent backups of their work. Reschedule: discuss the issue with the teacher if it is necessary to alter the final deadline. Plan to keep a backup of everything in future.

(c) Talk to them and emphasise that they are getting marks for their willingness to listen, negotiate and compromise. Use strategies such as the 'talking spoon' to allow all team members to have the chance to speak.

2. Encourage students to come up with a variety of possible solutions and to negotiate the best one.

(a) Talk to the team leader. Talk to the other team members; perhaps you are mistaken about no one else caring. Perhaps you dominated the early discussions and the others are not engaged in the project that you decided on. Be prepared to listen as well as talk.

(b) Talk to her. Offer to help. Explain how you feel in a positive way.

(c) You may need to talk less. Make sure that you listen to others' ideas and give them constructive feedback (not just negative criticism). Alternatively, are people not listening because you are too quiet and they do not know you have ideas to contribute?

(d) Why do you hate the project? Could you become more interested if you made an effort? You may have to overcome your feelings.

3. Planning, and listening to one another in the early stages of team building and planning.

Activity 4

Encourage students to think carefully, to justify their ideas and to express their opinions sensitively.

Activity 5

Encourage students to think carefully and to focus on solutions rather than on the problems.

⑦ Select evidence and present research

Guide to the skill

Selecting evidence is a vital skill for students to develop. They are often inclined to want to present *all* the information that they have found, whether or not it is relevant. It is important for students to ask themselves these questions:

- Will this help me answer the question?
- Is it relevant?
- Could I use it later in another piece of work, even if I can't use it here?

The skill of presenting research is closely related to the skill of developing a line of reasoning, but it also includes writing in clear English and meeting the assessment criteria. This section should therefore be used in conjunction with Section 4 (Developing a line of reasoning).

In terms of the assessment of Global Perspectives, presenting research includes writing the Individual Report. It is also relevant to the Explanation and the Reflective Paper for the Team Project, as both of these elements include the presentation of research.

Suggested answers: Level 1

These activities are introductory.

Select evidence

Activity 1

This activity can be used with every piece of research that students undertake.

Clear English

Activity 2

1. Encourage students to use their own language, and to make an effort to complete the activity. Even a partial attempt is good, and can lead to increased confidence and a greater willingness to try. As with the other skills in this section, the important thing is that students gain the confidence to try. The following answers are suggestions only.

(a) Having lots of cheap natural gas will make us use more gas, which will make climate change worse. What we need to do is stop carbon emissions completely.

(b) Growing populations, climate change and pollution make water scarcity worse. There ought to be enough water for everyone.

(c) (Water) scarcity is not the main cause of violence. Conflict is actually caused by several things, including inequality.

Presenting your research

Activity 3

When giving feedback on this activity, focus on how well students have:

- selected relevant information, ideas and arguments
- used their own, clear English to express ideas
- structured their ideas
- referenced their sources

Suggested answers: Level 2

These activities build on those in Level 1. It may be possible to move straight from Level 1 to Level 2; alternatively, there may be value in taking a more cyclical approach, coming back to Level 2 after some introductory work on other skills.

Organising thoughts into a line of reasoning

Activity 4

Encourage students to give reasons that really move the debate on, evidence that is properly supportive of the reasons, and to think about a logical structure and the meaning. It is better to have one good reason that really supports the conclusion than to have lots of unrelated information that is arranged without logic or meaning. Some sample answers are given below.

Reason: We need a new airport. Evidence: There isn't an airport. Mini conclusion: I think an airport would be good so we don't have to drive two hours before we fly on holiday. Conclusion: We should build a new airport here.	✗ This student has tried, but has not managed to make logical links or to move the discussion on. Ask them why we need an airport. Is it just for holidays? Does 'We need a new airport' really give us a reason to believe that 'an airport would be good'? Why should the airport be here and not in the neighbouring city?
We have a lot of international trade and business here, but the airport has only one runway so we can't land enough aeroplanes. Also, it was built in the 1960s, so it is dingy, ugly and not suited to the needs of the 21st-century traveller. So we should build a new airport here. Reason: Trade and business; only one runway. Mini conclusion: Can't land enough aeroplanes. Reason: It was built in the 1960s. Mini conclusion: It is dingy, ugly and not suited to the needs of the 21st-century traveler. Conclusion: We should build a new airport here.	✓ This is a well-structured line of reasoning, with good use of mini conclusions; the ideas are also linked well, with 'so' and 'also'. Encourage this student to research some precise information about the trade and business, and the number of aeroplanes needed versus the number that can land. Evidence on its own is not always good, but the right evidence, well used, can improve an argument. This student could also think about why the airport should be here and not in a different place. That would give another line of reasoning.

Activity 5

Encourage students to check their research as objectively as possible. One strategy would be to use different colours to underline each different aspect. For example, causes and consequences could be underlined in red, while perspectives might be underlined in green, and linking words such as *so*, *because* and *therefore* in blue.

Where appropriate, use peer assessment. This works most effectively when students are giving advice and feedback for improvement, rather than when they are giving marks or passing judgement.

Suggested activities: Level 3

These activities are intended as extension.

Causes, consequences, possible solutions

Activity 6

Encourage students to apply their skills and to see the value of improving draft work.

Activity 7

Encourage students to give reasons that really move the argument on, to use evidence and examples that are realistic and relevant, and to present different perspectives and opinions thoughtfully.

Download the most recent Cambridge mark schemes, and encourage student to use these mark schemes to assess and improve their own work.

It may be useful to do one or two of these options as timed essays, as if they were practice examination papers rather than practice Individual Reports.

Activity 8

Encourage students to apply their skills to make positive improvements to the work. Make sure that they think about what they have done to improve it and that they are ready to apply this learning to the next piece of work they do.

Reflection

Reflection is an important part of the course. Allow students have sufficient time to reflect.

Conflict and peace

Introduction

What causes conflicts? How should we deal with the consequences of conflicts? How do we bring about peace? In an increasingly populated, increasingly globalised world, these are some of the fundamental questions of our time. Actions in one country have an effect on countries around the world. Climate change is already contributing to shortages of food and water, which in turn can exacerbate existing conflicts and may even spark new ones.

Underlying their project work, students should have an awareness of the key issues relating to conflict and peace, but their knowledge in this area is not being tested in itself. Projects can focus on any area of conflict and peace, including specific conflicts, the role of the UN, the morality of war, conflict resolution or how to deal with refugees from war-torn areas, as long as there is an active outcome and there are cross-cultural perspectives. Throughout the Team Project sections, information is provided on some of the cultural perspectives embedded within the documents. This is to a great extent information based on glimpses of a cultural perspective – a single openly expressed belief, or an unstated belief or a choice of words which betrays a (subconscious) belief, which could form part of a cultural perspective. Teasing out these glimpses is a different activity from deliberately researching the beliefs of a particular group of people from a particular cultural perspective. Nevertheless, it is good practice.

Suggested resources

http://www.un.org/en/peacekeeping/	A United Nations page with links to a number of relevant issues related to peacekeeping.
http://www.unwomen.org/en/what-we-do/peace-and-security/conflict-prevention-and-resolution	A United Nations page relating to the role of women in conflict prevention and resolution.
http://www.unv.org/what-we-do/thematic-areas/peace-conflict-resolution.html	A United Nations page giving examples of the role volunteers can play in peacekeeping and conflict resolution.
http://www.nature.com/news/conflict-resolution-wars-without-end-1.17070	A complex but interesting article on conflicts as complex systems. Some students may be able to skim read this for relevant material, but others may need the central ideas simplified for them.
http://www.bbc.co.uk/news/world-middle-east-26116868	A clear account from a British perspective, which aims to be objective, of the causes of, and events in, the conflict in Syria.
https://www.worldwatchmonitor.org/	WorldWatch Monitor reports the story of Christians around the world under pressure as a result of their faith. It has a clear perspective that should be taken into consideration.
http://www.islamic-relief.org.uk/	Islamic Relief UK is an independent NGO underpinned by Islamic faith. It has a clear perspective that should be taken into consideration.
https://www.amnesty.org.uk/syria-turn-lights-back-0#.Vo0zHvmLSbg	Amnesty International is a charity organisation focusing on human rights. In this article, the charity is petitioning about lights in Syria; the graphic is interesting. Other parts of the Amnesty International website are also useful.
http://www.thestar.com/opinion/commentary/2014/08/11/international_law_should_give_both_sides_pause_in_israelpalestine_conflict.html	*The Star* is a good quality Canadian newspaper. This article is fairly complex, but many students should be able to skim read it for key information.

Suggested answers to the activities

Activity 1

1. Encourage students to read the comments for gist rather than worrying about the detail of the complex language. They are looking only for issues. The following are suggestions only. As long as students can justify their answers, other answers are acceptable.

   (a) Conflict resolution, solutions for peace

   (b) Causes of conflict, the case for war

   (c) Causes of conflict, conflict resolution

   (d) Causes of conflict, paths to peace

   (e) The case for war, role of individuals, nations and NGOs in conflict

2. Suggested answers (others are possible if they can be justified):

   (a) This comes from the UN's own perspective, and this is made up of the cultural perspectives of people who are well educated, who believe in the UN's work as a force for good in the world and who generally take a global perspective. There are alternative cultural perspectives which regard the UN as a bad thing – as anti-democratic, interfering, over-bureaucratic, meddling in national affairs etc.

   (b) This is a personal perspective rooted in a cultural perspective which believes that it is acceptable / realistic / useful / right to respond to terrorism with war (as opposed to other ways of opposing or dealing with terrorism). This is a particular kind of rhetoric made popular in the US and Europe after the 2001 terror attacks in America.

   (c) No specific cultural perspective – attempting to be objective. This might imply an educated or academic cultural perspective.

   (d) What sort of cultural perspective this is depends on who 'we' are. This could be a perspective based on fear, worry or concern about predicted conflict in the speaker's own area. But it is also the kind of thing that people in the West might say with reference to less economically developed countries, and that would rest on the belief that 'we' have the right or duty to do something about problems even if they do not affect our nation or us personally. This might be a colonial or neo-colonial perspective based on power politics, or it might be a perspective based on religion or charity.

   (e) This particular cultural perspective is academic, educated and cynical.

3. Encourage debate and discussion.

Activity 2

1. Encourage discussion.

2. Note that dictionary skills – whether the dictionaries are online or in print – are invaluable, while online translation tools can deskill students and tend to provide poor translations. Suggestions are given below, but encourage students to consider a range of definitions.

Conflict	A serious disagreement or argument; a battle or war.
Peace	Quiet, tranquillity; the absence of war; an agreement or treaty leading to the end of a conflict.
Resolution	The action of solving a dispute or contentious matter.
Peacekeeping	Keeping peace, often using military force to keep a treaty or agreement between two nations in conflict.
Moral ideals	Beliefs about how the world should be. Justice is an example of a moral ideal.
National security	The idea that governments should defend the nation; a term for the defence of a nation against threats. In the USA, the term is also used to refer to international relations.
War	Armed, hostile conflict between groups, nations or states.
The United Nations	An international organisation, with its headquarters in New York, formed in 1945 to promote international peace, security and economic development. Most countries in the world are members of the United Nations.

Activity 3

Encourage students to think, discuss and work together to extend their understanding.

Note that each of the perspectives mentioned is highly complex, and most of them are only glimpsed in the documents. It would be necessary to find out much more to have a full understanding. But we can ask questions and do research to help ourselves understand these perspectives.

Encourage students to approach cultural perspectives by asking questions such as:

- What beliefs do these people share?
- What does this cultural perspective value most highly?
- Where do their beliefs come from?
- How do these people see the world?
- How do these people understand their place in the world?

Document 1

This is rooted in cultural beliefs about democracy, and its value. These beliefs have their roots in the European Enlightenment which privileged the equality of all men and the value of reason. (It is worth noting that, in Autumn 2015, the UK parliament voted in favour of air strikes in Syria. This does not change the moral value of the air strikes themselves, but does mean that the decision to make them was made democratically).

Document 3

There are a number of different cultural perspectives present in this document – although not all have the same voice. There is the cultural perspective of the traditional tribes – seen thorugh the belief that land is common to all and not something which can be owned and passed down as an inheritance within a single family.

The settlers – former slaves – had absorbed cultural beliefs and practices from the US. They did believe that land could be owned, and believed in the need for laws and a written constitution – written down by them, favouring them, and taking priority over the unwritten agreements of the traditional tribes.

We get a glimpse of the cultural perspective of a ruling elite which sees personal gain and luxury as of prime value and certainly more important that the benefit of the people. This is a cultural perspective shared by ruling elites around the world and across the ages – this land / estate / country is mine to benefit from and I am entitled to all that it produces. Others – inferior people – are there to serve me.

We get a glimpse of the cultural perspective of child soldiers – young people who cannot remember peace and whose belief systems have been formed by war, atrocity and violence.

Document 4

Written from the cultural perspective of someone who believes that we shoud find ways to address the negative consequences of our consumer decisions. We see a glimpse of the cultural perspective of those who use mineral resources to fund war – are these cynical people, idealists chasing a dream? We can't tell.

Activity 4

Encourage students to think and debate. You may wish to use the suggestions below to provoke discussion.

1. Although the image of conflict resolution is labelled as successful, this is clearly intended for humorous effect. However, the cartoon does raise some serious issues. Who is affected by the conflict? Are there children, friends or neighbours who might suffer the consequences? It raises questions about the way in which we might describe a resolution as successful, despite the evidence. It also asks us to consider the people who might be involved in conflict resolution. Who has been trying to resolve this conflict? The two people involved or a third party?

2. The cartoon shows a personal perspective with an individual conflict, however the issues could be applied to nations in conflict, and to the international consequences. Think about attempts by senior figures from around the world trying to broker peace in Gaza, Syria, Northern Ireland and other conflict zones. How effective can third party conflict resolution be if the main participants are not fully engaged with or committed to the process?

Activity 5

Encourage students to think and debate. You may wish to use the suggestions below to provoke discussion.

1. Should nations such as the UK, the USA or Russia become involved in conflicts in other areas of the world? Is it ever acceptable to use force against nations that are not directly attacking your nation? Is joining a fight likely to be an effective way of finishing the fight, or is this more likely to escalate the conflict, making it more complicated and longer lasting?

2. A democratic parliament voted against sending troops Syria, but troops from that country have been engaged in warfare there. Should anything override this kind of a democratic vote? If so, what?

3. Encourage discussion.

Activity 6

1. [9]

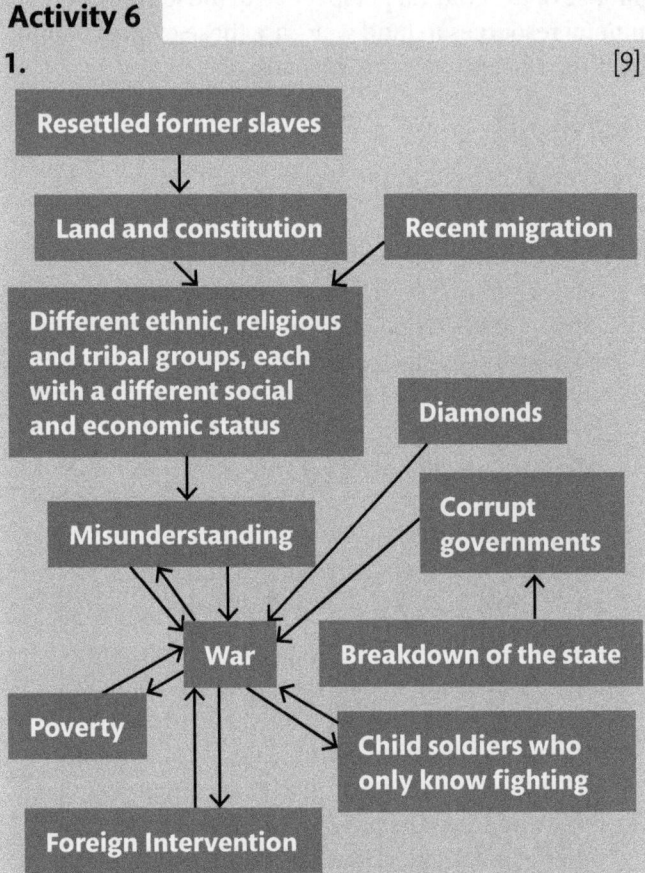

Resettled former slaves → Land and constitution → Different ethnic, religious and tribal groups, each with a different social and economic status

Recent migration → Different ethnic, religious and tribal groups

Different ethnic, religious and tribal groups → Misunderstanding

Diamonds → Corrupt governments

Misunderstanding ↔ War

War ↔ Breakdown of the state

Corrupt governments → Breakdown of the state

Poverty ↔ War

War ↔ Child soldiers who only know fighting

War ↔ Foreign Intervention

2. (a) Evidence could be gathered by: sending people – journalists, doctors, charity workers, academics, teachers, etc. – to assess the situation; talk to the people; reading newspapers; looking on the internet – at blogs and photos, and on social media sites.

(b) The situation in Liberia is extremely complex. Anyone you send would only have a view of part of the situation, so you would need to piece together the whole picture. Each individual you send or talk to would have their own perspective, and in a war situation this can be very emotional and detached from reality. People may have emotional reasons to lie about their own guilt, and to present the other side as worse than it is. Anyone in a war zone may also be in physical danger. Religious beliefs and disagreements can confuse the picture, too. Communications are difficult in war zones, and post, internet, phones, etc. may not be working. Anything online could be unreliable because of bias, the need to conceal the truth, emotional involvement, etc. Newspaper content might be censored or funded by one side or another.

3. (a) The refugee would have escaped from a threatening and frightening situation. This person would have personal knowledge, but would not have seen the whole picture. They are a first-hand witness, but this does not make them reliable. This person will also have emotional attachments and a bias towards one group: what would bring a successful peace for this person may be a disaster for others. So this person's answers are emotive and therefore not fully reliable.

(b) The refugee limits the options. The claim 'The only way . . .' is a very strong one but it is not supported here. It seems inconsistent to say that the only way to bring peace is to fund weapons, especially nuclear weapons. Furthermore, having been to a place is not the same as having a clear understanding of a complex situation with all its causes and consequences. As a result, the refugee's reasoning does not seem very logical.

Activity 7

1. Key issues: minerals such as tantalum – used in electronic devices – fund conflict and human rights abuses.

Consequences: Congo is poor because of this conflict, despite having great mineral wealth.

Different perspectives: child soldier, rebels, US lawmakers and corporate leaders, purchasers.

Possible courses of action: reduce the reliance of the electronics/technology industries on conflict tantalum.

2. Encourage research, debate and discussion. Diamonds are thought to be a luxury jewellery item, but in fact they are used in many technological applications. Diamond can be increasingly cheaply synthesised but many of these processes use diamond grit as a source of carbon. Tantalum is not yet commercially synthesised.

Activity 8

1. Encourage students to research the issues that may affect each individual. Answers will vary. Suggested answers:

A politician in Ethiopia: There has been conflict in Ethiopia, which a politician will have to manage. There is conflict in Sudan, a neighbouring country, which sometimes threatens Ethiopia, and there are many Sudanese refugees in Ethiopia. A politician will need to manage the demands these refugees place on a poor nation. There is also simmering conflict. As the populations grow and as demands on the available water grow, this conflict will need to be managed.

School student: A range of conflicts with other individuals, conflicts with parents, conflicts with teachers. Some students may be in conflict about whether they can continue to study; other young people may not have the chance to go to school because they are involved in armed conflict as child soldiers.

Syrian child: Children in Syria are likely to be living in fear, dealing with bombing, fighting and regular loss of family and friends. The conflict has destroyed the country's infrastructure, affecting health care, closing schools and cutting off power supplies. Many Syrian children are (at the time of writing) refugees: they have lost their homes and maybe their families. Some have been sent away on their own to try to get to safety, which can make them vulnerable to abuse and other forms of conflict.

Toddler in Glasgow: Conflict with, and possibly conflict between, parents; occasionally conflict over toys with other children. Scotland is (in 2015) still divided about whether it should become independent from the UK, which might affect the child. Glasgow has some fairly poor socio-economic conditions, which may lead to conflicts – but, overall, this toddler is fairly lucky.

Business leader in Washington DC: Conflict over how much tax to pay to the government. Conflicts around the world may affect the business, and affect business decisions.

2. and **3.** Encourage debate and discussion. Answers will vary. In 2. encourage students to research and discuss factors that could affect cultural perspectives – that is, beliefs shared by groups of people. Discuss also how these factors could affect the beliefs. For instance, a Syrian child is likely to be a Muslim, they are likely to have lost a family member, and may well have lost their home. They may currently want people to stop bombing them, want lost loved ones to come back, want an education – all of these may be combining with beliefs learned from those around them to form a cultural perspective formed in pain.

Activity 9

1. to **6.** Encourage students to apply their skills, and to set up their lines of enquiry carefully.

Activity 10

1. and **2.** Answers will vary. Encourage students to think carefully about what is likely and what is not. Encourage students to discuss different cultural beliefs that underlie different perspectives.

Activity 11

Encourage discussion, and encourage students to think carefully about the most likely consequences.

Reflection 12

Reflection is an important part of the course, so it is important to allow class time for this activity. It may be useful to use a learning journal, as this might allow for some ongoing written dialogue about the issues. The key here is to avoid simple praise or giving a student's thoughts a value; instead, try to engage a student in discussion over time and include questions in your written response that will push the student to the next level, and expect them to respond.

Reflection 13

Encourage students to think carefully and to take this activity seriously, as this kind of reflection is an important part of the assessment.

② Disease and health

Introduction

In the West, we tend to take good health and good healthcare for granted, blaming ill health on the poor choices we make as individuals. However, there are many places in the world where good health is not a matter of lifestyle choices, but the result of forces beyond an individual's control.

Underlying their project work, students should have an awareness of the key issues relating to disease and health, but their knowledge in this area is not being tested in itself. Projects can focus on any area of disease and health, including specific health challenges, questions about who should pay for healthcare, the division between rich and poor, issues relating to who should take responsibility for an individual's health, or specific projects to improve health, as long as there is an active outcome and there are cross-cultural perspectives.

Suggested resources

http://science. howstuffworks.com	The Discovery channel includes a number of short videos on medical health and related issues.
http://www. redcrossblood.org/ donating-blood/donor-zone/games/blood-type	A game relating to blood type and blood donation.
http://www.newyorker. com/tech/elements/ the-moral-dilemmas-of-doctors-during-disaster	An article discussing the moral dilemmas for doctors during disaster.
http://www.unicef.org/ malaysia/campaigns_wffc. html	A Unicef page with information on campaigns in Malaysia.
http://www.ready.gov/ kids/games/data/dm-english/wildfire.html	Health-related games.
http://www.nlm.nih.gov/ medlineplus/games.html	Health-related games.
http://www.livescience. com/health/	A range of articles related to disease and health.

http://kidshealth.org/teen/ diseases_conditions/	Information about many of the diseases and health conditions that can affect teenagers. The page is aimed directly at teenagers, so the language and concepts are accessible.
http://www.nejm.org/ infectious-disease	The material on this site is challenging, but it offers a great deal of relevant information. Many students may be able to isolate relevant facts and statistics, even though they may not understand the whole.

Suggested answers to the activities

Activity 1

1. Encourage students to read the comments for gist rather than worrying about the detail of the complex language. They are looking only for issues. The following are suggestions only. As long as students can justify their answers, other answers are acceptable.

   (a) Equality, access to healthcare

   (b) Health effects of lifestyle choices, funding healthcare, whose responsibility is health?

   (c) Health and economic development

   (d) Preventative healthcare, whose responsibility is health?

   (e) Equality, access to healthcare, effects of poor health, funding healthcare

   (f) Funding healthcare, whose responsibility is healthcare?

2. Suggested answers (others are possible if they can be justified):

(a) This seems to be part of a dominant bureaucratic perspective which believes that statistical information is valuable and which prioritises information that can be expressed statistically. A counter to this perspective would be an anti-bureaucratic perspective which holds that many of the most important aspects of life cannot be measured or expressed as statistics.

(b) This is part of a cultural perspective found in the UK (and probably other Western nations) which passes people the blame for their health issues. It is part of a culture of blame, although it often expresses itself in terms of responsibility. It is linked to tabloid and semi-tabloid newspapers such as the *Daily Mail*. This perspective is not always well thought through – people in the UK who choose to smoke or drink tend to pay more tax so they do contribute more to their healthcare. Furthermore, it is hard to know where to draw the line – although not exercising is unhealthy, exercise can lead to injury and the need for healthcare.

(c) From a transnational global organisation – the cultural perspective will be educated, global but (probably) Western dominated, bureaucratic and data driven.

(d) It is hard to know exactly what the cultural perspective is – this could be 'Outraged of Tunbridge Wells' – a cultural figure who writes to newspapers to express outrage (and who exists in one form or another in many cultures). Alternatively, this could be a medical doctor coming from a cultural perspective of education, information, making decisions on the basis of facts.

(e) This is from a cultural background in which it is normal to pay healthcare bills rather than having universal access to healthcare which is free at the point of use. There is a cultural perspective relating to frustration with inequality and lack of opportunity.

(f) As e. but with a different specific opinion. It expresses the belief that your health is your own responsibility.

3. Encourage discussion and debate, and let students know that they are free to follow their own interests.

Activity 2

Note that dictionary skills – whether the dictionaries are online or in print – are invaluable, while online translation tools can de-skill students and tend to provide poor translations. Suggestions are given below, but encourage students to consider a range of definitions.

Preventative healthcare	Measures taken to prevent disease, rather than treating it.
Measles	An infectious, viral disease causing fever and a red rash, usually in children. It can be fatal, but can usually be prevented by a vaccine.
National Health Service	A health service in the UK that is funded through tax payments and is free at the point of use. This kind of health service is known as a Universal Health Service.
Vaccination	Inoculation with a mild form of a disease to prevent a serious form of the same disease.
Lifestyle choice	A choice a person makes about how to live and behave.
Malaria	An infectious disease characterized by cycles of chills, fever, and sweating. It is transmitted to humans via bites from infected mosquitos.
Acute respiratory infection	A serious infection, often in the lungs, that prevents normal breathing.
Health insurance	An arrangement where a person pays regular sums of money to an insurance company, and the insurance company then pays for medical treatment if and when it is needed.

Activity 3

Encourage students to continue to discuss the definitions as they play, to consolidate their understanding.

Note that each of the perspectives mentioned is highly complex, and most of them are only glimpsed in the documents. It would be necessary to find out much more to have a full understanding. But we can ask questions and do research to help ourselves understand these perspectives.

Encourage students to approach cultural perspectives by asking questions such as:

- What beliefs do these people share?
- What does this cultural perspective value most highly?
- Where do their beliefs come from?
- How do these people see the world?
- How do these people understand their place in the world?

Document 1

Antonia comes from a cultural perspective which prioritises caring for others and the value of human life. It is an educated perspective which assumes that others will also have enough education to understand data.

Julian simply provides a fact.

Qing Yu expresses a rather cynical cultural perspective, which suspects what the government says and does. There is an assumption here that it is acceptable to criticise the government – there are cultural perspectives where this is not the case.

Document 2

This is based on the belief that children should have a fair beginning in life.

Document 3

These views are similar to views actually expressed in debates on free healthcare in the UK and in the US during the Obamacare debate.

Activity 4

Encourage students to think and debate. You may wish to use the suggestions below to provoke discussion.

1. Answers will vary.
2. 2002 is a long time ago, but in some areas life is much worse now for children than it was then, so it is still relevant. Some aspects may have improved in some areas.
3. Consider war, abuse, smoking in the presence of children, decisions about diet, etc.

Activity 5

1. These are opinions expressed by unknown sources, so we cannot be sure of their reliability.
2. No, the consequences are extreme and unlikely. It is quite possible, for example, to be in favour of free healthcare and still oppose specific kinds of healthcare, such as abortion. There is no evidence

to suggest that 'free' (tax-funded) healthcare would depress the economy. The reasoning is incoherent, ranting and contradictory.

3. C's reasoning is quite good to start with. It is logical and thoughtful, explaining how 'free' healthcare works. The analogy with demanding that the government provide us with diamonds is problematic, however. Diamonds are luxury goods, whereas an individual's health is a necessity. The government would not benefit from giving out diamonds, but it does benefit from having a healthy population because the result is increased productivity. Allow other reasonable interpretations and opinions here.

4. Encourage discussion.

Activity 6

1. **Facts:** 'Around 75% of deaths among people aged 10–24 in the US are caused by unintentional injuries or violence.'/'More than half of child deaths in developing countries in 2001 were caused by acute respiratory infections, measles, diarrhoea, malaria, and HIV/AIDS.'/'. . . in 2001 99% of child deaths were in developing countries.' These points can all be verified, so can be shown to be correct or incorrect.

   Opinion: 'It doesn't really matter if these young people are dying from preventable accidents or preventable diseases – it's just wrong.' This is Antonia's belief, and it cannot be verified as either true or false.

2. The category 'people aged 10–24' includes some adults and leaves out some children. To really understand the differences in child mortality, we would need to have statistics from exactly the same group of people: children.

3. Encourage students to apply their research skills.

4. It is a fact as it can be verified. It might be possible to argue that the information about causes of heart disease and strokes is opinion because there is no absolute certainty, but it is expert opinion, backed by scientific evidence.

5. Long term studies of two groups of young people, comparing smoking rates between those who can see branded packaging and those who cannot. It would be hard to control for other factors. Alternatively, compare smoking rates of young people following the introduction of non-branded, plain packaging with rates prior to this. Again, there may be difficulties in controlling for other factors.

6. It is an opinion as it cannot be verified. Of course, this is a mildly humorous reference to the fact that there is corruption in Britain, even though we don't call it that, and that the British don't believe that corruption exists, even though government ministers accept money to influence democratic decision-making.

Activity 7

1. to **6.** Encourage students to apply their skills, and to set up their lines of enquiry carefully.

Activity 8

1. Encourage students to research the issues that may affect each individual. Answers will vary. Suggested answers:

Labourer: Unsanitary conditions leading to illness; lack of healthcare; poverty; poor nutrition leading to illness.

School student: Illness due to air pollution.

Pregnant woman: Lack of antenatal care; lack of doctors and midwives; high infant and maternal mortality rates.

Toddler: Generally poor diet by the standards of an MEDC country, leading to high levels of heart attack, etc.; high incidence of alcoholism in Glasgow, which may affect the toddler's parents and thus lead to problems for the toddler, or it may later affect the toddler; lower life expectancy than that of toddlers in Edinburgh, London or other parts of the UK.

Business leader: A business leader in Washington, D.C., USA will have a good level of health insurance and is likely to be well-nourished and to live in good circumstances, so they will be shielded from most ill health. However, they may have lifestyle-related health issues such as stress-related illness or illness related to over-indulgence in food or alcohol. They may also travel a lot, and be exposed to a variety of diseases.

2. Encourage students to think carefully and discuss different cultural perspectives and the beliefs that underlie them. Remind them that the first answer they think of is not necessarily the best one.

3. Encourage students to think carefully about their answers, and to discuss and to justify their ideas. Answers will vary.

Activity 9

Answers will vary. Encourage students to think carefully about what is likely and what is not.

Activity 10

Encourage discussion, and encourage students to think carefully about the most likely consequences.

Reflection 11

Reflection is an important part of the course, so it is important to allow class time for this activity. It may be useful to use a learning journal. This might allow for some ongoing written dialogue about the issues. The key here is to avoid simple praise or giving a student's thoughts a value; instead, try to engage a student in discussion over time and include questions in your written response that will push the student to the next level, and expect them to respond.

Activity 12

Encourage students to think carefully and to take this activity seriously, as this kind of reflection is an important part of the assessment.

③ Human rights

Introduction

Human rights are a key issue in the world today, along with the responsibilities they engender.

In the West, we tend to take human rights for granted and assume that everyone agrees that these are fundamental rights for all humans.

Underlying their project work, students should have an awareness of the key issues relating to human rights, but their knowledge in this area is not being tested in itself. Projects can focus on any area of human rights, including the law, specific human rights campaigns, abuses, activism, or issues relating to the universalism of human rights, as long as there is an active outcome and there are cross-cultural perspectives.

Suggested resources

www.amnesty.org http://www.amnestyusa.org/news/multimedia	Amnesty International is one of the world's leading human rights NGOs. These sites include a wealth of print and video material.
http://www.humanrights.com/	This site offers a free education package for each educator.
http://www.youthforhumanrights.org/	This site has useful videos on human rights, which are useful for listening practice and well targeted at a young audience. The material is somewhat sentimental and takes a very American or Western view, but offers opportunities for discussion.
https://www.hrw.org/	Human Rights Watch is a leading human rights NGO.
http://www.fundsforngos.org/featured-articles/worlds-top-ten-human-rights-organisations/	This page contains information on the world's top ten human rights organisations.
http://journal-neo.org/2015/06/17/eritrea-human-rights-and-neocolonial-propaganda/	This article argues against a UN assessment of the state of human rights in Eritrea and takes the perspective that UN human rights are often neo-colonial propaganda.
http://www.latrobe.edu.au/research/research-impacts/researchers/videos/the-global-opposition-to-universal-human-rights	A short video summarising some of the opposition to universal human rights.
http://www.developmenteducation.ie/blog/2014/02/debating-human-rights-universal-or-relative-to-culture/	A discussion of the arguments against universal human rights.

Suggested answers to the activities

Activity 1

1. Encourage students to read the comments for gist rather than worrying about the detail of the complex language. They are looking only for issues. The following are suggestions only. As long as students can justify their answers, other answers are acceptable.

   (a) How universal are human rights? (Some students may raise the issue of women's rights.)

   (b) Individual rights vs. social stability, civil rights vs. national security, limits on human rights

   (c) Limits on human rights

   (d) How universal are human rights?

   (e) Where do human rights come from?

2. Suggested answers (others are possible if they can be justified):

   (a) Transnational charity, educated, attempts to take a global overview (although others may see this as imposing beliefs). Comes from a cultural perspective which prioritises the value of helping others and the belief that women should have equal rights.

(b) This is an Egyptian newspaper, which does not give away much of its own cultural perspective. We get a glimpse of a political cultural perspective in which the priority is to be seen to provide swift justice to terrorists and where 'justice' is equated to punishment (rather than preventing terrorism or ensuring due process of law). We get a glimpse of the cultural perspective of Amnesty's regional director, which values human rights above all else.

(c) There is a political cultural perspective here which prioritises a country's sovereignty over human rights and justice.

(d) This is an academic, philosophical expression of international law by a transnational organisation. This view firmly believes in human rights as universal – whatever other cultural practices there are in your country, every single human being has human rights because they are human. The roots of this view are in ancient Greek philosophy and Enlightenment philosophy.

(e) This is a normal confused person with no particular cultural perspective – faced with philosophical concepts for the first time!

3. Encourage discussion and debate, and let students know that they are free to follow their own interests.

What is it that interests you about where human rights come from, Kwame?	✓ This question will help Kwame to pinpoint what interests him and give him the opportunity to articulate difficult concepts.
That doesn't allow you to consider cross-cultural perspectives, does it, Kwame?	✗ This statement puts control of the work back with the teacher, and undermines Kwame's own thinking.
What global or cross-cultural perspectives can you think of for that one, Kwame?	✓ This question can focus Kwame's thinking on the global perspective, or give him the opportunity to share thoughts that hadn't occurred to the teacher.

Activity 2

Note that dictionary skills – whether the dictionaries are online or in print – are invaluable, while online translation tools can deskill students and tend to provide poor translations. Suggestions are given below, but encourage students to consider a range of definitions.

Human rights	Rights that we should have because we are human. These rights are written down in the Universal Declaration of Human Rights and many countries have included these rights in their laws.
Legal rights	Rights that we have because the law says that we have them.
Natural rights	Rights that everyone has under 'natural law'. These rights cannot be rejected by any laws. This idea is about 300 years older than the idea of human rights.
Freedom to	The freedom to do as you please: to marry, live, work, establish a political party, and believe as you wish. This is sometimes called 'positive liberty'.
Freedom from	The freedom from hunger, oppression, poverty, or other external factors. This is sometimes called 'negative liberty'.
Civil rights	The rights and liberties of each individual, usually political and social, because they are the citizens of a particular country. These include the right to vote and freedom of speech.
Universal	Applies to everyone throughout the world.
National security	There are lots of different interpretations of national security. The basic idea is that the government takes control of the safety of the nation. This includes setting up an army for defence, but also taking action against rebels, spies and terrorists.

Activity 3

Encourage students to think, discuss and work together to extend their understanding.

Note that each of the perspectives mentioned is highly complex, and most of them are only glimpsed in the documents. It would be necessary to find out much more to have a full understanding. But we can ask questions and do research to help ourselves understand these perspectives.

Encourage students to approach cultural perspectives by asking questions such as:

- What beliefs do these people share?
- What does this cultural perspective value most highly?
- Where do their beliefs come from?
- How do these people see the world?
- How do these people understand their place in the world?

Document 1

A global, supranational organisation which prioritises the values embedded in human rights, and the belief that these are universal (i.e. everyone has them), and that they can be imposed if countries do not accept them. This thinking has its roots in Greek philosophy and Western Enlightenment philosophy.

Document 2

@government minister comes from a (political) cultural perspective which believes that human rights are something that you can earn or deserve, and prioritises protecting the public and being popular with voters over people's inherent dignity.

@member of the public – merely asks questions, but is probably questioning the cultural perspective that some people who break the law are more criminal than others. In Europe at least we share a cultural perspective which assigns more blame to criminals of low socio-economic status. Breaking and entering seems to be a worse crime than fraud or speeding.

@victim – this is a cultural perspective based in fear and ignorance and pain, which prioritised vengeance and punishment.

@ law professor – this is a cultural perspective based in education and understanding of the principles of the law in Western liberal democracy. It probably assumes that these values are universal.

Note that all of these people could come from the same country. They may all share a cultural perspective in the sense of believing in the rule of law and the equality of all before the law. But their different levels of education, power, influence and willingness to question assumptions leads them to having different cultural perspectives within the overall perspective that they share.

Document 3

This comes from a Chinese newspaper. The Chinese cultural perspective generally has roots in Confucian thinking, and tends to prioritise social stability and the value of social institutions and the family over the value of the individual.

The overriding value here is that national sovereignty overrides human rights, and that human rights are an issue for individual countries and should not be used as a political tool.

We also see a belief that different countries may have different criteria for human rights, which hints at a cultural perspective which fundamentally disagrees with the Western view that human rights are universal and applicable to everyone.

There is a clear dislike of being told what to do by other countries, and a belief that the US should address its own human rights issues before acting as an international judge.

(Compare this with the cultural perspective of some British politicians, as seen in Activity 1c – some, although by no means all, British politicians object to the authority of the European Courts and the Human Rights Act, believing that they undermine British sovereignty. Here, too, a specific national take on rights is proposed – so a dislike of others' political interference and a desire to determine the rights of one's own citizens is not limited to China)

Document 4

This comes from Eritrea, which has its own background of having been colonised and struggling to develop as an independent nation in the aftermath of colonisation. There are residual attitudes and beliefs about the effects of colonisation and the motivations of former colonisers which can be glimpsed here – and could be researched.

This cultural perspective also sees UN human rights reports as politically motivated propaganda rather than as an attempt to ensure that everyone has the human rights to which they are entitled as human beings.

(Note that it is possible for a culture (e.g. Western) to have a genuine belief in the value of human rights, whilst also using them as a political tool).

Activity 4

Encourage students to think and debate. You may wish to use the questions below to provoke discussion.

1. and **2.** Are there times when you should not say what you think, even though you have the right to?

3. Consider these groups of people: murderers, terrorists, illegal immigrants, spies, women, children. Should their rights ever be limited? Do we sometimes need to make decisions for people that might infringe their rights?

4. What about in wartime?

Activity 5

Encourage students to apply their skills.

Activity 6

1. and 2. Encourage students to think, discuss and debate. Answers will vary.

3. The most important thing is that students think about and justify their answers. Remind them that 'I agree' is not the same as 'this is effective reasoning'. Suggested answers:

   @governmentminister: Makes a lot of assertions without backing them up. We can question whether protecting the public really means taking away all rights from criminals.

   @memberofthepublic: Raises important questions that form a reasonable response to @governmentminister because they identify some forms of breaking the law that a government minister would not want to see as 'criminal'. Highlights the weakness of @governmentminister's position, but does not go beyond asking questions to formulate own reasoning.

   @victim: A rant, containing unfounded assertions and apparently motivated by emotion not reason. Contradictory (criminals go free/better off in prison) and illogical.

   @lawprofessor: Factually accurate, moderate, logical, and gives reasons for a conclusion. This is the best reasoning.

Activity 7

1. The article discusses the relationship between human rights and national sovereignty. Ultimately, it concludes that sovereignty is necessary to protect human rights. The article argues that the USA has double standards and should sort out its own human rights abuses. It also argues that UN human rights come from an attempt by Western countries to maintain influence after they lost their colonies.

2. and 3. Encourage debate and discussion. Answers will vary. The article makes some good points, but there is a degree of sophistry in the link between human rights and human rights of a nation, with conflation and equivocation, changing meaning all the time and subtly changing the nature of the debate.

Activity 8

1. Encourage students to research the issues that may affect each individual. Answers will vary. Suggested answers:

   Detainee: Detention without charge; possibly innocent people held with serious terrorists; possibility of torture; generally poor conditions.

Human rights activist: Depends on the country and what they are in prison for. May well be deprived of most rights, possibly tortured, just because they campaign for the rights of others. Consider Liu Xiaobo, Narges Mohammadi, Nelson Mandela, for example.

Amnesty International worker: Focused on combatting human rights abuses. May be lucky enough to come from a safe background with few rights abuses, but many have experienced human rights abuses themselves.

Murderer: Deprived of right to liberty. Question as to whether this person should be deprived of the right to vote.

Person deciding what to buy: When buying items, many people like to consider the human rights abuses that go on in the production of the goods they are buying. These can include slave labour, child labour, and backgrounds of conflict in which human rights abuses are rife.

2. Encourage students to think carefully and discuss the different cultural perspectives these people may have and the beliefs that underlie them. Remind them that the first answer they think of is not necessarily the best one.

3. Encourage students to think carefully about their answers, and to discuss and to justify their ideas. Answers will vary. As seen in Document 3, there is room for real discussion about whether human rights are only a matter for nations or whether they should be a global issue.

Activity 9

1. to 6. Encourage students to apply their skills, and to set up their lines of enquiry carefully.

Activity 10

Answers will vary. Encourage students to think carefully about what is likely and what is not.

Reflection 11

Reflection is an important part of the course, so it is important to allow class time for this activity. It may be useful to use a learning journal. This might allow for some ongoing written dialogue about the issues.

Activity 11

Encourage students to think carefully and to take this activity seriously, as this kind of reflection is an important part of the assessment.

4 Language and communication

Introduction

Our language is a deep-rooted part of us, how we think and who we are. The word *language* comes from the Latin *lingua* meaning 'tongue'. In many languages, the words for 'language' and the words for 'tongue' are the same, and in English we still speak of having a 'mother tongue'. Language facilitates communication, but can also be a significant barrier to our ability to communicate with others.

Underlying their project work, students should have an awareness of the key issues relating to language and communication, but their knowledge in this area is not being tested in itself. Projects can focus on any area of language and communication, including language and culture, the effects of having to work in a second language, improved communication technologies, one world language, changing language use, or gendered language, as long as there is an active outcome and there are cross-cultural perspectives.

Suggested resources

http://www.els.edu/en/ManyLanguagesOneWorld	An essay competition.
http://www.businessinsider.com/why-there-wont-be-a-universal-language-2014-7?IR=T	An explanation of why there is no universal language and why there can never be one.
http://www.debate.org/opinions/should-there-be-one-global-language	Various opinions about whether or not there should be one global language. Useful for the evaluation of the quality of reasoning and the evaluation of source material.
https://greatlanguagegame.com/	A game in which students have to identify different languages by their sounds.
http://blogs.scientificamerican.com/guest-blog/why-does-a-southern-drawl-sound-uneducated-to-some/	An interesting article on how we perceive different accents.
https://www.youtube.com/watch?v=-stQoViotts	An amusing video of a Scottish comedian talking about Australian accents.

Suggested answers to the activities

Activity 1

1. Encourage students to read the comments for gist rather than worrying about the detail of the complex language. They are looking only for issues. The following are suggestions only. As long as students can justify their answers, other answers are acceptable.

    (a) Should there be one world language?

    (b) Language and thought

    (c) Language and thought

    (d) Globalisation vs. localisation, should there be one world language?

2. Suggested answers:

    (a) This comes from the cultural perspective of someone whose first language is English, and who takes a narrow view of the value of learning another language – this is a common cultural perspective amongst first language English speakers, but not universal.

    (b) This is an academic cultural perspective, which studies the way perspectives develop.

    (c) This is an academic, psychological perspective.

    (d) This is an academic, historical cultural perspective.

3. Encourage discussion and debate, and let students know that they are free to follow their own interests.

Activity 2

Encourage students to work this out for themselves, using their own knowledge of different languages.

Activity 3

Encourage students to think, discuss and work together to extend their understanding.

Note that each of the perspectives mentioned is highly complex, and most of them are only glimpsed in the documents. It would be necessary to find out much more to have a full understanding. But we can ask questions and do research to help ourselves understand these perspectives.

Encourage students to approach cultural perspectives by asking questions such as:

- What beliefs do these people share?
- What does this cultural perspective value most highly?
- Where do their beliefs come from?
- How do these people see the world?
- How do these people understand their place in the world?

Document 1

There is not much information here about cultural perspectives, but, 'Internet World Statistics' implies a perspective in which statistics shape the world – or are at least valued.

Document 2

From 'Common Sense Advising,' 'Consumers' and 'Can't read, won't buy,' we can see that this document comes from a business and marketing cultural perspective, which values gathering information in order to improve business. This perspective values sales – it can be contrasted with an academic perspective.

Document 3

The cartoon visualises teens and parents as having different cultural perspectives and different world views, formed through different languages. There is no specific information on what those cultural perspectives are – but there is room for exploration of different generational cultural perspectives as part of students' project research.

Document 4

This is from an academic, feminist cultural perspective (where feminist means aiming for gender equality).

Activity 4

Suggested answers:

1. No. It is true that Document 1 shows us that there are more English- and Chinese-speaking internet users, so it may be worth companies considering whether to have English or Chinese versions of their site. However, part of the reason behind this statistic could be that there are simply more sites in English and Chinese, so these see the most traffic. Also, 'all' is an extreme claim. Document 2 shows that people prefer to spend time on (and presumably buy things from) sites in their own language. So this would be a reason for companies to use the languages of people they hope will buy their products. This may well be English and Chinese, but a French company selling only in France, for example, would do well to express their site in French.

2. You would need to know how many people in the world speak each language. This would help you to decide, for example, whether English is used more online because there are more English speakers, because people use English as a second language or just because most of the sites are in English. You would also need information on whether there are more sites in English and Chinese than in other languages, and about the proportion of each population that has access to the internet. This would help you to decide what the figures mean. For instance, if you find out that there are many more Russian speakers than Korean speakers in the world, but that most Koreans have internet access whereas many Russians do not, you would be able to interpret the statistics more accurately.

3. Look up population figures on government sites or on those of reliable supranational organisations like the UN. The UN could also be a good place to look for relative internet access statistics. You could search, for example, phrases such as, 'Global + comparison + internet access' or 'Russia statistics internet access'.

Activity 5

Suggested answer:

'Son, we're learning to speak teenage': This cartoon deals with issues of communication between the generations, and the way that older people (parents, teachers, etc.) have to learn to speak with their children, possibly learning new words, new grammar rules, and discovering new ways of seeing the world. It also probably plays on the idea that any attempt by settled, older people to learn 'teenage' is probably doomed and possibly ridiculous. This cartoon raises issues such as how adults communicate with teenagers, how the world is reinvented in new ways by new people looking at it with new perspectives, and how people with fundamentally different ways of seeing the world can communicate with each other. It also raises questions about when a variant of a language starts to become a language in its own right. Ask students to design a teenage vocabulary dictionary to share with adults, and investigate the causes of 'teen speak' – is it linked to social media?

Suggested answer:

1. The key point made in this article is that male generics do matter because they reinforce a system of thinking – a cultural perspective – and therefore a social system in which the male is privileged over the female.

2. Sherryl Kleinman works specifically on gender equality, so she has expertise and has thought carefully about the issues. This would make her a reliable source. She has a clear perspective of her own, and is likely to see information in the light of her perspective, but this does not make her unreliable in the same way that a reason to lie would.

3. The parts of the article that list male generics are facts. We can verify that these expressions are used and can even use print and audio evidence to give a geographical range for their use. It is a fact that in 1986 Douglas Hofstadter wrote a parody of sexist language. We would be able to verify that Kleinman has reported the contents of the parody accurately, so this could be considered factual. However, the parody itself is not factual; it's an imaginative prediction of consequences. So there is a substantial factual basis to the article. Yet it is also strongly influenced by opinion: 'The worst, from my observations, is the popular expression, "you guys"' is clearly a personal opinion; 'It makes a difference, if I think of myself as a "girl" or a "woman"' is also an opinion, as it is possible to argue against it (although it is tempting to think of this as a fact because there is such clear supporting evidence). Even some of the questions and suggestions convey the author's opinion that male generics are a problem: 'And can you think of one, just one, example of a female-based generic?' With these points in mind, the article is primarily opinion, but based on facts.

4. It is likely that people's reactions to the quality of reasoning in this article will be determined by whether or not they agree with it, and this will depend at least partly on whether they are male or female, whether or not they live in a traditional society, and whether or not they have had experience of language affecting or limiting their realities.

   Some of the objective points students can look for here include the following:

   - The passage does quite a good job of highlighting for us just how often we use male generics, and how we do use the male to refer to 'the entire universe of human beings'.

   - The author gives reasonable evidence of 'you guys' as occurring across the USA.

   - 'And even if it were regional, that doesn't make it right.' This is a fair point, but just because the expression 'you guys' is used across the USA, this doesn't make it wrong either. The author does show later why she thinks it is wrong, but here her point is rather rhetorical. Pointing out that there are regional things we'd like to get rid of doesn't really add to the argument (although be prepared to listen to students who argue that it does, as long as they can justify their ideas).

   - 'One consequence of male based generics is that they reinforce the system in which "man" in the abstract and men in the flesh are privileged over women.' This seems reasonable: it's plausible, possible, and many of us have seen evidence of it. It is quite well justified by the idea of words as 'tools of thought' and the suggestion that words can be used to maintain or to change reality. (It might be worth encouraging students to think of the kind of language that is applied to naughty or mischievous children and how it is different for girls and boys. If appropriate in the context of your school's culture, consider how girls and boys are insulted, the language used for men and women who are sexually active with a number of partners, and the language used to talk about male and female politicians. You could even look at what is said about male and female politicians: how often does the press concentrate on what female politicians are wearing rather than what they are saying?). There is an alternative view here, that words are just words and don't mean much, that these terms are just general and that women shouldn't get so upset about them. This is, of course, precisely the view that the article is arguing against.

   - 'There could be serious consequences for referring to a man as a "woman". . .' This is an unspecific prediction, but it seems reasonable, plausible, and consistent with evidence we can observe in many countries.

   - The main value of this passage seems to be that we should want our society to be inclusive, treating all people as being of equal value. Some may read the passage and think that it is about putting men down; a counter-argument would be that this is only true if they believe it is an insult for a man to be considered equal in value to a woman.

Activity 7

1. Encourage students to research the issues that may affect each individual. Answers will vary. Suggested answers:

   Migrant: Likely to speak Arabic as a first language and possibly English as a second language, so they will need to learn a new language. In the meantime, they cannot communicate, cannot work at the level they are educated to (or will struggle in school), and cannot easily make friends.

   School student: Will need to learn English, which is very different from Chinese. May wish to surf the internet, but much of the world's content is in English and the Great Firewall of China means that much of it is difficult or impossible to access from China.

   Physics student: Will need to work in English to progress, as most scientific papers and conferences are published in English, and many opportunities are in the English-speaking world. If this student cannot improve their English, they will probably have a less successful career.

   Business leader in Brazil: Will need to speak English to communicate with business partners around the world.

   Business leader in Washington, D.C., USA: Less likely to be bilingual or multilingual and will expect English to be the business language. On the other hand, this may mean that this leader may struggle with intercultural communication, because learning a language can help to understand another culture.

2. and 3. Encourage debate and discussion. Answers will vary. Encourage students to consider the different factors that might affect these individuals' cultural perspectives and the beliefs they may hold.

Activity 8

1. to 6. Encourage students to apply their skills, and to set up their lines of enquiry carefully.

Activity 9

Answers will vary. Encourage students to think carefully about what is likely and what is not.

Activity 10

Reflection is an important part of the course, so it is important to allow class time for this activity. It may be useful to use a learning journal. This might allow for some ongoing written dialogue about the issues. The key here is to avoid simple praise or giving a student's thoughts a value; instead, try to engage a student in discussion over time and include questions in your written response that will push the student to the next level, and expect them to respond.

Reflection

Encourage students to think carefully and to take this activity seriously, as this kind of reflection is an important part of the assessment.

5 Poverty and inequality

Introduction

What causes poverty? What effects does inequality have on health, education, the ability to earn a living, and cultural life? How should we deal with the consequences of poverty? How responsible should we feel for the relative poverty and well-being of people across the world? Does it make a difference if we wear clothes or use gadgets produced by people working in terrible conditions?

Underlying their project work, students should have an awareness of the key issues relating to poverty and inequality, but their knowledge in this area is not being tested in itself. Projects can focus on any area of poverty and inequality, including the effects of poverty and inequality on specific communities, the economic effects of globalisation, the relationship between poverty and development, or the minimum wage, as long as there is an active outcome and there are cross-cultural perspectives.

Suggested resources

https://www.oxfam.org.au/what-we-do/inequality/	This page from the well-known charity Oxfam features links to a range of other useful pages.
http://www.un.org/millenniumgoals/	A UN page with an accessible explanation of the Millennium Development Goals.
http://billmoyers.com/2014/07/11/three-steps-we-can-take-to-solve-poverty-from-someone-who-knows-firsthand/	An account of poverty in the USA, and suggested solutions. Some of these are specific to the USA, but others have wider application.
http://www.relevantmagazine.com/god/mission/features/23810-can-we-really-solve-poverty	An article, with a Christian perspective, from 2010 by the president of World Vision.
https://www.muslimaid.org/what-we-do/education/	A charity page with a variety of useful links.
http://sites.my.xs.edu.ph/joseph-pua-14/social-science/poverty-causes-effects-and-how-we-can-solve-it	This page features accessible interviews with people who earn very little.
http://qz.com/242352/the-philippines-now-has-100-million-people-and-just-about-as-many-problems-and-possibilities/	An accessible article with lots of information about the Philippines, its population and poverty.
https://www.usaid.gov/frontiers/2014/publication/section-1-extreme-poverty-philippines	A discussion about extreme poverty in the Philippines. A good source of useful information.
https://www.imf.org/external/np/exr/facts/mdg.htm http://www.imf.org/external/np/exr/facts/sdg.htm	Information from the International Monetary Fund on the Millennium Development Goals and the Sustainable Development Goals that follow them. The content is quite challenging, but students should be able to extract useful information.

Suggested answers to the activities

Activity 1

1. Encourage students to read the comments for gist rather than worrying about the detail of the complex language. They are looking only for issues. The following are suggestions only. As long as students can justify their answers, other answers are acceptable.

   (a) Minimum wage, equal opportunities

   (b) Equality, effects of inequality

   (c) Causes of global recession and increase in poverty

   (d) Poverty and human rights

   (e) Effects of poverty on health

2. Suggested answers:

(a) This comes from the perspective of ordinary, working people around the world.

(b) This is a description, which seems to be aiming for objectivity. (Note that there are cultural perspectives which think that global organisations like OECD have an agenda, and strongly oppose the work they do).

(c) This comes from a thoughtful journalistic cultural perspective. This perspective prioritises the attempt to be analytic and objective, communicating an understanding of a complex problem. It can be contrasted with the cultural perspective of those who choose to blame bankers, and with a more sensationalist type of journalistic perspective.

(d) This is a cultural perspective from a global organisation which is attempting to be objective, but which actually believes quite firmly that poverty is social, political and cultural as well as economic. There is a belief that international organisations and international governments can and should act to affect the lives of those around the world. There is a belief that poverty should be addressed. It sees poor people as suffering from the circumstances of poverty rather than as the agents of their own poverty – poor people can be helped out of poverty. This can be contrasted with cultural perspectives which view poor people as poor because they don't work hard, or because they are inferior – 'the undeserving poor.'

(e) This cultural perspective values happiness over wealth, but recognises that money can buy important things.

3. Encourage debate and discussion.

Activity 2

Note that dictionary skills – whether the dictionaries are online or in print – are invaluable, while online translation tools can deskill students and tend to provide poor translations. Suggestions are given below, but encourage students to consider a range of definitions.

Absolute poverty	A condition characterized by the severe deprivation of basic human needs, including food, safe drinking water, sanitation facilities, health, shelter, education and information.
Relative poverty	The condition in which people lack the minimum amount of income needed in order to maintain the average standard of living in the society in which they live.
Inequality	An unfair situation in some societies where some people have more opportunities, better education, better access to healthcare, etc. The term is increasingly used to refer to the gap between the very rich and the rest of the population.
Millennium Development Goals	Eight international development goals that were established after the Millennium Summit of the United Nations in 2000. The first seven goals focus on: eradicating extreme poverty and hunger; achieving universal primary education; promoting gender equality and empowering women; reducing child mortality; improving maternal health; combating HIV/AIDS, malaria and other diseases; and ensuring environmental sustainability. The eighth goal calls for the creation of a global partnership for development, with targets for aid, trade, and debt relief.
Global credit crisis	A worldwide period of economic difficulty experienced by markets and consumers. In 2008 and the following years, banks did not lend enough money to businesses – they did not give them credit. As a result, the businesses had cash flow problems and many had to close down.
Economic development	The improvement of a community's financial well-being and quality of life through the creation of jobs, increasing standard of living, growing incomes and making sure that the government gets more tax revenue to fund public projects.

Social poverty	Social poverty looks at the conditions that create an individual's or a population's circumstances, and the state of mind that can develop as a result. It includes the social consequences when individuals or populations suffer from a combination of linked problems such as unemployment, poor skills, low incomes, poor housing, high crime environments, bad health and family breakdown.
Cultural poverty	A lack of exposure to the arts, literature, film, theatre and other important cultural forms of expression.

Activity 3

Encourage students to think, discuss and work together to extend their understanding.

Note that each of the perspectives mentioned is highly complex, and most of them are only glimpsed in the documents. It would be necessary to find out much more to have a full understanding. But we can ask questions and do research to help ourselves understand these perspectives.

Encourage students to approach cultural perspectives by asking questions such as:

- What beliefs do these people share?
- What does this cultural perspective value most highly?
- Where do their beliefs come from?
- How do these people see the world?
- How do these people understand their place in the world?

Document 1

This comes from a rather socialist cultural perspective, focused on fairness and equality.

Document 2

A seems to come from a cultural perspective which believes that people who are poor in a rich nation could do better if they tried, and must therefore be poor through their own fault.

B comes from a cultural perspective which prioritises a free market economy as the most valuable thing. This particular individual seems not to be inclined to

check facts and is not logical, so assumes a cause and effect because of a pre-existing belief in a free market economy.

C All we know is that this person values accuracy.

D We do not know much about this person's cultural perspective – just that they see employees also as consumers.

Document 3

The cartoon aims to highlight different cultural perspectives regarding ambition, what to do with power and how realistic it is to attain power, with a focus on disparities between people of different gender and wealth.

Activity 4

1. and 2. Encourage students to apply their skills and research these points. Remind them to include a recent date in the search terms.

3. You would need to check. It may be that no health insurance is available for this amount in the USA, in which case this would be a fact; alternatively, it may be that you can get health insurance for this monthly premium, but that it doesn't provide much/enough cover, in which case this is an opinion that is exaggerating the truth for effect.

4. Encourage students to think about the most useful search terms if researching online. Another method might be to contact health insurance companies.

5. Although it is hard to disagree with this opinion, it *is* an opinion because it can't be verified. It might be better to call it a definition.

6. Encourage students to check carefully and thoroughly.

Activity 5

1. Opinion. It is an unverifiable belief about what should happen, not a prediction of what will or is likely to happen.

2. Encourage students to think about their answers from the perspectives of both employers and workers.

3. Encourage students to think carefully about what is likely.

4. Encourage students to think carefully about what is likely. Will businesses *really* fail if they have to pay their employees more?

5. These are opinions from unknown sources, so we can't know how reliable they are. We can only make judgements on their quality, for example, whether they reason well or whether we can cross-check their points.

6. No. The causes and consequences suggested are extreme and to a certain extent unlikely. There is a significant body of evidence, for example, that suggests that bad lending and excessive risk-taking in the banking system were prime causes of the last recession.

7. This argument seems logical, although it is perhaps unlikely that a rise in the minimum wage will prevent people from opposing a rise in prices.

8. Encourage debate and discussion.

Activity 6

1. They show that there is a strong correlation between poverty and living in a polluted area, even in a city in one of the richest countries in the world.

2. Encourage research and debate. In many countries, this is likely to be true. In the case of cities such as Shanghai and Beijing pollution is so bad that it affects both rich and poor.

3. Encourage students to think carefully about search terms they might use.

4. Encourage research and discussion. It is likely that there is a vicious circle between poverty and pollution. It may also be that rich people can afford to move to less polluted areas, and that they have the means to keep those areas less polluted.

Activity 7

1. The effects of inequality and poverty on life chances; our perception of our opportunities.

2. Encourage discussion.

Activity 8

1. Encourage students to research the issues that may affect each individual. Answers will vary. Suggested answers:

Labourer: Likely to have migrated because of poor economic circumstances and likely to be living in an insanitary part of town. It may be a long commute to work, which will be tiring, or it may not be easy to find work.

School student: Likely to suffer more from illness than students from privileged homes; unlikely to have the advantages of extra tuition, sports clubs, etc. May not be as well-nourished as more privileged students.

Young migrant mother: Depending on the country she is in, this young mother is likely to suffer serious poverty and inequality, although this is not guaranteed. Her asthma is likely to make it harder for her to work, and it is hard to work and look after children, especially if you do not speak the language.

Builder: Many builders are self-employed and only get paid when they work. As building involves physical labour, it is difficult or unwise to continue to work with a bad back. As a result, the builder may have to choose between health and income.

Sales person: Immediate unemployment after the business has closed is likely to lead to economic difficulties, depending on the person's financial circumstances. In a declining town, new work may be hard to find, so the person will need to think about moving to a town or city that offers more opportunities. However, this may be difficult with an elderly mother to look after.

2. and 3. Encourage debate and discussion. Answers will vary.

Activity 9

1. to 5. Encourage students to apply their skills, and to set up their lines of enquiry carefully.

Activity 10

Answers will vary. Encourage students to think carefully about what is likely and what is not.

Reflection

Encourage students to think carefully and to take this activity seriously, as this kind of reflection is an important part of the assessment.

6 Sport and recreation

Introduction

What role does sport play in the life of an individual or a nation? How should we deal with issues in international sport? Is recreation a luxury for the rich or a necessity for the wellbeing of us all?

Underlying their project work, students should have an awareness of the key issues relating to sport and recreation, but their knowledge in this area is not being tested in itself. Projects can focus on any area of sport and recreation, including corruption, the role of sporting governing bodies, the morality of doping, health benefits of hobbies, or inequalities between rich and poor nations, as long as there is an active outcome and there are cross-cultural perspectives.

Suggested resources

http://stress.about.com/od/funandgames/a/The-Importance-Of-Hobbies-For-Stress-Relief.htm	An overview of the benefits of hobbies.
https://www.yahoo.com/parenting/hobbies-for-kids-with-real-psychological-benefits-106537821202.html	An article about how children can benefit from hobbies, including information on specific hobbies.
http://abcnews.go.com/Health/story?id=118258&page=1	A more detailed, albeit still accessible, explanation and exploration of the benefits of hobbies.
http://www.theroar.com.au/2015/03/16/womens-sport-must-step-out-of-the-shadows/	An article with a clear perspective on women's sport. The article is focused on Australia but can be applied more widely.
http://www.abc.net.au/news/2011-03-04/sporthicks/44640	An article about the damage hero worship in sports can do to young males. An interesting read, though you may wish to edit some of the references to bad behaviour.

Suggested answers to the activities

Activity 1

1. Encourage students to read the comments for gist rather than worrying about the detail of the complex language. They are looking only for issues. The following are suggestions only. As long as students can justify their answers, other answers are acceptable.

   (a) Doping in sport, international cooperation/competition

   (b) Corruption in world sporting bodies

   (c) International cooperation/competition, sport and national pride, supporting youth development

   (d) International cooperation/competition, sport and national pride

   (e) Sport and health, benefits of hobbies

   (f) Supporting youth development, sport/hobbies and community

2. Suggested answers:

   (a) There is not much information on this perspective – but it does imply that winning is more important than fairness.

   (b) The cultural perspective of the passage is journalistic, with an emphasis on fact finding and reporting, and just a hint of valuing the scandalous. There is an implied belief that accepting bribes and being corrupt is bad (and possibly also an undertone of enjoyment of the powerful being caught being naughty). There is a glimpse of the cultural perspective of Fifa officials, who do seem to think that it is ok to take bribes (especially if you can get away with it).

   (c) This comes from a cultural perspective which believes that sport it good, elite national sport is valuable and that our country being the top international players is very important. These things may be more important than the alternatives, such as school sport which encourages fun exercise which would combat obesity.

(d) There is no much information here about the cultural perspective – possibly middle class, does not value sport but does value order.

(e) This comes from a cultural perspective which sees value in sport and hobbies other than winning and competition. It tends to value a psychological and educational approach.

(f) This comes from a cultural perspective which assumes that television stations are there to benefit the population (and could be contrasted with perspectives which see television as a tool for the government to use to control the population, or as private industry which needs only to make money...)

3. Encourage debate and discussion.

Activity 2

Note that dictionary skills – whether the dictionaries are online or in print – are invaluable, while online translation tools can de-skill students and tend to provide poor translations. Suggestions are given below, but encourage students to consider a range of definitions.

Encourage students to look up, research and debate the differences between the concepts. Encourage them to think of different examples for each concept.

Activity 3

Encourage students to think, discuss and work together to extend their understanding.

Note that each of the perspectives mentioned is highly complex, and most of them are only glimpsed in the documents. It would be necessary to find out much more to have a full understanding. But we can ask questions and do research to help ourselves understand these perspectives.

Encourage students to approach cultural perspectives by asking questions such as:

- What beliefs do these people share?
- What does this cultural perspective value most highly?
- Where do their beliefs come from?
- How do these people see the world?
- How do these people understand their place in the world?

Document 1

The cartoon takes a critical stance regarding football, corruption and the chances of Fifa arriving at fairness.

There is not much information about that cultural perspective.

Document 2

Keira comes from a cultural perspective which values sport and hobbies for their positive effects on people.

Hassan comes from an anti-sport cultural perspective, which believes that school sports humiliations are more damaging than any benefits they may bring.

Bina comes from a cultural perspective which values sport as being for all.

Document 3

The cultural perspective focuses on the value of one's own country being dominant in international sport, and believes that going back to basics with gymnastics is the way to success in all sports. Note that the author's focus is on Malaysia – but the general cultural perspective that holds international sporting success as important for one's own country is found in many countries.

Activity 4

1. The cartoon raises the issue of how corruption in sport is linked with general political corruption. Can we improve corruption in sport with a new law when everything around sport is corrupt?

2. Encourage discussion and debate.

3. Encourage students to justify their opinions.

4. Encourage students to think carefully about the search terms they use and to apply their skills.

Activity 5

1. Opinion, as it cannot be verified. This opinion can be supported with evidence and further opinions, but it is possible to disagree and argue that the examples given are not fundamental aspects of human nature.

2. '. . . if we introduce this as a policy, there will be far fewer problems with dissatisfied, unhappy people' / 'we'll have fewer issues with gangs, street violence and crime' / 'it will also make us more equal'. Each of these points predicts a consequence of introducing this policy.

3. 'It's wrong that they make children do sport at school.' Here, the word 'wrong' places a value on the idea of making children take part in sport. (Note that the phrase 'It's so embarrassing and humiliating' expresses personal dislike, but does not put a value on it in the way the word 'wrong' does.)

4. **Facts:** 'Only a small proportion of young people become elite athletes in national teams.' This can be verified.

'It's supposed to feed into national sport.' It might be possible to check whether there is a government policy that says that school sport should feed into national sport, in which case this could be a fact. Otherwise, it's simply an opinion about what school sport should achieve.

Opinions: '. . . the problem with school sport is that it's all about competition, and being the best.' / '. . . the rest of us get bored and give up.' / '. . . sport and exercise should be for everyone.' / 'We all need to be fit.' These are opinions with which it is possible to disagree. Some may argue that the final example is a fact, however it is possible to argue against it by saying that it might be healthier if we were all fit, but writers and teachers and office workers and drivers don't *need* to be fit. The point can also not be verified. Remind students not to confuse commonly held opinions with facts.

5. to **8.** Encourage discussion and debate, and remind students to apply their skills. Expect them to justify their opinions.

Activity 6

1. Malaysia must put more emphasis on the development of athletics, partly to avoid embarrassing failures in international competitions, but also because athletics, which is cheap to develop, will provide the skills to support the development of other sports.

2. Encourage students to discuss, debate and justify their views.

Activity 7

1. • Fact
   • Prediction
   • Opinion
   • Fact
   • Opinion (backed up with facts)

2. Encourage students to apply their skills.

Activity 8

1. Encourage students to research the issues that may affect each individual. Answers will vary. Suggested answers:

Working parent: Finding time for sports or recreation; finding money for sports and recreation; needing the benefits of sports and recreation to deal with the stress; spending time with the child(ren); engaging in sports and recreation as a family activity.

School student: Different national sports; different national attitudes to sport. A girl in Dubai will have different issues to those a boy in Dubai has; for example, her parents may think that sports clothing is immodest. Dubai is too hot for many sports, although the facilities available to the wealthy allow quite a range. In Beijing, the pollution can make outdoor activity unhealthy, but the air quality is improving.

Fourteen-year-old girl: Stress and strain on her body; hours of training; sacrificing social life and struggling with education in order to achieve her goals.

Politician: Finding time for personal health and recreation; making decisions about laws relating to the nation's sporting life.

Elite athlete: In addition to training, performing and being in the public eye, it may be tempting to become involved in illegal practices, such as giving information to people who should not have it, or making sure the event ends in a particular way.

2. and **3.** Encourage debate and discussion. Answers will vary.

Activity 9

1. to **6.** Encourage students to apply their skills, and to set up their lines of enquiry carefully.

Activity 10

Answers will vary. Encourage students to think carefully about what is likely and what is not.

Activity 11

Encourage discussion, and encourage students to think carefully about the most likely consequences.

Reflection

Reflection is an important part of the course, so it is important to allow class time for this activity. It may be useful to use a learning journal. This might allow for some ongoing written dialogue about the issues. The key here is to avoid simple praise or giving a student's thoughts a value; instead, try to engage a student in discussion over time – include questions in your written response that will push the student to the next level and expect them to respond.

Reflection

Encourage students to think carefully and to take this activity seriously, as this kind of reflection is an important part of the assessment.

7 Tradition, culture and identity

Introduction

What are our traditions? Why do we keep them, even when we migrate? Does our culture define us or can we choose our own identity? What do traditions mean to us? Does the effect of globalisation on minority cultures matter? What are the consequences of the loss of tradition? What happens to us when we move between cultures? These are some of the key questions relating to tradition, culture and identity.

Underlying their project work, students should have an awareness of the key issues relating to tradition, culture and identity, but their knowledge in this area is not being tested in itself. Projects can focus on any area of tradition, culture and identity, including specific traditions and their role in culture and identity formation, the effects of technology on culture, the relationship between everyday culture and high culture, or the effects on individuals of moving between cultures, as long as there is an active outcome and there are cross-cultural perspectives.

Suggested resources

http://video.nationalgeographic.com/video/movies/cultural-differences-ggtu	An interesting video on cultural differences, showing young boys from Sudan travelling to the USA.
http://www.debate.org/opinions/does-fashion-influence-culture	A site where individuals can post comments for or against particular questions, in this case whether or not fashion influences culture.
http://tckid.com/what-is-a-tck.html	Interesting information about third culture kids – children who are raised in a country with a different culture from that of their parents.
http://inhabitat.com/extraordinary-living-bridges-are-made-of-growing-roots-and-vines/	An article about living bridges, which are part of a fragile village culture in India.

Bride and Prejudice	A 2004 film directed by Gurinder Chadha. It retells Jane Austen's *Pride and Prejudice* in the context of India and the Indian diaspora. This film could be used to discuss a range of issues to do with tradition, culture and identity.
Quartet	A 2012 film directed by Dustin Hoffman. It features a lovely scene where an elderly opera singer and a teenage boy compare the merits of opera and rap, and the way they each express emotion. This film could also be used to ask other questions about culture and tradition, such as the role of art forms such as opera, the role of the elderly in society, the role of music in society, and the concept that love stories are for the young.

Suggested answers to the activities

Activity 2

Intangible cultural heritage	Traditions or living expressions inherited from our ancestors and passed on to our descendants, such as oral traditions, performing arts, social practices, rituals, festive events, knowledge and practices concerning nature and the universe, or the knowledge and skills to produce traditional crafts.
Culture	The ideas, customs, and social behaviour of a particular people or society. Culture also refers to the arts and other examples of human intellectual achievement.
Identity	Who a person or group is, and the characteristics that make them who they are and distinguish them from others.
National identity	The sense of a nation as a whole, represented by traditions, language and culture. The phrase can also refer to the feeling of belonging to a nation.
Global identity	The sense of belonging to the whole world, and of defining yourself as a citizen of the world.
Tradition	Beliefs, customs and practices that are handed down from generation to generation.
Reality	Things as they actually exist.

Art	The use of skill and imagination to produce beautiful objects.

Activity 3

Note that each of the perspectives mentioned is highly complex, and most of them are only glimpsed in the documents. It would be necessary to find out much more to have a full understanding. But we can ask questions and do research to help ourselves understand these perspectives.

Encourage students to approach cultural perspectives by asking questions such as:

- What beliefs do these people share?
- What does this cultural perspective value most highly?
- Where do their beliefs come from?
- How do these people see the world?
- How do these people understand their place in the world?

Document 1

There are a range of different cultural perspectives glimpsed here. The cartoon contrasts the beliefs that culture is what people do in everyday life with 'high' culture.

Chavez takes a political perspective.

Tan takes a literary perspective, seeing language as shaping the world.

Bernstein comes from a perspective which believes that 'idiot' culture should not drown 'high' culture.

Document 2

There is an attempt to be objective. There is not very much information on the cultural perspective.

Document 3

Anti-globalisation comes from a cultural perspective which believes that individualistic, different national identities are valuable. A high value seems to be placed here on the role of shopping in national and cultural identity.

@global-girl comes from a multi-cultural background, and suggests that she might have a range of cultural (and national) perspectives.

@lovemynationbecauseimtoldto comes from a cultural perspective which rejects Western cultural hegemony – that is, disapproves of Western ideas being imposed on all. This view does not accept national identity as something real.

Activity 4

1. For example:

    Chavez: Culture as a way of living and believing, which can include all aspects of society.

    Bernstein: 'idiot culture', in which the weird and stupid is mainstream culture and is actually admired, but doesn't reflect the whole culture.

    Cartoon: The 'decline of culture' tends to refer to culture as high-minded art, thinking, intellectualism, intelligentsia, etc. as opposed to more ordinary enjoyments.

2. **For example:** Culture is highly personal because the culture we live in becomes part of us, and affects our beliefs, the way we see the world, and our ambitions for ourselves. However, it can never be *only* personal because culture is by its nature bigger than an individual: it's a shared way of being. Yet culture and nation are not quite the same either. It is important to many nations that people share a culture and a way of seeing the world because this can unify a nation and make people want to work together. Today's nations are often multicultural. Making policies that are fair to all the cultural groups and that also create a national, unifying culture is an important job for national governments. Globally, cooperation can be easier if each party makes an effort to understand the culture of the others. For example, cooperation between the UK and China works better when each nation tries to understand what is important to the other and how its people see the world.

Activity 5

1. You need to know what sort of programmes make up 'local content'. For example, if the local content programmes are mainly news, current affairs and sports, this will not be a very good measure of how local culture is represented on television. This might give a local perspective on local, national and international affairs and on sporting competitions, however culture – in terms of the way people live, the way they use language and the things they see as important – tends to be more strongly represented in drama, soap operas, plays, detective stories, films and so on. If most of the television content is American, for example, then the people of New Zealand will be picking up American ideals, American ambitions, American language and American assumptions – that is, television will be representing American culture, rather than local New Zealand culture.

2. You need to know how much the BBC is watched in comparison with other channels and how much local content other channels offer, how much of this is prime-time programming and how you define local culture. For example, if other channels with different cultural biases have more viewers, then the BBC's high proportion of local content programmes does not necessarily indicate that people see their own culture represented. If the local content is shown significantly less at prime time and more in the middle of the night, then it's likely that people aren't seeing their own culture represented on television as much. On the other hand, if the local content is on at prime time and people watch it more than other channels showing non-local content, then people probably do see their own culture represented. How you define local culture is an important issue in the modern world. For example, do Scottish programmes aired in England count as local? What about northern European crime drama? Danish, Swedish and Norwegian crime drama has become very popular in the UK, possibly because the countries share elements of culture. Encourage students to think about these issues with regard to their own country and culture.

3. Yes, this is fairly reliable. The government has access to information and to experts, and is a reasonably accountable democratic government that would normally try to find and publish the truth.

4. This would be problematic because total air-time programming and prime-time programming are two different things. More people watch at prime time – just after school, just after work, at weekends – so this is a particularly important time in terms of deciding whether a culture is well represented. If 75% of total air time is local compared with only 10% of prime time, then most people will not be seeing a lot of local content and are therefore less likely to see their own culture represented.

Activity 6

1. It's actually quite hard to decide whose reasoning is most effective here. @anti_globalisation is rather extreme, predicting disastrous consequences and offering a false dilemma: either we fight globalisation or 'it will bring about the end of everything we value'. On the other hand, globalisation is increasing the similarities between locations around the world. There certainly are parts of the cities named that are very similar: the same chains of shops, the same style of shopping malls, and so on.

However, as @global_girl points out, there are also parts of these cities that are still very different, with their own identities. @global_girl makes some good points, especially in her second contribution, but she doesn't really provide reasoning, just observations and opinions. In addition, her first contribution contains assumptions that need to be explored, such as 'shopping and tourist districts are not culture'. In fact, you could argue that these areas *are* part of a city's culture; she seems to have an unstated belief about what culture is that she doesn't fully articulate. Her next sentence attacks @anti_globalisation without any evidence: we don't know whether or not @anti-globalisation has explored beyond the tourist districts. In her second contribution, however, @global_girl does respond directly to @lovemynationbecauseimtoldto and does give personal evidence to show that identity isn't fixed. These are strengths, but someone else could easily come back and give a different personal example to show that, for them, identity *is* fixed.

@lovemynationbecauseimtoldto has interesting points and gives examples to support the idea of national identities breaking down. The ideas do make logical sense and, even though it's not expressed here, they have theoretical backing. In addition, it is possible to verify that many modern nations are composed of several 'shifting cultural groups'. However, there is no support for the claim that the identities are breaking down everywhere because they were never real. There are other possible explanations as to why they might be breaking down. So, overall, @lovemynationbecauseimtoldto probably has the strongest reasoning, but it still needs a lot more support.

Activity 7

1. Encourage students to research the issues that may affect each individual. Answers will vary. Suggested answers:

Labourer: Assuming this is a rural labourer, city culture is very different from rural culture.

American student: Chinese and American cultures are very different: different things are important, different things offend people, business is done differently, the food is different, and festivals are different. Unless the student can read Chinese, they won't be able to read simple things like signs.

Film maker: Funding will be an issue, as will the question of an audience. Should the films be made in English for a global audience? Is that a form of betrayal of the local culture?

Toddler in Glasgow: Has a higher chance than toddlers elsewhere in the UK of belonging to a low status socio-economic group; less likely to have access to business culture or to art, theatre, film, live music and other forms of enabling culture.

Last speaker of minority language: It must be very lonely! Who are you if there is no one like you to recognise your identity and carry it into the future?

2. and 3. Encourage debate and discussion. Answers will vary.

Activity 8

1. to 6. Encourage students to apply their skills, and to set up their lines of enquiry carefully.

Activity 9

Answers will vary. Encourage students to think carefully about what is likely and what is not.

Reflection

Reflection is an important part of the course, so it is important to allow class time for this activity. It may be useful to use a learning journal. This might allow for some ongoing written dialogue about the issues. The key here is to avoid simple praise or giving a student's thoughts a value; instead, try to engage a student in discussion over time – include questions in your written response that will push the student to the next level and expect them to respond.

Reflection

Encourage students to think carefully and to take this activity seriously, as this kind of reflection is an important part of the assessment.

Water, food and agriculture

8

Introduction

Food and water, like air, are fundamental to our existence. Yet with more than seven billion people, only one earth, and massive inequalities in resource distribution, how can we ensure that everyone has fair access to food and water?

Underlying their project work, students should have an awareness of the key issues relating to water, food and agriculture, but their knowledge in this area is not being tested in itself. Projects can focus on any area of food, water and agriculture, including specific droughts, floods or famines, the role of science and genetic modification, the role of technology, food waste, or how to deal with poor food choices, as long as there is an active outcome and there are cross-cultural perspectives.

Suggested resources

http://www.monsanto .com	Monsanto is a company that provides pesticides and genetically modified seeds. This is the site of a controversial company and its clear perspectives should be considered.
http://www.oxfam.org. uk/blogs/subject/food-security	Oxfam is a leading anti-poverty charity. Its site offers a range of blogs relating to world food security.
http://foreignpolicy .com/2014/09/18/ water-wars/	Foreign Policy is a global magazine. This article uses complex language but contains some useful ideas.
http://www.aljazeera .com/indepth/features /2011/06/2011622193 147231653.html	Al Jazeera is a global news organisation. This accessible article provides information about water scarcity and conflict.
http://www.climate.org/ topics/agriculture.html	A page about the effects of climate change on agriculture, including some useful links and facts.
http://www.greenpeace. org/usa/sustainable-agriculture/issues/gmos/	Greenpeace is a leading environmental campaigning organisation. This page outlines the issues with genetic modification.

Suggested answers to the activities

Activity 1

1. Encourage students to read the comments for gist rather than worrying about the detail of the complex language. They are looking only for issues. The following are suggestions only. As long as students can justify their answers, other answers are acceptable.

   (a) Self-sufficiency

   (b) Water as a human right, water use

   (c) Sustainable farming

   (d) Affordable food

   (e) Access to clean water

2. Suggested answers:

   (a) This is a national perspective. It comes from a cultural perspective which values national independence.

   (b) This cultural perspective is fundamentally economic, seeing the world in economic terms. It values economic motivations – and seems not to understand any other kind of motivation.

   (c) This is a 'green' or 'environmentally friendly' perspective, which believes in the benefits of sustainable farming.

   (d) This is a journalistic, reporting cultural perspective. There is an emphasis on facts, with some prediction – and possibly a bit of fear mongering to boost sales.

   (e) This is the perspective of millions of poor parents around the world.

3. Encourage debate and discussion.

Activity 2

Note that dictionary skills – whether the dictionaries are online or in print – are invaluable, while online translation tools can de-skill students and tend to provide poor translations. Suggestions are given below, but encourage students to consider a range of definitions.

Self-sufficiency	Being able to provide for your own needs. For a country, this means providing all the food it needs.
National security	In the context of this topic, this refers to the safety of the country, and its ability to provide enough food in case of war.
Drought	A long period of unusually low rainfall.
Flooding	A situation where there is much more water than usual, and water overflows onto land.
Sustainable farming	The production of food, fibres or other products using safe, environmentally sound practices, in a way that can be continued over time without over-using resources.
Market forces	The economic factors affecting the price of, demand for, and availability of goods.
Price discrimination	Charging customers different prices for the same product or service. The seller may charge each customer the maximum price that he or she is willing to pay.
Pipeline	A long pipe, typically underground, for transporting oil, gas, etc. over long distances.

Activity 3

Encourage students to continue to discuss the definitions as they play to consolidate their understanding.

Note that each of the perspectives mentioned is highly complex, and most of them are only glimpsed in the documents. It would be necessary to find out much more to have a full understanding. But we can ask questions and do research to help ourselves understand these perspectives.

Encourage students to approach cultural perspectives by asking questions such as:

- What beliefs do these people share?
- What does this cultural perspective value most highly?
- Where do their beliefs come from?
- How do these people see the world?
- How do these people understand their place in the world?

Note that Europeans (and possibly others!) generally share a cultural perspective which sees water, food and agriculture as problems for LEDCs, especially for 'Africa', without differentiating 'Africa' into its various parts. There are, of course, very real problems in this area for LEDCs, many of which are on the African continent. But there are also very real problems in this area in HEDCs, many of which can get lost in concern about others. So the documents have been chosen to highlight that this really is a set of whole-world problems, including rich-world.

Document 1

This is a journalistic perspective, with an attempt to represent different cultural perspectives. We get glimpses of the perspective of the government needing to protect waterways and of the cultural perspective of the farmers – who mistrust government interference, who want to make a profit and are frustrated because government regulators have 'changed the rules'. There is a sense of unfairness.

Document 2

This comes from an economic cultural perspective which values price as a means of distributing resources. It doesn't seem to prioritise fairness or equal access to resources – but would probably argue that by using price mechanisms we can arrive at a *more* fair distribution of resources than we have at present.

A: Values fairness and equality.

B: This is an attempt to be objective, but seems to come from a cultural perspective which portrays poor people as 'other', and has a fairly low opinion of this 'other'. This indicates that this person does not see themselves as poor.

C: Values equal access of all to essentials.

Document 3

This is a semi-scientific, mainly journalistic cultural perspective, which makes scandal whilst trying to appear to value social fairness.

Document 4

Comes from a cultural perspective which supports farmers for humanitarian and national interest reasons.

@whodofthoughtit comes from a less well educated cultural perspective, which does not value logical argument. He believes that poor people (ie 'others') should have access to food, so has some social awareness, but distances himself from this other. He also values the status of his own country as contrasted with 'countries' such as Africa (which is, of course, a continent). This is not an empathetic perspective.

@Sweetpea attempts to empathise with farmers. Other than that, we have little information about her cultural perspective.

Activity 4

1. There have been increasing periods of drought.
2. Encourage debate and discussion.
3. Encourage discussion of likely consequences.
4. Encourage students to apply their skills.

Activity 5

1. It seems like a reliable source, which aims to share knowledge and has access to experts. It is partnered with reliable institutions such as the World Bank (although the World Bank may have a specific agenda, its backing lends this organisation credibility).
2. A's reasoning seems to be a reaction based on emotion rather than reason. It is important to treat all people as 'fully human' however poor they are, but whether or not the source is treating poor people as less than human is open to debate. For example, the source could be read as wanting to give poor people better access to water than they have currently. The consequences are rather extreme.
3. These consequences, while not certain, do seem likely. These will not be the consequences for all poor people, but B doesn't claim they will.
4. Encourage candidates to think, to refer clearly to the reasoning and to justify their opinions.

Activity 6

1. The fad for bottled water began as a way to be healthy – drinking bottled water instead of alcohol at lunch. However, drinking bottled water when water is free is unreasonable, and raises issues of social justice because many people don't have access to clean water at all.
2. Encourage candidate to apply their skills.
3. Encourage discussion and debate.

Activity 7

1. The newspaper isn't completely sensationalist because it attempts to be moderate – 'The government needs to seriously consider its policies. . .' – whereas a sensationalist newspaper might say something like 'Government failing farmers', 'Frantic farmers flee flocks' or 'What will we eat when war comes?' The article is also quite thoughtful, analysing causes and consequences. On the other hand, it talks about 'Our farmers', which is an emotional tactic, and fails to analyse fully the issues of food security, so while the paper is not completely sensationalist, it does not appear to be very serious either.

2. In the short term, the consequences of getting food from abroad may be positive for developed countries: cheaper food, better trade links, and the opportunity to sell other products abroad. However, for less developed countries, 'export agriculture' can lead to the need to import food for eating, which is expensive, and can mean that people are hungrier or more malnourished than if they grow food locally for local people to eat. It can also mean that local people have less disposable income for other things, such as education, consumer goods, and so on. Longer term, and in terms of food security, a country that relies on imports for food is likely to be vulnerable. Encourage candidates to think about how they would attack a country that depended on imported food. Attacking their food supplies would be one key way, and you wouldn't even have to be at war with a country that supplied food for this to be a real problem. Furthermore, war is not the only threat. What happens if oil prices rise so much that transporting food becomes prohibitively expensive but you no longer have people with farming skills (for example, because you've built offices and homes on the farms)?

3. @whoduvthoughtit is not very reliable. The basic facts are wrong: Africa is not a country and not all countries in Africa are poor.

4. The consequences that @whoduvthoughtit suggests are too extreme to be realistic. If meat and milk were more expensive, poor people would not have 'nothing to eat'; they might have to eat less meat and milk but there is nothing to suggest that grain, lentils, soya, eggs or vegetables would be unaffordable. The claim 'we'd be a poor country like Africa' is far too extreme and unrealistic. There is no logical reason why an increase in the price of meat and milk would make a whole country poor.

5. @whoduvthoughtit's reasoning is poor. It touches on one important issue – that poor people need to be able to afford to eat – but does so in an exaggerated way. The response fails to back up opinion with reasons and facts, and is emotional, illogical, ranting and lacking in empathy. For example, it doesn't suggest a reason why farmers should sell their products at less than the cost of producing them and directs an unfair emotional response at farmers. It doesn't consider the idea that farming is not a job but a lifestyle and a business. Farmers may feel that they lack the skills to do a different job or they may love their land and the work they do. More importantly, this attack on farmers misses the point: if farmers go out of business, food security becomes a serious issue.

6. This depends partly on how well @Sweetpea actually knows John and his circumstances. A 'friend's stepdad's old school friend' could be a distant connection, so this is very much second-hand evidence. This makes it a fairly unreliable source because this sort of testimony gets distorted and exaggerated. Alternatively, @Sweetpea might regularly spend time on the farm and have more first-hand evidence, which would be more reliable. We'd also need to question how typical John is.

7. @Sweetpea is giving an example that explains her opinion that we should take the plight of farmers more seriously. In so doing, she gives some reasons related to John's situation which might apply to other farmers: 'There is no money to be made', 'he's struggling', 'he can't just choose another job', ' Farming is in his blood, and the land is part of him'.

Activity 8

1. Encourage research and discussion.
2. Encourage discussion and debate.

Activity 9

1. to **6.** Encourage students to apply their skills, and to set up their lines of enquiry carefully.

Activity 10

Answers will vary. Encourage students to think carefully about what is likely and what is not.

Activity 11

Encourage discussion, and encourage students to think about what is really likely.

Reflection

Reflection is an important part of the course, so it is important to allow class time for this activity. It may be useful to use a learning journal. This might allow for some ongoing written dialogue about the issues. The key here is to avoid simple praise or giving a student's thoughts a value; instead, try to engage a student in discussion over time and include questions in your written response that will push the student to the next level, and expect them to respond.

Reflection

Encourage students to think carefully and to take this activity seriously, as this kind of reflection is an important part of the assessment.

1 Belief systems

Introduction

What is a belief? How much do our beliefs matter? To what extent should we accept other people's different beliefs? What is the power of belief?

Underlying their report, students should have an awareness of the key issues relating to belief systems, but their knowledge in this area is not being tested in itself. Reports can focus on any area of belief systems, including specific belief systems, religious and political tolerance, the power of belief to effect change, or the reasons why we believe different things, as long as there is a clear global research question, discussion of causes, consequences and perspectives, and a proposed solution.

Suggested resources

http://www.worldvaluessurvey.org/WVSContents.jsp?CMSID=Findings	Interesting maps showing the different beliefs prevalent in different parts of the world.
http://topdocumentaryfilms.com/power-of-belief/	An interesting video in which a sceptic and a scientist examine magical thinking and various superstitions and supernatural beliefs. A useful resource for getting us to question our beliefs. Note that the video is longer than it initially claims.
https://www.ted.com/talks/carol_dweck_the_power_of_believing_that_you_can_improve/transcript?language=en	Carol Dweck discusses positive beliefs about learning and their effects on learning.
http://www.skeptic.com/eskeptic/12-03-07/#feature	An article comparing the effects of scientific understanding on belief in supernatural and paranormal phenomena. Much of the content is accessible and a useful source of information.
http://www.livescience.com/16748-americans-beliefs-paranormal-infographic.html	An article about Americans' beliefs in the paranormal. The page includes links to other articles that explain the science and psychology behind these beliefs.
https://www.ted.com/talks/wade_davis_on_the_worldwide_web_of_belief_and_ritual/transcript?language=en	Wade Davis talks about a range of different belief systems. A good introduction and a good basis for further research into one of these belief systems.
http://www.skeptic.com/reading_room/conspiracy-theories-how-to-determine-true-conspiracies-from-false/?gclid=CIb3iaSpycgCFcZuGwod4sAPlw	A sceptical look at conspiracy theories.
http://www.theweek.co.uk/62926/conspiracy-theories-the-worlds-top-ten-secret-plots	Information about specific conspiracy theories, with some links and references to other sites. A useful resource for discussion about how you test and weigh evidence before deciding what to believe.

Suggested answers to the activities

Activity 1

1. Encourage students to read the comments for gist rather than worrying about the detail of the complex language. They are looking only for issues. The following are suggestions only. As long as students can justify their answers, other answers are acceptable.

   (a) Tolerance of others' beliefs

   (b) Scientific belief, religious belief, role of evidence in belief

   (c) Role of evidence in belief

   (d) Power of belief

   (e) Tolerance of others' beliefs, can a belief be wrong?

2. Suggested answers: others are possible if they can be justified:

B, C, D, F

A, C

E

3. Encourage debate and discussion.

Activity 2

1. Encourage students to understand that these are all forms of belief, but there are differences in the nature of these forms, as well as differences in how they are supported or justified. Knowledge has a strong justification in evidence, while religion has a strong justification in faith.

Belief	An idea that you hold with conviction or believe to be real. This can be any kind of idea, for example, religious, scientific, moral, or political.
Faith	Complete trust in someone or a strong belief in a particular religion. Often held to be belief without evidence or belief despite the evidence.
Superstition	A widely held but irrational belief in supernatural effects. Not based on knowledge or reason, and often relates to behaviour that is supposed to bring good or bad luck.
Knowledge	A belief based on reason, evidence and scholarship. Some argue that a belief must be certain and true in order to count as knowledge, but deciding whether or not a belief is true can be problematic; we can often only use evidence and reason to arrive at a highly probable idea of what the truth is.

2. Encourage discussion and debate. Moral standards are beliefs about what we should do and how we should treat each other. If, for example, other people hold moral beliefs that allow murder, it might be reasonable to argue that tolerating such beliefs would lead to a fall in moral standards. However, many populist newspapers talk of any change or acceptance of others' beliefs as an unacceptable fall in moral standards, when in fact that change might be positive.

Activity 3

1. Use the words below to fill in the gaps

Most of us want the freedom to believe whatever we want. But there must be some restrictions. If we believe in religious freedom for ourselves, we must **tolerate** other people's religious views. This includes the idea that we should not **discriminate** against other people on the basis of their beliefs, for example when choosing employees.

When should our beliefs be restricted by the facts? Religious belief is characterised by **faith**, so religious believers sometimes hold their beliefs despite the **facts**. **Scientists**, on the other hand, tend to believe only what can be supported by facts and evidence. It is important to be able to **distinguish** clearly between beliefs which need **proof** and those which do not. For instance, it would not make sense at all to believe that the sky is green.

Activity 4

1. **(a)** Beliefs relating to benefit fraud, immigration, crime, immigration, what the Government spends money on (including foreign aid, Jobseekers' Allowance and pensions). Encourage students to state the beliefs clearly.

(b) Encourage students to express clearly the contrast between the facts and the beliefs.

2. to 4. Encourage discussion and debate.

Activity 5

1. Intellectual integrity (or honesty) is linked to beliefs based on things you can observe (often especially linked to the scientific method). 'Just belief' refers to faith, where there is no evidence to support the belief. This could be faith in God, faith in oneself, or trust in another person. Some aspects of life, such as religion, require belief without evidence; people who believe both in God and in the need for proof can feel very conflicted.

2. Belief is a personal issue, especially when it comes to religion. However, it also matters on a national level. For example, if people really believed that they should lead a healthy lifestyle (rather than believing that burgers and a film are better than salad and some exercise), the national health would be better, and this would contribute to economic productivity. People who show intolerance towards those who hold different beliefs to themselves can contribute to violence and social problems on a national level. This is even more significant globally, when nations go to war over their differing beliefs.

Activity 6

1. The study shows that people's beliefs about the drink had a real effect on their test scores. People who believed the drink made a significant difference to mental performance scored significantly higher than the control group in the test, as did people who believed the drink was bought at full price. On the other hand, people who believed that the drink provided only a slight improvement tended to perform less well than the control group, and believing that the drink was bought at a discount made their scores even worse.

2. Piece of information: How a group who had not had the energy drink scored compared with a group who had had the drink.

   How it would help: If the people who had had the drink showed a higher performance, then it would be possible to conclude that the drink had a real effect, assuming a control group had been included. If the people who had not had the drink performed just as well, then it would be possible to conclude that the effects of the energy drink were merely psychological.

Activity 7

1. You would need to know whether the mother regularly left her children alone and for how long. Leaving a five-year-old child once for two minutes is very different from regularly leaving babies for two hours, for example, and taking children from a mother for a minor slip might do more harm than good. You would also need to know more about the mother's behaviour generally. If she was generally neglectful, struggling with addiction, or even abusive, then @Suki would probably have helped the children by removing them from a painful situation; however, if she was generally loving and kind, then the children might have suffered by being taken away. Evidence about what happened to the children afterwards might also help to determine whether @Suki's intervention has done more harm than good. Did the children find a loving home? Did they complete their education? Did they get good jobs and become loving parents? If they did, the decision might have been a good one; if they did not, it may be more difficult to establish the cause of their problems – whether these are due to their early experiences with a struggling mother, their removal from her, or their experiences following their removal.

2. (a) 'Our behaviour depends on our beliefs.' This is an opinion, as it cannot be verified. You can also argue against it, for example by saying that our behaviour might depend on instinct, reason or on the law rather than on beliefs.

   (b) '... we shouldn't tolerate beliefs that cause harm.' This is a value judgement, which is a kind of opinion. It cannot be checked or verified, and it deals with morals and how things should be, so it's about values.

3. Cleaning our teeth seems like a good example of a personal, non-threatening behaviour affected by beliefs. However, you could argue that we clean our teeth because our parents told us to or because they feel better if they are clean, and you could also show that some people don't clean their teeth even though they believe it would keep them healthy. So this might not be as good an example as it seems.

4. @deepthinker's response is reasonable because it is true that beliefs don't harm anyone if you keep them to yourself. On the other hand, some people are offended by the different beliefs others hold. Is this harmful? And who is inflicting the harm in this case? It might be true that beliefs lead to actions, but they don't always lead to the same actions. For example, two people might believe that immigrants cause problems, but one might stay at home quietly and the other might preach hatred. So it is reasonable for @deepthinker to distinguish between beliefs and actions.

5. @thatsallthereis's reasoning is very ineffective. It attacks the arguers instead of the arguments with the phrase 'You all are wishy-washy liberals'. It then goes on to restrict the options with the idea that 'either we tolerate all beliefs, or we tolerate none', which doesn't make sense as we clearly do tolerate our own beliefs, even if we don't tolerate those of others. The next part of @thatsallthereis's argument is very poor, featuring extreme, unconnected consequences, and a contradiction of the first part of the reasoning.

Activity 8

1. Encourage students to research the issues that may affect each individual. Answers will vary. Suggested answers:

Migrant: May believe that Germany will be a better place than war-torn Syria, but may find that refugee camps and hostility from the local people, combined with cold weather and general strangeness, is even worse than home (or they may be correct in their belief, if they find themselves in a supportive, friendly place); likely to be Muslim (although there are also Christians fleeing from Syria), while Germany's population is mainly Christian, so may encounter religious intolerance. (Note that, while Germany is a mainly Christian nation, it has a large minority of Muslims, and there is currently (in 2015) political division within Germany in relation to this. PEGIDA is fighting against the islamification of Europe, but there is a strong counter-movement of people protesting against PEGIDA and welcoming refugees.)

Female head of state: Likely to have to contend with men – and other women – who believe that leadership is a male privilege or characteristic.

Woman who wants to wear a hijab in Paris: Likely to face discrimination. There is a strong movement to ban the hijab in France. The justification for this is that France is a secular society and does not allow religious symbols to be prominent, whether they are Christian or Muslim. However, this is underpinned by a group in society who are not tolerant of others' beliefs.

Woman who does not want to wear a hijab or a niqab in Riyadh: Likely to face serious consequences because of the strong belief – and law – in Saudi Arabia that women must be covered in public.

Physics professor: Conflict perhaps between the scientific belief in the need for evidence, and faith in God. Many physicists who believe in God have come to a resolution in their minds that these are two different kinds of belief, and that they are not contradictory.

Activity 9

1. to 6. Encourage students to apply their skills, and to set up their lines of enquiry carefully.

Activity 10

Answers will vary. Encourage discussion and debate, and remind students to think carefully about what is likely and what is not.

Biodiversity and ecosystem loss

2

Introduction

What is biodiversity? Why should we preserve it? How much do ecosystems matter? How can we save them? Is it worth sacrificing prosperity in order to protect them?

Underlying their report, students should have an awareness of the key issues relating to biodiversity and ecosystem loss, but their knowledge in this area is not being tested in itself. Reports can focus on any area of biodiversity and ecosystem loss, including specific ecosystems and their benefits, specific species that are endangered, the possibilities for change, or the relationship between economic and environmental concerns when we are talking about biodiversity and ecosystems, as long as there is a clear global research question, discussion of causes, consequences and perspectives, and a proposed solution.

Suggested resources

http://www.bee-leader.eu/en/bees-biodiversity-project	Information about a project to reduce the loss of bee colonies.
http://www.chinadaily.com.cn/regional/2015-10/08/content_22153281.htm	An article on Chinese efforts to improve biodiversity and look after coral reefs.
http://www.theguardian.com/environment/2015/jun/17/bees-are-worth-billions-to-farmers-across-the-globe-study-suggests	An article from *The Guardian* newspaper about the value of bees to agriculture. The text consists largely of facts and figures but is accessible.
http://www.theguardian.com/environment/biodiversity	A list of articles from *The Guardian* newspaper on the subject of biodiversity, organised by month. A range of global biodiversity issues is covered, and the photography is impressive.
http://www.sciencedaily.com/releases/2015/10/151014142135.htm	A report on the ways in which biodiversity can help ecosystems survive extreme weather. A challenging read, but many students will be able to pick out the main ideas.
http://www.abc.net.au/pm/content/2012/s3498341.htm	An Australian Broadcasting Company programme on links between declining biodiversity and the rise of asthma and allergies.

Suggested answers to the activities

Activity 1

1. Encourage students to read the comments for gist rather than worrying about the detail of the complex language. They are looking only for issues. The following are suggestions only. As long as students can justify their answers, other answers are acceptable.

    (a) Value of different ecosystems, human consequences of ecosystem loss

    (b) Effects of human activity on ecosystems

    (c) Relationship between economics and environmental concerns

    (d) Human consequences of ecosystem loss

    (e) Relationship between economics and environmental concerns, role and value of biodiversity

    (f) Relationship between economics and environmental concerns, changes we need to make

2. Suggested answers:

    (a) A, C

    (b) A, B, E

    (c) A, D, F

Activity 2

Note that dictionary skills – whether the dictionaries are online or in print – are invaluable, while online translation tools can de-skill students and tend to provide poor translations. Suggestions are given below, but encourage students to consider a range of definitions.

Biodiversity	The variety of life on earth; the number and variety of different species in a particular habitat. This includes plants, animals, insects, fungi, bacteria, etc.
Ecosystem	A complex set of relationships between the living and non-living parts of a natural habitat.
Mangroves	Salty, seawater swamps dominated by trees or shrubs with tangled roots that grow at least partly above ground. The trees can also be called mangroves.
Habitat loss	The destruction of a natural habitat, a place where a particular kind of creature lives, so that that creature can no longer live there. Habitat loss can be caused by human activity or extreme weather events.
Deforestation	The clearing of trees; turning a forest into cleared land. Also used to refer to the overall loss of forests.
Reforestation	Planting of trees; turning cleared land back into forest.
Conservation	The protection, preservation, management, or restoration of wildlife and of natural resources such as rivers, forests, soil, habitats, and ecosystems.
Financial incentives	Benefits in terms of money used to persuade people to behave in ways that they normally would not.

Activity 3

Encourage students to think, discuss and work together to extend their understanding.

Activity 4

1. The trees 'act as a buffer against the wind and heavy rains, breaking their intensity just before they make landfall'.
2. Mangroves form 'a vital part of the natural cycle in coastal lagoons. Fish and other marine creatures like prawns use the deep roots as breeding areas. The forests protect coastal communities from abrupt tidal shifts and storms, while slowing shore erosion'.
3. to 5. Encourage students to apply their research skills and encourage discussion.

Activity 5

1. Hong Kong suffers from long-term habitat loss caused by human activity, although to some extent this is now being reversed, having been helped by the introduction of the country parks. The local people do not appreciate their biodiversity and, instead, see it as a threat. One ongoing threat is the use of rare animals in traditional Chinese medicine.

Activity 6

1. We need to know whether Adam's uncle simply has memories of DDT use and its consequences, or whether he has expert knowledge about DDT use and its consequences, for example, as a scientist, teacher or historian. We also need to know whether he tends to be truthful or whether he is prone to exaggeration.

2. Adam tends to exaggerate: 'politicians **never** think their decisions through', 'killed **all** the birds', 'now there are **no** bees', 'going to be a **total** disaster'. This makes him less reliable. We might assume that Adam is quite young and not himself an expert, as his main source of information is his uncle. This also makes him less reliable. We need to know whether Adam has done any research into bees and pollination, and whether he might have a reason to lie or to tell only part of the truth.

   Dinesh presents argument and prediction rather than information and we therefore have limited information about his reliability. We need to know whether he has researched this issue, whether he is an expert, and whether he has any reason to support one view in particular. For example, is he working for an organisation like Greenpeace?

3. Adam tends to exaggerate quite a lot, which undermines a basically sound line of reasoning. It would be easy to dismiss Adam as a result of his exaggeration rather than listening to his ideas.

   '... [DDT] just killed all the birds...' This is too extreme. DDT may have killed many birds, but we still have birds today so this is not a realistic consequence. However, the idea that DDT had harmful consequences for birds is reasonable.

   '... there are no bees...' This is also too extreme. Pesticides are killing significant numbers of bees, but 'no bees' is not yet a consequence, and is unlikely to be.

'... this is going to be a total disaster.' The problem with this point is that it is too general and too vague, and therefore seems more exaggerated than it is. The consequences of insufficient bees to pollinate food crops will indeed be serious; disaster might not be an exaggeration here. It is likely that there will be food shortages, that prices will rise, and that people will go hungry – and this may lead to riots, civil unrest, political instability, conflict, and humanitarian crises. It is also likely that people will find ways to protect or bring back bees, move towards wind-pollinated crops, employ people to pollinate plants using paintbrushes (as they currently do in some plant nurseries) and find new ways to ensure that plants can be pollinated.

4. Dinesh suggests some reasonable consequences, but doesn't really show why these consequences are likely, or why they are more likely than rules about use of biodiversity helping to protect it. He also both states and implies that these are consequences are negative ones, but does not explicitly explain *why* they are negative.

   '[Making a set of rules about how our biodiversity can be used] will result in a price tag on biodiversity.' It is possible that setting rules could lead to costs and prices being applied. This would certainly be one way of enforcing the rules; for example, 'Yes, you can cut logs / use that plant for medicines, but you will have to pay $20 billion'. This would be a very complex process with many complex steps of causes and consequences. Dinesh seems to have a problem with this because of a further consequence: that the rich will be able to exploit the poor. However, there is an alternative: the rules could be set up to protect the interests of poorer countries.

   '... we'll only conserve the things we understand the value of.' This seems a very likely consequence, as it would be hard to persuade people to take losses now for the sake of resources that they think have little value. An alternative consequence would be that we conserve all ecosystems and biodiversity equally, but this seems much less realistic, as we have limited resources to do so.

   'It will be a way of rich countries gaining commercial benefit while poor countries are exploited.' This is also possible and even, sadly, likely. It is probable that rich countries would have a large role to play in setting up any rules, and might not even recognise that they were setting them up for their own benefit. An alternative consequence is that the rules are well set up to protect the interests of poor countries in their diverse ecosystems, though this might be hard to achieve due to conflicts of interest in poor countries.

5. Adam's example of DDT is exaggerated and vague, and needs to be based more on evidence. It doesn't show that politicians never think their decisions through, but it does show that unintended consequences can be a problem. The example of the bees is also useful and relevant, but again more evidence is needed. For example, which pesticides kill bees? Have many studies been done? Is this a vague rumour or scientifically supported? How serious is the problem? How widespread is the problem? Is it a problem only faced by rich countries? In addition, Adam states that 'Thirty percent of our food needs to be pollinated'. Where does this figure come from? What does Adam want to achieve with this fact? Adam uses emotion when he talks about 'total disaster' and 'There are already enough hungry people'. Here, he is using sensationalism to appeal to our fears. Overall, Adam has a good idea of a problem, but he doesn't use give reasons or use evidence well. He is too vague and prone to exaggeration to make a clear point.

6. Dinesh doesn't give any evidence at all. His reasoning would be better if he had some evidence to support the consequences he predicts. Each of the consequences he suggests is a reason why making a set of rules about the use of biodiversity is a 'terrible idea'. Why these consequences and not others? Dinesh uses emotion when he talks about poor countries being 'exploited'. He is appealing to a sense of injustice and unfairness. His argument is better structured and reasoned than Adam's, but still problematic.

Activity 7

Encourage debate and discussion.

Activity 8

1. to **10.** Encourage students to apply their skills, and to set up their lines of enquiry carefully.

Activity 9

Encourage students to apply their skills and to undertake additional research if necessary.

Reflection

Reflection is an important part of the course, so it is important to allow class time for this kind of activity.

Changing communities

3

Introduction

What is a community? Who is in a particular community? What makes a strong community? How are communities changing around the world? Will changing populations, changing religions, changing working lives, and the changing social and economic roles of women change communities? Will this necessarily be a bad thing?

Underlying their report, students should have an awareness of the key issues relating to changing communities, but their knowledge in this area is not being tested in itself. Reports can focus on any area of changing communities, including specific communities and their challenges, the effects of de-industrialisation on communities, the possibilities for change, loneliness and isolation, or the changing religious and cultural make-up of communities, as long as there is a clear global research question, discussion of causes, consequences and perspectives, and a proposed solution.

Suggested resources

http://www.iied.org/urban-communities-are-devising-their-own-solutions-build-resilience	A report from the International Institute for Environment and Development about the ways in which communities are changing in response to specific difficulties relating to climate change. The report describes a community-led response.
http://www.theguardian.com/australia-news/2015/may/07/remote-aboriginal-communities-still-in-limbo-despite-release-of-major-reforms	A report on reforms affecting Australia's Aboriginal communities, which includes a short, interesting video.
http://www.abc.net.au/local/videos/2014/08/18/4069130.htm	A video report about a photographer who uses his art to contribute to local communities.
http://says.com/my/news/from-broken-bridges-to-paved-roads-how-impian-malaysia-is-changing-lives-in-rural-sarawak	A report and video about initiatives to promote development and change communities in less developed parts of Malaysia.
http://www.establishmentpost.com/multiculturalism-uniquely-singaporean-identity/	An exploration of Singaporean society as multicultural.

Suggested answers to the activities

Activity 1

1. Encourage students to read the comments for gist rather than worrying about the detail of the complex language. They are looking only for issues. The following are suggestions only. As long as students can justify their answers, other answers are acceptable.

   (a) Shrinking cities

   (b) De-industrialisation, different local communities within a nation

   (c) Community control and decision making, community response to climate change

   (d) Online communities

   (e) Religion and community

2. Suggested answers:

   (a) C, D

   (b) A, B, C

   (c) E

Activity 2

Note that dictionary skills – whether the dictionaries online or in print – are invaluable, while online translation tools can de-skill students and tend to provide poor translations. Suggestions are given below, but encourage students to consider a range of definitions.

Demographics	Statistical information about a population; the study of populations through statistics.
De-industrialisation	Reduction in the amount of industry; the decline of manufacturing in a community.
Modernisation	Making something modern.
Rural	Relating to the countryside (rather than towns and cities).
Secularisation	Changing something – usually a country, a school or an institution – so that it is no longer controlled by or closely associated with religion or religious institutions.
Social enterprise	Businesses that use business strategies to tackle social problems.
Social isolation	A state or process in which people, groups or cultures lose communication with others.
Urbanisation	An increase in the proportion of people living in cities rather than in the countryside. It can mean the movement of people from the country to the city. It can also mean the growth and spread of cities.

Activity 3

1. Encourage students to continue to discuss the definitions as they play, to consolidate their understanding.

Activity 4

1. and 2. Encourage students to think carefully about possible consequences, and what is really likely. Encourage discussion.

Activity 5

1. Opinion, as it cannot be verified: it's what Javier believes.

2. Whether this is fact or exaggeration depends on the scale of the urbanisation and the resources available. It is possible that so many people are arriving and so few resources are available that the pressure on the city's resources is genuinely unmanageable. The word 'unmanageable' sounds extreme and exaggerated and is often used simply to mean 'difficult'. If it is possible to verify that the pressure is unmanageable (as opposed to difficult to manage), then it is a fact. However, it is more likely that it is merely difficult to manage and that some people who used to have good access to the resources now have to make sacrifices. So this is probably an exaggeration.

3. Encourage students to think carefully about search terms.

4. **Opinion:** 'We can't prevent urbanisation.' / 'It's happening so we have to deal with it.' / '... [we don't have slums] because the government made strict rules about land use'.

   Prediction: If governments and city leaders make good decisions, urbanisation will be a good thing.

5. Encourage students to think carefully about search terms, what sort of site would be useful, and the use of images as sources of information.

6. Encourage students to apply their skills, thinking carefully about search terms and the sort of information they need.

7. Opinion, as it cannot be verified: Ngoc's claims are supported, but you could agree or disagree with them.

8. This could be either fact or exaggeration (it is actually taken from reports that seem to be factual, but encourage students to think through the possibilities and to make checks). Encourage students to think carefully about search terms and what sort of site would be useful.

Activity 6

1. **Key issue:** In developed countries, many cities are shrinking and declining.

   Causes: Populations are shrinking in developed nations; people are moving from smaller cities to bigger cities with strong economies and communities.

   Consequences: Economic decline in small cities, which leads to more people moving away; crime can flourish.

Possible solutions: Use incentives to attract businesses to smaller cities or manage the decline (this article argues that the consequences of managing decline are better); provide cheaper accommodation where people want to live; return declining areas of older cities to nature.

2. Encourage students to apply their skills, to think about their search terms carefully, and to consider the kinds of information they need.

Activity 7

1. 'loneliness', 'isolation of the elderly', 'spending cuts to services'.

2. 'The mobilisation of local and social entrepreneurship', 'Building on what's already there', 'Bridging gaps between neighbours'.

3. Encourage students to look up terms they do not understand, and encourage debate and discussion about the ways that that these mechanisms might help to address the three key challenges.

4. and 5. Encourage students to apply their skills.

Activity 8

1. Encourage students to research the issues that may affect each individual. Answers will vary. Suggested answers:

    Labourer: May have to live in a place that does not yet have suitable infrastructure, such as running water, electricity or effective transport links; there may be more work, or better paid work, than there was at home.

    School student: Too many students in each class; students arriving with diverse needs that might take up the teacher's time and attention; (possibly) insufficient infrastructure; parents may have more money but less time. Increased diversity may stimulate thought, empathy, new ideas and understandings. For students who have recently migrated, the bigger city may be challenging but the standard of education may be better.

    Owner of a new computer business: May benefit from a rapidly growing customer base but may find a great deal of competition, high overheads, and insufficient infrastructure.

    Commuter: Crowded trains, buses and trams; a lack of trains, buses and trams going to the new residential areas.

    City leader: Good to be managing a growing city; an exciting challenge but a big one; will need to manage the demands on resources and plan for a bigger population.

2. Answers will vary. Encourage research and discussion. Suggested answers:

    Young person: May be difficult if family members are in shrinking cities and most career opportunities are in bigger cities; shrinking cities are a less vibrant place to build a careeer. On the other hand, accommodation is cheaper in a shrinking city, some jobs that can be done remotely, and some jobs – such as hairdressers, teachers, plumbers and lawyers – are always needed, even if in smaller numbers.

    Government policymaker: Will need to decide whether to try to attract businesses to shrinking cities or to manage the decline; will need to take the human cost into consideration.

    Someone who wants to set up a business: Shrinking cities have declining markets, and it may be harder to attract the right quality of workers if the younger, most competent candidates have moved to the bigger cities. However, costs are likely to be lower in a shrinking city.

3. and 4. Encourage debate and discussion.

Activity 9

1. to 6. Encourage students to apply their skills, and to set up their lines of enquiry carefully.

Activity 10

Encourage discussion, and encourage students to think carefully about the most likely consequences.

Reflection

Reflection is an important part of the course, so it is important to allow class time for this kind of reflection. It may be useful to use a learning journal. This might allow for some ongoing written dialogue about the issues. The key here is to avoid simple praise or giving a student's thoughts a value; instead, try to engage a student in discussion over time and include questions in your written response that will push the student to the next level, and expect them to respond.

Reflection

Encourage students to think carefully about their research materials, and to do more research if necessary.

4 Digital world

Introduction

Digital technology has changed the world almost beyond recognition in a very short space of time and will probably continue to do so for some time to come. This raises a number of questions, including whether or not the effects of digital technology on our brains and on our culture are positive ones. We also have to ask questions about fairness and access to this technology.

Underlying their report, students should have an awareness of the key issues relating to the digital world, but their knowledge in this area is not being tested in itself. Reports can focus on any area of the digital world, including specific digital developments and their global consequences, issues of fairness and access to high speed internet connection, the ways in which governments and businesses use our data, digital surveillance, or the effects of digital technology on trade or culture, as long as there is a clear global research question, discussion of causes, consequences and perspectives, and a proposed solution.

Suggested resources

http://www.bbc.co.uk/newsbeat/article/34328417/cyberbullying-worse-than-face-to-face-abuse-suggests-global-research	An accessible article giving information from a global study on online bullying.
http://nobullying.com/cyberbullying-bullying-statistics-2014-finally/	A page with recent cyberbullying statistics.
http://timesofindia.indiatimes.com/home/education/news/Cyberbullying-is-ragging-treat-it-as-such-CBSE/articleshow/46522406.cms	A suggestion from India about how to deal with cyberbullying by refusing to give students their grades.
http://www.interpol.int/Crime-areas/Cybercrime/Cybercrime	Information on cybercrime from the world's largest international police organisation.

http://www.forensicscolleges.com/blog/resources/cybercrime-on-rise-2015	Information about specific cybercrimes on the rise in 2015. The text is challenging, but many students will be able to extract key information from this report.
http://www.midanmasr.com/en/article.aspx?ArticleID=200	An article about the effects of digital technology on art.
https://search.wikileaks.org/?q=digital+surveillance	WikiLeaks search results relating to digital surveillance. WikiLeaks releases information that many governments would rather keep secret.
The Fifth Estate	A 2013 film relating to the WikiLeaks scandal and the life of Julian Assange.

Suggested answers to the activities

Activity 1

1. Encourage students to read the comments for gist rather than worrying about the detail of the complex language. They are looking only for issues. The following are suggestions only. As long as students can justify their answers, other answers are acceptable.

   (a) Effects of computer use on our brains, effects on culture

   (b) Effects of computer use on our brains, effects on culture

   (c) Digital surveillance, (possibly) international connectedness

   (d) Access to broadband/computers

   (e) Pace of change, effects on culture

   (f) International connectedness

2. Suggested answers:

   (a) B, F

   (b) C, E

   (c) A, D

3. Encourage debate and discussion.

Activity 2

Note that dictionary skills – whether the dictionaries are online or in print – are invaluable, while online translation tools can de-skill students and tend to provide poor translations. Suggestions are given below, but encourage students to consider a range of definitions.

1.

Digital	Digital describes electronic technology that generates, stores and processes data in terms of two states: positive and non-positive. Positive is expressed or represented by the number 1 and non-positive by the number 0. Thus, data transmitted or stored with digital technology is expressed as a string of 0's and 1's. Each of these state digits is referred to as a bit. http://whatis.techtarget.com/definition/digital

2.

3. Encourage the development of strong dictionary skills.

Activity 3

1. C

2. Encourage students to work together.

   (a) True.

   (b) False. Australia had relatively high broadband costs in 2011, but broadband was relatively affordable.

3. and **4.** Encourage research, debate and discussion.

Activity 4

1. Millions of people around the world are putting data onto social media sites like Facebook, and companies can use this data however they like without our permission.

2. to **5.** Encourage debate and discussion.

Activity 5

1. Encourage research and discussion.

2. Encourage debate and discussion.

3. Encourage students to think carefully about what sort of experiment would show when we make the most ethical decisions. For example, it would be possible to give groups of people ethical judgements to make while wearing or not wearing a tDCS cap. One difficulty might be how to decide what counts as a more ethical decision.

Activity 6

1. Encourage research and discussion. Suggestions include:

   (a) The boss may have access to a lot of online information about the employee, especially if the potential employee has not been careful about their privacy settings, or if their friends have tagged them in embarrassing photos. This is likely to be more the case in an HEDC where access to the internet is more affordable.

   (b) The internet will allow for research of the competition, simplify the process of setting up a business, and provide a sales route. Although the internet is more expensive in LEDCs, it can provide an even more important access to markets here.

   (c) This person may find that their emails and online activities are observed. They may raise security alarms at airports.

   (d) She needs a better internet connection on trains!

   (e) A child just starting school will need to develop the ability to keep learning new technologies.

Activity 7

Answers will vary. Encourage discussion and debate, and remind students to think carefully about what is likely and what is not.

Reflection

Reflection is an important part of the course, so it is important to allow class time for this kind of activity. It may be useful to use a learning journal. This might allow for some ongoing written dialogue about the issues. The key here is to avoid simple praise or giving a student's thoughts a value; instead, try to engage a student in discussion over time and include questions in your written response that will push the student to the next level, and expect them to respond.

5 Family

Introduction

Around the world, families are changing. Increasingly, more parents are having just one or two children, and increasing numbers of people are having no children at all. Parents are separating and re-marrying, creating complicated family relationships. Our very first, and perhaps most deeply rooted, sense of identity develops from our relationships with our families. So these changes in families are, in turn, changing how we see ourselves and how we see the world. How much will this affect the way we interact with the world?

Underlying their report, students should have an awareness of the key issues relating to families, but their knowledge in this area is not being tested in itself. Reports can focus on any area of family, including specific family structures and their benefits, changing socio-economic roles of parents, family values, the effects of migration, poverty and government policy on families, or aging families, as long as there is a clear global research question, discussion of causes, consequences and perspectives, and a proposed solution.

Suggested resources

http://worldfamilymap. ifstudies.org/2014/ articles/world-family- indicators/family- structure	Statistical data on families from around the world, including useful graphics.
http://blog. euromonitor. com/2013/07/special- report-the-family- structure-of-the-future. html	A report featuring predictions about family structure based on trends in data. The report includes helpful graphics and is useful for comparing predictions with what is actually happening, as well as spotting trends.
http://www. washingtonpost.com/ news/wonkblog/ wp/2013/04/04/ people-who-marry- young-are-happier- but-those-who-marry- later-earn-more/	Interesting statistics on the effects on happiness and income of marrying at different ages. The article also includes a useful mention of the difficulties in drawing conclusions from the data available.

http://www.icrw.org/ child-marriage-facts- and-figures	Information and statistics about the causes and consequences of child marriage. The ICRW also has many other articles relating to women and their role in families.
http://www. channelnewsasia. com/news/singapore/ changing-trends-in- family/1864600.html	Information about the changing family structure in Singapore, including the sandwich generation, where people are looking after their parents as well as their children.
https://publichealth. yale.edu/news/article. aspx?id=11240	Information on the effects of Chinese pensions on Chinese family structure and social life.
http://www. theglobeandmail. com/news/national/ new-family-structures- elbowing-their-way- into-collective-portrait/ article4556027/	An article about new family structures in Canada.

Suggested answers to the activities

2. Suggested answers:

   (a) B, D, F

   (b) C, (possibly) E

   (c) A, E

3. Encourage debate and discussion.

Activity 2

Note that dictionary skills – whether the dictionaries are online or in print – are invaluable, while online translation tools can de-skill students and tend to provide poor translations. Suggestions are given below, but encourage students to consider a range of definitions.

Marriage	A legally accepted relationship between two people, who share their lives and their home.
Maternity leave	A period in which a woman is legally allowed to be absent from work while she gives birth to a child and for a short time afterwards.
Paternity leave	A period in which a man is legally allowed to be absent from work to look after a young child.
Quality time	Time spent giving a child, partner or loved one your undivided attention. The idea is that the time spent together, which does not have to be long, is high quality and enjoyable.
Young caregiver	Also known as a young carer, this is a child who has primary responsibility for looking after someone, often a parent, who is ill or who has special needs.
Family priorities	The things that are most important for a particular family, or for families in general.
Family values	Values (supposedly) learned within a traditional family unit, typically those of high moral standards and discipline.

Activity 3

Encourage students to think, discuss and work together to extend their understanding.

Activity 4

1. Cartoon 1 raises the issue of how parents and children relate to each other and interact, and the effects of the generation gap in technological and online living. Cartoon 2 raises the issue of the effects of technology, which mean that children can do things their parents can't. How does that affect the relationship between them?

2. Encourage discussion.

3. Encourage debate and discussion.

Activity 5

Encourage research, debate and discussion.

Activity 6

1. This could be a fact, if you can verify that Anya's family never lets her do what she wants. There are some families where this might happen. However, it is more likely to be an opinion based the frustration of a few instances of not being allowed a free rein and then exaggerated, especially as Anya also says that her family are wonderful. We see another instance of probable exaggeration when she says, 'they are **always** arguing'.

2. **Facts:** 'I live with my mum.'/'It's just the two of us.'/ '... we watch films together and cook together.' / 'I help with the household chores...'/'... I make a mess too.' All these can be verified. (Note that 'I help with the household chores...' could be an unfounded opinion.)

   Opinions: 'Sometimes this is great...'/'Sometimes though, I wish we had a bigger family.' These points are about how Kofi feels, and cannot be verified as facts.

   Prediction: 'I think my mum will be lonely when I leave home.' Here, Kofi is talking about a future event.

   Value judgment: '... it's only fair...' This is about what Kofi ought to do; fairness is a value.

3. – 10. Encourage debate and discussion.

Activity 7

1. **(a)** Paternity leave is a good thing.

   (b) Employers will be less prejudiced against mothers when they are making employment decisions; fathers will have better relationships with their children; fathers will do more childcare later, when child is older; children will do better at school; the burden on the mothers will be reduced.

2. Encourage debate and discussion.

Activity 8

1. @outraged traditionalist seems to attack the whole magazine without referring to the arguments in the article at all. The comment comes across as a generalised rant, where no reasons are offered to support the opinions aired. @outraged traditionalist also misses the clear link between families and economics, so the comments are not really relevant.

   @equality guru seems more calm and measured, but doesn't really give any reasons for the opinions given, simply listing them instead.
   @equality guru agrees with the article and the comments are relevant, but there needs to be a greater use of logic and more reasons offered to support the opinions.

2. Encourage candidates to think carefully and logically.

Activity 9

1. Encourage students to research the issues that may affect each individual. Answers will vary. Suggested answers:

   Woman who has migrated from Indonesia to the UAE: Will miss her children; will be missed by her children; lives of both mother and children will be affected; may affect the children's education and life chances.

   Child who grows up with her grandmother: The generation gap between a grandmother and child is usually greater than that between a parent and a child. However, there is often less conflict between a grandmother and grandchild than between a parent and child.

   Chinese national: Likely to work long hours and have a work-life imbalance; may have to live in Africa, which will mean either upheaval for the family or loneliness; may have to travel a lot, which will put pressure on family life.

   Ten-year-old: Will experience a great deal of pressure on him to behave like an adult while still a child; may have to do without the guidance and protection that a mother can offer.

   Marriage counsellor: Will have a detailed insight into the problems in marriages and in families; should have strategies to deal with this, but may be difficult to cope with at times.

Activity 10

1. to 6. Encourage students to apply their skills, and to set up their lines of enquiry carefully.

Activity 11

Answers will vary. Encourage research, discussion and debate, and remind students to think carefully about what is likely and what is not.

Activity 12

Encourage students to apply their skills and to undertake additional research if necessary.

Reflection

Reflection is an important part of the course, so it is important to allow class time for this activity. It may be useful to use a learning journal. This might allow for some ongoing written dialogue about the issues. The key here is to avoid simple praise or giving a student's thoughts a value; instead, try to engage a student in discussion over time and include questions in your written response that will push the student to the next level, and expect them to respond.

6 Humans and other species

Introduction

How do humans interact with other species on the planet? Do other species have moral rights? How much does it matter how we treat other species? Are some species more important than others?

Underlying their report, students should have an awareness of the key issues relating to humans and other species, but their knowledge in this area is not being tested in itself. Reports can focus on any area of humans and other species, including stewardship, animal rights, the need for other species, ethical issues, or the differences between humans and other animals, as long as there is a clear global research question, discussion of causes, consequences and perspectives, and a proposed solution.

Suggested resources

http://www.livescience.com/33376-humans-other-animals-distinguishing-mental-abilities.html	A reasonably accessible article on the differences between humans and animals, in terms of their mental ability.
http://www.faithclimateconnect.com/	A Christian perspective on humans' relationship with the Earth.
http://uk.businessinsider.com/space-colonization-could-make-humans-evolve-into-multiple-species-2015-6#ixzz3gC93JWTD	An article about how living in space could lead to the evolution of humans into another species or subspecies.
http://www.herald.co.zw/caring-about-animals-dehumanising-people/	A Zimbabwean response to the killing of Cecil the Lion.
http://www.bornfree.org.uk/animals/african-elephants/projects/ivory-trade/	An article from the Born Free Foundation on the history and banning of the ivory trade.
http://www.takepart.com/article/2013/04/10/pink-poison-rhino-horn-stop-ivory-trade	An article about a pink dye that could save the lives of rhinos by making their horns worthless to poachers.

Suggested answers

Activity 1

1. Encourage students to read the comments for gist rather than worrying about the detail of the complex language. They are looking only for issues. The following are suggestions only. As long as students can justify their answers, other answers are acceptable.

   (a) Human-animal interactions

   (b) Differences between humans and animals, wild and domestic animals

   (c) Stewardship

   (d) Wild and domestic animals

   (e) Humans and plants, ethical issues, stewardship

   (f) Evolution

2. Suggested answers:

   (a) A, C (in the sense that religious beliefs are personal), F

   (b) D

   (c) B (in the sense that it is universal), C (in the sense that this can apply to a range of nationalities), E

3. Encourage debate and discussion.

Activity 2

1. **(a)** 'It's natural' means that something happens in the natural world or in the natural course of things. It is often used to make people feel better about things, especially if they feel guilty or ashamed. 'It's right' can mean that something is factually accurate, but it is often used to refer to something being morally acceptable. There is a tendency to confuse 'natural' and 'right', and also 'unnatural' and 'wrong'. However, something can be natural *and* wrong; for example, it's natural to want to kill for revenge or to covet beautiful things and even to simply take them, but these behaviours are regarded as wrong in many societies.

   (b) The difference between 'we have the right to' and 'it is right to' is a subtle one. Having the right to do something means being entitled or legally allowed to do it, whereas 'it's right' means that it is morally acceptable. For example, according to the Universal Declaration of Human Rights, we all have the right to freedom of speech. We have the right to express our personal opinions.

This is not the same as expressing our opinions always being the right thing to do. There are times when it is advisable or more morally acceptable to keep our opinion to ourselves. Equally, we may accept that humans have the right to make decisions about animals (although this is more contentious), however this does not mean that every decision we might make is the right one, or is morally acceptable.

(c) The difference between 'stewardship' and 'domination' is also quite small and some interpretations of these terms can overlap. However, 'stewardship' generally means managing or taking care of something for others; for example, the idea that we have stewardship of the Earth while we are alive and need to manage its resources for those who come after us. On the other hand 'domination' means controlling, mastering or exercising ruling power; it lacks the sense of taking care of something or of managing it carefully, and focuses instead on control and power. So those who think that humans have stewardship of the Earth tend to think that we should take more care of it than those who think that humans have domination over the Earth.

(d) A pet is a companion animal, often a dog or a cat, that lives with humans, is provided with food and water and does not usually work. A domestic animal is usually a farm animal or a working animal, one that lives alongside and is useful to humans. As with pets, humans provide domestic animals with shelter, food and water. Domestic animals include those that produce meat, milk and eggs, and those that pull carts. A wild animal lives in its natural habitat. It finds its own food, water and shelter.

Activity 3

Encourage students to think, discuss and work together to extend their understanding.

Activity 4

1. Food source, companionship, public service and rescue, service and therapy.

2. and 3. Encourage debate and discussion

4. Encourage debate and discussion.

5. **Suggested answer:** According to Document 1, 25% think that the most important role of animals is companionship. More people turn to their pets for a feeling of comfort than to their mothers, so pets are clearly very important to people (in US society). This importance is a good reason to ensure that they have good health care.

Activity 5

1. Opinion, as it cannot be verified. It may be based on value judgements such as 'eating meat is wrong' or on factual, statistical or predictive evidence.

2. **Facts:** 'It takes 7 kg of grain to produce 1 kg of beef.' / 'It also takes thousands and thousands of litres of water.' These points can be 'verified, though they are clearly subject to dispute and discussion, as we can see from Jacquie's response.

   Prediction: 'If we did [stop eating meat], there would be enough food for everyone.' Some students may argue that Keith is only talking about what *would* happen rather than what *will* happen. In some cases, this would be a valid point, but here Keith might just as easily have written, 'If we all stop eating meat, there will be enough food for everyone'.

   Value judgment: '... it's wrong to eat beef.' / 'It's murder.' These could also be classed as opinions, as value judgements are a specific kind of opinion.

3. Opinion because it is too general to be verifiable. If Jacquie was talking about a specific field, it would be possible to verify that the land wasn't good enough for grain production, but we can't do this for all land used for grazing. However, it would be possible to verify that *quite a lot of* this land would not support grain production, so we can say that Jacquie's opinion is well founded in fact.

4. Encourage discussion, relating it back to Activity 2.

5. to 6. Encourage research, debate and discussion. Encourage students to think about what is likely and what is less likely.

Activity 6

Encourage research, debate and discussion.

Activity 7

1. (a) Definition   (d) Opinion / value judgement

   (b) Fact   (e) Fact

   (c) Prediction   (f) Fact, opinion and value judgement

2. Encourage students to apply their skills.

Activity 8

1. to 6. Encourage students to apply their skills, and to set up their lines of enquiry carefully.

Activity 9

Encourage discussion, and encourage students to think carefully about the most likely consequences.

Activity 10

Encourage students to apply their skills and to undertake additional research if necessary.

7 Sustainable living

Introduction

What does it mean to live sustainably? Who is responsible for ensuring that we live sustainably? Do we really have to sacrifice a comfortable life? What if people think I'm poor because I don't drive a flash car? How can we change attitudes to consumption so that sustainable living becomes possible?

Underlying their report, students should have an awareness of the key issues relating to sustainable living, but their knowledge in this area is not being tested in itself. Reports can focus on any area of sustainable living, including specific proposals for sustainable projects, specific species that are endangered, the possibilities for change, investigations into individual and collective efforts, or the need for international action, as long as there is a clear global research question, discussion of causes, consequences and perspectives, and a proposed solution.

Suggested resources

http://www.un.org/ sustainabledevelopment/ sustainable-development-goals/	An overview of the UN's sustainable development goals, the successors to the Millennium Development Goals.
http://mg.co.za/ article/2015-03-20-00-how-to-make-waste-work	A report on an eco-warrior from South Africa about how waste can be made to work.
http:// thoughtleader.co.za/ readerblog/2011/08/19/ the-sustainability-farce/	An opinion piece that talks about sustainability as a farce if it does not include measures to help the poor.
http://www.thestar. com.my/Metro/ Community/2015/06/25/ Serving-up-food-for-thought-Penang-Green-Carnival-is-all-about-sustainable-living/	A report from Malaysia about the Penang Green Carnival, which aimed to help people understand how their lifestyles affect food sustainability. The report mentions a competition to design a recycled object, an idea that could be adapted in class.
http://www.thestar. com.my/News/ Nation/2015/10/18/Haze-schools-to-close-again/	A report from Malaysia about how air pollution is forcing schools to close. The report offers plenty of material for discussion. Should schools close? Is it worth sacrificing air quality for industrial and economic growth?
http://www. thanhniennews.com/ society/hcmc-may-have-to-cut-down-150yearold-trees-in-central-park-for-metro-line-52551.html	A report from Vietnam about old trees endangered by metro development. This report offers plenty of material for discussion in terms of environmental and economic sustainability. Can the economy be sustained without suitable transport links?
http://www.abc.net.au/ news/2015-09-11/staying-steadfast-to-build-an-unusual-sustainable-home/6768442	An article about a sustainable home built in Australia.
http://www.theguardian. com/sustainable-business/sustainable-living-behaviour-change-growth	An article from *The Guardian* newspaper about the need to change behaviour rather than attitudes. The language is quite challenging but the arguments are logically set out and most students should be able to understand the gist.

Suggested answers to the activities

Activity 1

1. Encourage students to read the comments for gist rather than worrying about the detail of the complex language. They are looking only for issues. The following are suggestions only. As long as students can justify their answers, other answers are acceptable.

   (a) Lifestyle and status

   (b) Using finite resources, whose responsibility is sustainability?

   (c) Changing attitudes

   (d) Using finite resources, lifestyle and status

   (e) Government legislation, reducing waste

   (f) Sustainable development

2. Suggested answers:

   (a) A, D

   (b) B, C (this may be a specifically British perspective, but it may also have a more global relevance), E (regional company)

   (c) F

3. Encourage debate and discussion.

Activity 2

1	Sustainable living	A lifestyle that uses as few resources as possible, and causes as little environmental damage as possible.
2	Pollution	Presence of harmful substances in the air, water or general environment.
3	Consumption	Using resources, goods and services.
4	Green	Generally used to refer to someone or something which aims to be sustainable or environmentally friendly.
5	Consumer	A person who purchases goods or services.
6	Sustainable development	Growth and development which meets the needs of the present without using up all the resources that people will need in the future. Includes the idea that social, environmental and economic progress are all possible within the limits of earth's natural resources.
7	Recycled	Converted from waste into a usable product.
8	Government initiative	A course of action started by the government that begins a process of change.

Activity 3

Encourage students to continue to discuss the definitions as they play, to consolidate their understanding.

Activity 4

Encourage students to apply their skills, and to debate and discuss.

Activity 5

Document 2 outlines the key problems in achieving a sustainable lifestyle: people do not always know what it means to live sustainably; people do not want to make sacrifices if others do not; people want governments to take the initiative; people need centralised systems such as transport links.

Activity 6

1. (a) A blog on a newspaper is linked to the newspaper's name and to its legal obligations. The writers are likely mostly to use opinions, but also to have a track record of writing well, checking their facts (or getting an editor to do this) and working within legal limits. Personal blogs may be excellent, well researched and well reasoned, and many experts do have personal blogs. However, *anyone* can have a personal blog, so they may feature rants, mistakes, personal attacks, inaccuracies, long-winded and boring accounts, and a host of similar problems.

   (b) This blog is published by a reputable newspaper, so its facts are generally likely to be reliable. On the other hand, it's an opinion piece rather than a factual or researched one, so most of the facts and information it contains are common knowledge, which can be unreliable. We wouldn't argue that there is a grand show of fireworks at the start and end of the Olympics or New Year celebrations in many cities. Whether India invests heavily in nuclear power plants or electricity-driven trains is not common knowledge and it is unclear here whether the author means 'India doesn't invest at all heavily' in these or 'India doesn't invest in these at all'.

2. Yes, the causes of pollution the author suggests are reasonable. Households might play a larger role than the author allows.

3. Removing these kinds of power plants, industries and vehicles would go quite a long way towards solving pollution-related problems (and climate change) but this wouldn't undo the damage that has already been done and is continuing to have an effect. They might be replaced with other harmful solutions or the removal might trigger serious economic problems that seem worse than the original pollution. So the consequence is fairly likely and reasonable, but not as simple as the author makes it sound.

4. (a) Some good reasons are given, but little evidence. The author is mostly trying to persuade us that the suggestion 'that this single night of revelry is anti-environment and a major cause of pollution is blatantly unfair'. Reasons given include: 'Blaming firecrackers for pollution is typical of our habit of misrepresenting the truth and directing the blame in the wrong direction'; 'The real reasons for pollution are ... four wheelers'; that not enough is done to move towards a clean environment; and that if everyone else is allowed to have firecrackers, there is no reason why India shouldn't. The first three of these points do persuade us to accept the idea that blaming firecrackers for pollution is unfair; the last is simply a version of, 'all my friends are allowed, why aren't I?' Also, it might be that Sydney, Singapore and London would be better off reducing their use of pyrotechnics.

   (b) Emotion is used alongside reasons. For example, calling people who are against a noisy Diwali intellectuals plays on people's fear of being seen to be stupid. The rhetorical questions at the end of paragraphs 2 and 3 are intended to play on people's feelings of righteous grievance and injustice.

   (c) Largely, this piece offers opinion presented as opinion; however, the following could be taken as opinions disguised as facts: 'Almost everyone is against a noisy Diwali; most of all the intellectuals...'; 'Not at all.'; 'Worldwide, firecrackers are the preferred way to celebrate any happy occasion.'

5. Encourage students to think this through, organising themselves as independently as possible. Do students want a class discussion, or group or pair discussions? Would they rather write about this or talk about it? Can they remember how to set up discussions, with class rules, and manage it themselves? What measures should they take to ensure that people are talking about the right things?

Activity 7

Encourage students to apply their skills, to think carefully about what is likely, and to undertake research.

Activity 8

1. to 6. Encourage students to apply their skills, and to set up their lines of enquiry carefully.

Activity 9

Encourage students to apply their skills and to undertake additional research if necessary. Remind students to think carefully about what is likely and what is not.

Reflection

Reflection is an important part of the course, so it is important to allow class time for this activity. It may be useful to use a learning journal. This might allow for some ongoing written dialogue about the issues. The key here is to avoid simple praise or giving a student's thoughts a value; instead, try to engage a student in discussion over time and include questions in your written response that will push the student to the next level, and expect them to respond.

8 Trade and aid

Introduction

What are the benefits and disadvantages of trade and aid? Should rich countries give aid at all? What about if the recipient is corrupt or making choices that the donor disagrees with?

Students should have an awareness of key issues relating to trade and aid underlying their report, but their knowledge is not being tested in itself. Reports can be based in any area of trade and aid, including specific proposals for aid projects, different types of aid including disaster relief and the relationship between trade, aid and development. There must, however, be a clear global research question, discussion of causes, consequences and perspectives, and a proposed solution.

Suggested resources

http://www.cgdev.org/ blog/1385-billion-question-when-does-foreign-aid-work	Interesting article looking at when aid works, and how much it works, rather than focusing on whether it works or not. Quite challenging, but most students should be able to get some information and ideas from it.
http://www.usglc.org/kids-discuss-global-leadership/ ?gclid=CM2TtbORysgCFYy RGwodv-kJxA	Accessible video – American children give reasons why America should give foreign aid – largely because this will allow the US to develop overseas markets. Much in here to discuss.
http://www.abc.net. au/news/2015-05-13/ foreign-aid-cuts-under-new-budget-africa-indonesia/6465264	Details of Australian cuts to foreign aid in 2015.
http://europe.chinadaily. com.cn/china/2015-10/16/ content_22204214.htm	Report on plans to reduce Chinese poverty, with references to specific aid – should be seen in conjunction with the Chinese economic boom and increase in trade.

Suggested answers to the activities

Key vocabulary and language exercises

Economic development	Economic development means focusing on development that generates money. This can include creating jobs, but usually focuses on national measures such as Gross Domestic Product (GDP).
Human development	Human development focuses on development that prioritises human freedoms, the development of democracy, equality, improvement of the human condition, and human achievements.
Inequality	Usually, the size of the difference between rich and poor. This can be measured in income, wealth, opportunity, power, access to education, justice, etc.
Disaster relief	Responding to catastrophes and disasters, such as earthquakes, floods, famines and wars. This includes humanitarian aid, such as food, shelter and clothing.
Neo-colonialism	The ways in which rich, powerful countries control and influence poorer countries. This is usually done through economic and political influence rather than by war, occupation and direct political control, (as in traditional colonialism) – although war does still play a role, especially in the Middle East and Afghanistan.
Free trade	International trade is left to operate freely, without government restrictions.
Protectionism	Governments regulate international trade to protect their own domestic industries.

Activity 3

Refer to Document 1.

1. Cartoon 1 – 'Poverty, exploitation and aid'. Personal perspectives might include individual opinions about poverty, exploitation, and the usefulness of aid in trying to prevent poverty. National perspectives: countries may be harmed by trying to use aid to prevent poverty / governments are unlikely to be successful in attempts to use aid to hold back poverty / governments should address the way they exploit the poor rather than providing aid / governments are posturing when providing aid rather than addressing the real problems.

Global Perspectives: Countries and NGOs and supranational organisations need to work together to address the exploitation which drives poverty, rather than using aid to stop it.

Cartoon 2 – This cartoon expresses a range of different personal perspectives on the issue of inequality. People in MEDCs agonise over food and guilt, while people elsewhere have a different perspective – there are more important issues. One national perspective would be to sort out priorities for national action on pressing world problems, and to persuade people to buy into these priorities. One global perspective would be to consider the issues that really matter to people around the world and persuade individuals to buy into the solutions to these, rather than emoting over very personal issues such as their dinner. Alternatively, you could argue that the whole cartoon is based in one person's personal perspective – there may be people who value the arms trade, for example, because it feeds their families, or who would rather have slave wages than no wages. How do we feel about these perspectives?

Cartoon 3 – 'Thank God – it's a panel of experts'. Personal perspectives: people in the disaster stricken place are likely to be unimpressed by a panel of experts instead of food, shelter, clean water. However, the experts are likely to have a different personal perspective – they will probably believe that their contribution is highly valuable (as research, in directing relief efforts, etc). National perspectives: Governments are likely to believe that experts have a valuable contribution, and it makes them look good. The country must be seen to be doing something. Global perspectives: It would be rash to send aid without expert coordination – if each nation just sent relief supplies without relying on the expertise of specialists, the relief effort would probably be ineffective.

2.

Cartoon 1. Issues here include: is aid any use? Can it help with poverty or will it simply be crushed? Should we rather address exploitation? If so, how? How else can we deal with poverty?

Cartoon 2. What is the best way to provide disaster relief? Do we waste resources on useless panels of experts (and other attempts to help) when water is needed, or are experts essential to guiding relief efforts? Should relief efforts be guided by locals or by global experts? Are 'experts' just self-serving?

Cartoon 3. How can individuals in MEDCs best help those in need? Is food more important than justice, debt, arms or slave wages? To whom? In what circumstances? In what ways can addressing our eating habits and food management in MEDCs have an effect on those in LEDCs? How can individuals have an effect on global justice, debt, arms, and slave wages? Is emotional agonising over LEDC problems effective? How can it be translated into effective action? Whose perspectives / opinions on LEDC problems should we listen to?

3. Encourage students to express their reflections and to justify their choices thoughtfully.

Activity 4

Refer to Document 2.

1. Opinion / value judgement. You can agree or disagree with this, argue it either way. This cannot be verified, and so it's an opinion, not a fact. Also, it deals with unfairness, so it's dealing with values, which makes it a value judgement.

2. Christian Aid is likely to have experience, expertise and access to research evidence and first-hand eyewitness accounts of the effects of aid and trade. This gives them some reliability. On the other hand, they are a religious charity which gives a priority to helping people via aid, so they are likely to be biased somewhat, and perhaps give more weight to evidence which accords with their perspective. So there is no reason to believe that they are lying about Kofi Eliasa, for example, or any other facts – but we need to bear in mind that there might be other facts to take into consideration.

Activity 5

Refer to Document 3.

1. a) We need to know whether the celebrity organising the concert has a good track record of making valuable use of proceeds from relief concerts – will the money transfer be efficient? What sort of projects will it fund? How much of the money that I give will actually go to the disaster relief fund? Will I share the values of the projects? If the celebrity has a history of taking (too much of) the money for themselves, or taking too long to donate the money, or of funding projects that aren't much use, then we would be better off donating in a different way. However, if I share the values of the celebrity, and if they get relief to people quickly without the bureaucracy of the big NGOs, then this could be a good way for me to donate. Also, I'd have to ask if I like their music. If I don't, I would be better off just donating money.

b) We need to know exactly what projects the Red Cross is funding, and whether these are likely to be useful and accord with my values. I also need to know how efficient they are compared to the celebrity concert. I might also ask what I get out of donating to the Red Cross – does it matter to me whether I get a concert or just knowledge that I've helped?

2. a) There isn't an easy answer to whose reasoning is better – both give reasons and evidence, are quite thoughtful, make reasonable points, and suggest plausible consequences. @musiclover makes a good point when they say that disaster concerts can raise money quickly – there is plenty of evidence for this. It is plausible to suggest that a concert can raise more money than a celebrity simply donating – although we may be more convinced of their genuineness if they also donated a significant sum of money. @musiclover does raise the question of values – is it selfish to want to feel good about giving or to hear music. We may argue that people are more likely to be generous if they feel they get something from it. @cynicalrealist begins with loaded questions, which raise plausible possible alternative consequences, but aren't well argued in themselves. It is possible that money from disaster concerts ends up in the wrong place, but to really make this point they would need evidence and examples of when this has happened. The argument that disaster concerts distract from real charity is more reasonable. This relies on the idea that it's wrong to sing and dance when people are mourning – this could be argued for or against, but it is a reasonable value to use here. It's also reasonable to say that (at least sometimes) charity disaster concerts do become about us and how we feel rather than about the people in need. We could argue about whether this matters if help gets to the people in need. A weakness in this argument is that there's no reason given why charities should be leading charity campaigns rather than celebrities.

b) @cherryblossom's answer to @cynicalrealist is highly ineffective. It attacks @cynicalrealist rather than engaging with their argument. @cynicalrealist does make some thoughtful points about whether concerts for disaster relief are the best way to help people, but @cherryblossom does not deal with these at all.

Activity 6

Refer to Document 4.

1. Suggested answers:

   (a) Instability and conflict in Africa are threatening China's economic links with Africa. There are increasing political and security risks.

   (b) China's diplomacy is adapting and China is re-evaluating its development policies

   (c) China is mediating conflicts and assisting with peacekeeping and security. China is enhancing the social aspects of its development policies.

2. Encourage students to apply their skills.

Activity 7

Encourage students to apply their skills, to think carefully about what is likely, and to research.

Activity 8–9

Encourage students to apply their skills, and to set up their lines of enquiry carefully.

Activity 10

Reflection is an important part of the course, so it is important to allow class time for this activity.

① Demographic change

Introduction

There are many different approaches to discussing demographic change. The Student Book provides one possible approach. Teachers should feel free to take a different approach if it will suit their class better, but the focus of any teaching should always be the Global Perspectives skills. The written examination will test skills, rather than subject knowledge.

Demographic changes are important because of their effects on individual lives, business decisions, national policy and international relations. We need fewer people in the world to reduce the impact of climate change and to reduce the burden we are placing on the world's resources, yet individual countries need growing populations to maintain economic growth and to support aging populations. There are a wide range of issues, from the way we react to individual loneliness caused by changing family and social structures to the way we deal with movements of populations.

Suggested resources

http://www.helpage.org/	An NGO focused on issues relating to age.
https://www.ted.com/speakers/hans_rosling	A link to a number of TED talks by Hans Rosling on demographics.
http://www.populationcontrol.org/INDEX.ASP	An organisation with an agenda. Note in particular the link to the article about the family planning adviser who has 19 children.
http://mariestopes.org/	Family planning.
http://www.un.org/africarenewal/magazine/may-2013/africa%E2%80%99s-youth-%E2%80%9Cticking-time-bomb%E2%80%9D-or-opportunity	This article is challenging, but students should be able to gain some information, and there are links to a range of related issues.
http://unstats.un.org/unsd/demographic/	Links to UN statistics on demographic change.

Suggested answers to the activities

Activity 1

1. Encourage students to read for gist rather than worrying about the detail of the complex language. They are looking for issues only. The following are suggestions. So long as students can justify their answers reasonably, other answers are acceptable.

   (a) Demographics and development.

   (b) Government intervention in changing demographics, increasing professional population.

   (c) Increase in professional women.

   (d) Demographics and economics.

2. Identify at least one comment or question which comes from:

   (a) B, C (personal in that it is about a specific person), D (using demographics for personal gain).

   (b) C (national in that it is about changes in one country)

   (c) A

3. Encourage debate and discussion.

Key vocabulary and language exercises

Activity 2

It cannot be emphasised enough that dictionary skills – whether online or in print – are valuable, and that online translation tools de-skill students and generally provide poor translations. There are no specific answers.

Activity 3

1. If we invest in baby products now, we will make lots of money.

2. If the government provided incentives for educated workers to move out of the capital, develop thriving economic communities would develop all around the country.

3. If I had stayed in the town where I was born I would have enjoyed a fulfilling career in banking.

Skills practice exercises

1. Encourage students to skim-read for gist. Issues mentioned include the following.

    (a) Total world population: unsustainable pressure on resources

    (b) Youth population: youth unemployment, social unrest, disconnect between young people and government.

    (c) Older population: cost of supporting older population, aging healthily.

2. Encourage debate and discussion

3. **(a)** Possible solutions for NGOs: promote family planning, equip people in Sub-Saharan Africa with 21st century skills, providing education and training, investing in human capital, preventing non-communicable diseases (NCDs)

    (b) Possible solutions for individuals: family planning, education, providing best nutrition for your children when they are very young,

    (c) Possible solutions for national governments: providing development aid, involve young people in decision-making, provide jobs, and be transparent about what they are doing to reduce corruption, redesigning pension systems, remaining engaged with society,

4 and **5.** Encourage students to apply their skills and be thorough.

Question 1

a) The older people are in the US, the more likely they are to believe that vaccination should be required.   [1]

b) The younger people are in the US, the more likely they are to believe that humans evolved over time, the more time people have spent in education, the more likely they are to believe that humans evolved over time.   [2]

c) Accept a range of different possible causes. Credit the quality of the explanation.   [3]

d) Accept any reasonable answer. Use Cambridge's most recent generic mark schemes.   [6]

Suggested answers might include: The issues are personal for people who live there - people who need more doctors or teachers, for example. Also personal for those young people who do not wish to live in shrinking agricultural communities full of older people... However, the problems are primarily regional. They are not representative of the whole of the USA, but this particular part of it. The problems are also highly significant for this region, because it could end up in a situation of reversing development. The problems are national and global because there is a trend across the USA and other developed countries for some regions to be declining.

Question 2

a) We need to know why people left, and what the local government is doing to attract people and to develop jobs. We need to know whether sufficient young people want to live in rural areas, and whether there will be sufficient schools, etc. to attract a younger population.   [6]

b) Long term study charting the links between population and recession / growth

    Investigate other possible causes of population decline, such as a drive for family planning, or reasons why near neighbours would not migrate to Russia – such as war.   [8]

    Large scale surveys asking people about reasons why they are having smaller families, why they are emigrating etc.

Question 3

a) 'People aren't going to have more children,' is a prediction because it is talking about something that will (or will not) happen in the future.   [2]

b) This is a fact which can be verified with statistics.   [3]

c) Accept any reasonable answer – either @Educated Mother or @Spindrift Seafoam could reasonably be seen to be the most effective.   [15]

@Educated Mother sets out a very logical argument, giving reasons, intermediate and main conclusions. If we accept that the country needs more people, her conclusion follows logically. It might be possible to question whether we really need more people – perhaps instead we need older people to work for longer. Her conclusion will be provocative to many – but she does set out logically the advantages of encouraging immigration. On the other hand, she does not consider any disadvantages of immigration, or that they might outweigh the advantages. She provides facts and opinions and uses measured language.

@our country first provides a rant without logic or fact. It is exaggerated and unrealistic (but often to be found in the populist press) It is contradictory to suggest that immigrants are taking our jobs and sponging on benefits as well as being in the 'luxury' of prison. It is based only on exaggerated opinion.

@Spindrift Seafoam provides a short but logical argument based on facts but it does not deal with the practicalities of the suggestion.

Question 4

a) Accept any reasonable answer. Use Cambridge's most recent generic mark schemes.   [24]

2 Education

Introduction

There are many different approaches to discussing education. The student book provides one possible approach. Teachers should feel free to take a different approach if it will suit their class better, but the focus of any teaching should always be the Global Perspectives skills. The written examination will test skills, rather than subject knowledge.

Education is important because of the role it plays in the development of individual lives and careers as well as its significance in the development of a nation. Globally, access to high quality education is one of the most vital issues. It will determine the fates of individuals and the rise and fall of super economies. One key issue which is not often discussed is that wealthy nations in the West are not developing their education systems sufficiently, and therefore their populations cannot compete in the global economy with the skilled populations in emerging economies.

Suggested resources

http://worldliteracyfoundation.org/	Accessible, contains information, is fundraising so has a clear agenda.
http://www.unicef.org/statistics/index_countrystats.html	Access to education statistics by country.
http://en.unesco.org/gem-report/	Challenging but full of information about different aspects of education.
https://www.ted.com/topics/education	A range of TED talks about different aspects of education.
https://www.ted.com/speakers/andreas_schleicker	Andreas Schleicher's TED talks on education systems. Fascinating, difficult in places, but contains plenty of information that can be accessed at different levels.

Suggested answers to the activities

Activity 1

1. Suggested answers, other answers are possible if they can be justified.
    (a) Education–business partnerships
    (b) Equality in education, quality of education
    (c) Assessment, possibly purpose of education
    (d) Quality of education
    (e) Purpose of education, right to education

2. Suggested answers, other answers are possible if they can be justified.
    (a) C, D (personal in so far as it is a first person account), E
    (b) D (national in so far as it is a government minister talking about national issues)
    (c) A, B

3. Encourage debate and discussion, and encourage students to apply their skills.

Activity 2

It cannot be emphasised enough that dictionary skills – whether online or in print – are valuable, and that online translation tools de-skill students and generally provide poor translations. Suggestions are provided, but encourage students to consider various definitions.

1. No specific answers – encourage students to think and to research.

Activity 3

1. If we invest in education now, the next generation will be able to compete in the world economy.

2. If the government provided incentives for businesses to invest in education, this would improve education systems and provide workers with the skills businesses need.

3. If I had only worked harder at school, I would have a better life now.

Skills practice exercises

Activity 4

Refer to Document 1

(a) 85.4%

(b) Encourage students to compare personal experience and to research accurate statistics.

(c) Encourage debate and discussion.

(d) Encourage debate and discussion.

(e) Comparative studies will show general patterns, but this cannot necessarily be applied to individual families.

(f) Encourage students to apply their research skills.

(g) Encourage students to apply their research skills.

(h) Encourage students to compare a range of different aspects of the primary systems in two countries.

(i) Encourage debate and discussion – especially encourage students to think about systems that are different from the one they grew up in.

(j) Encourage students to research and to apply their skills.

Activity 5

(a) 'My family needs the money I can earn' is probably a fact, as it can be verified by looking into Tishan's family finances. However, people do have differing opinions about needing money, and these are sometimes based on values. Some families, for example, would do without things to put a child through education because they believe that education is valuable, whereas others do not see the value of education, and believe more strongly that they 'need' the money from a working child/young person. So this isn't as clear-cut as it initially seems.

(b) 'I'd love to study to be a doctor' is an opinion because it is a personal belief that cannot be verified. 'It's a good job' is an opinion because it expresses Tishan's belief, but can't be verified – it would be reasonable to either agree or disagree about this being a good job, based on expectations, personal preferences, personality, etc. You could say that it's a value judgement, because it's placing a value on the job, but it's a social and economic value rather than a moral value. 'It's like living in a box when I dream of the sky,' is an opinion, because it expresses the way Tishan feels. This cannot be checked or measured or verified, and it wouldn't necessarily be the same for anyone else. 'It seems so unfair that some of my friends are at school and hating it, while I can't go.' This is an opinion because it can't be verified, and also a value judgement because it deals with the value of fairness.

(c) Encourage students to justify their views.

(d) Colin's value judgement: 'Schools should be free (but only for people who work hard and get good results)'. This is a value judgement because it is talking about how the world should be, placing a value on education. Colin's prediction: 'Then no one would waste time or misbehave, and those of us who want to learn could get on with it.' Colin is predicting that this would be a consequence of making schools free only to those who work hard and get good results.

(e) Ruby's opinions: 'I'm lucky to have parents who value education'; 'This is the wrong education for me'. Both of these are expressions of her feelings. Ruby's value judgement: 'I should be able to choose my own future'. This is a statement about how the world should be, placing a value on personal freedom of choice.

(f–i) Encourage debate and discussion.

Economically productive is better because you're working in the economy.	✗ This does not add anything, but explains a little what economically productive means. Why is this better than personal fulfilment?
Being economically productive is good, because it means that are contributing to your country.	– This does give a reason why being economically productive is good but not why it is better than personal fulfilment. The comparison has not been made.
It's more important to be economically productive than personally fulfilled. This is because your personal fulfilment is only about you, but if you are economically productive it helps the whole country.	✓ This does give a reason and makes the comparison. You could argue against this reason but that is fine. We are not expecting logically perfect arguments. However, this is still looking at a personal perspective, thinking about how an individual is helping the country, not looking from the national perspective.

From a national perspective, it is more important to train people to be personally fulfilled than economically productive. This is because people who are personally fulfilled will work much harder and give more to the country than people who are just doing jobs.	✓ This is a thoughtful answer which gives a reason which adds to the discussion, and makes the comparison. It also raises a point for discussion – is it really a choice between being economically productive and personally fulfilled? Could a government ever really take the risk that training people to be happy would lead to economic productivity?

Activity 6

(a) i) Not true. In 2030, 2% of the graduates in the world will be from the UK, and 23% from India – this is an important difference.

ii) Not true. The article predicts that these two countries will have a smaller share of the global talent pool, but they may still have more graduates than currently.

iii) True.

(b) Emerging economies such as China, India, Brazil and Argentina are increasing the numbers of graduates they have, and increasing their share of the global graduate pool. Countries which are currently wealthy are decreasing their share of the global graduate pool.

(c) Encourage debate and discussion – one likely consequence is that countries such as China and India will have an economic advantage because they will have access to huge numbers of knowledgeable and skilled people. This will help to develop a range of economic sectors – especially in areas such as biotechnology, information technology, etc. – but this does assume that graduates have the skills that the economy needs.

Activity 7

Reflection is an important part of the course, so it is important to allow class time for this kind of activity.

Suggested answers to examination practice

Question 1

a) Problem solving, team working, communication. [1]

b) Encourage clear explanation. [2]

c) No, this is not a reasonable conclusion to draw. We can only know that 12% of business leaders think that numeracy is in the top three skills they want from employees. Most of them may think that numeracy is in the top four. So maths may still be important – and indeed in many countries success in a mathematics qualification is a necessary requirement for employment. [3]

d) High literacy, high enrolment in primary and secondary schools. [2]

e) For four marks, require consideration of personal, national and global aspects of education. A well-developed discussion of one or two of these aspects could score three marks. [4]

Question 2

a) Reward likely predictions of consequences [2]

b) Reward reasonable ways of testing the prediction, using Cambridge's most recent generic mark schemes. [5]

Question 3

a) It's an opinion which cannot be verified, and can be argued against. 'Mass education doesn't work in the modern world.' Is this a fact or an opinion? Justify your answer. [3]

b) Peter might be biased because he cannot find a job, and blames the education system instead of himself, thus lacking objectivity. [2]

c) It is reasonable to say that either Peter or Imi provides the most effective reasoning. [15]

Peter gives some good reasons for why the education system is not working – it is reasonable to suggest that learning information will not help young people to problem solve, to be creative or to communicate well, which is what employers want. However, it doesn't necessary follow that 'the system is rubbish' because he cannot find a job. There may be other reasons why he did not do well. The suggestion to return to masters and apprentices might be interesting, but Peter has not given reasons for it. Most of his language is measured, except when he talks about his own situation. He mostly gives opinions, but with some support.

Andi does make a good point about the gap between the privileged and the less privileged, but overall the reasoning is very poor, because it attacks Peter for being privileged instead of answering his argument or preparing his own argument. The language is emotive and exaggerated, and the opinions are quite extreme.

Imi is measured and thoughtful, and proposes a reasonable solution to a problem. There are no major weaknesses in her argument. However, there are no real reasons to support this solution.

Question 4

Use Cambridge's most recent generic mark schemes.

3 Employment

Introduction

There are many different approaches to discussing employment. The Student Book provides one possible approach. Teachers should feel free to take a different approach if it will suit their class better, but the focus of any teaching should always be the Global Perspectives skills. The written examination will test skills, rather than subject knowledge.

Employment is important because of the role it plays in the fulfilment of individual lives and as an indicator of the economic health of a nation. Increasingly, people are having to move from their homes to find employment – whether that is moving to a more thriving city, or migrating to another country entirely, and this has serious social consequences.

Suggested resources

http://www.fastcompany.com/3046332/the-new-rules-of-work/what-work-will-look-like-in-2025	Ideas about the future of work.
http://www.theguardian.com/careers/careers-blog/job-market-future-20-years-time	Challenging, but contains ideas and information which many students will be able to extract.
https://www.ted.com/talks/larry_smith_why_you_will_fail_to_have_a_great_career?language=en	A TED talk on following your passions to gain a great career.
https://www.ted.com/talks/andrew_mcafee_what_will_future_jobs_look_like?language=en	A TED talk on the automation of future jobs.
http://data.worldbank.org/indicator/SL.IND.EMPL.ZS	A range of statistics from the World Bank.

Suggested answers to the activities

Activity 1

1. Accept any answer which can be justified.
   (a) Fairness
   (b) Unemployment, job as identity, young people.
   (c) Unemployment, young people.
   (d) Job creation
   (e) Equality, profit
   (f) Equality, fairness
   (g) Young people

2. Identify at least one comment or question which comes from:
   (a) A, B
   (b) C, D, E, F
   (c) C, D, G

3. Encourage debate and discussion. Candidates should apply their research skills.

Activity 2

1. It cannot be emphasised enough that dictionary skills – whether online or in print – are valuable, and that online translation tools de-skill students and generally provide poor translations. Suggestions are provided, but encourage students to consider various definitions.

1	Employee	A worker.
2	Employer	Someone who provides workers with a job.
3	Entrepreneur	A person who sets up a business, taking the risks and gaining any rewards.
4	Multi-national corporation	A large business which operates in many different countries.

5	Recession	A period of general economic decline. A local, national or global economy stops growing and may shrink. This usually comes together with high unemployment.
6	CEO	Chief Executive Officer – the highest ranking person in a company.
7	Affirmative action	Action which favours groups of people who usually suffer from negative discrimination.

2. The local area used to have a lot of small, local businesses, run by local **entrepreneurs**. However, two **multinational corporations** have recently arrived. In some ways this is an advantage for the community, because there is less **unemployment**. On the other hand, people who used to own their own companies, now have to **apply for a job** and work for someone else. Probably the biggest problem is that all the senior management jobs go to foreigners. We need **affirmative action** to ensure that local people are fully represented at management level.

Skills practice exercises

Activity 3

1. Men tend to enjoy the top positions in society, but also the worst positions in society.

2. **(a)** Poorly educated men in rich countries are struggling to adapt to changes in the labour market.

   (b) Cultural attitudes must shift (young men accept being hairdressers, etc., young men work harder at school). Policymakers also need to lend a hand, because foolish laws are making the problem worse. Even more important than this, we need to improve the education system, and young men need more positive role models.

3. Encourage students to debate and discuss, and to write responses with full justification.

4. **(a)** The region's economies do not create enough jobs for skilled workers.

   (b) Many employers prefer make workers, and those who prefer female workers often offer only unskilled jobs.

5–7. Encourage debate, discussion and research.

Activity 4

1. Encourage students to research what they need to know and do.

2. Encourage students to think carefully. Suggested answers include: they need to know whether the company really exists, is likely to remain in business, is suitable for them, whether the income will cover the costs, whether they will be happy away from family and so on.

Activity 5

1. Fact – it can be verified.

2. This is a fact about the company's intentions.

3. It is not in conflict. Nineteen48 recognises that it needs to make a profit in order to make charitable donations.

4. Suggested answers include:

   (a) Opinion – it can be disagreed with and cannot be verified.

   (b) Accept either Savannah Susie or Puteri 24_7 as most reasonable. Savannah Susie identifies a problem and a solution. She is reasonable and measured, mostly. It would be possible to challenge whether the men are sitting around waiting for a solution or wishing for the past, but what she says is reasonable. Septimus Drake suggests an unrealistic solution – sending women back to the kitchen would not solve the problem that certain groups of men in rich countries lack the necessary education to do the work available, or that much of the work available is 'women's work'. His attitude may well be part of the problem. His language is emotive and his reasoning is exaggerated and over stated. Puteri 24_7 identifies a problem and analyses it extremely clearly with reasons and conclusions and measured language. However, the solutions suggested by Puteri 24_7 are not practical in the modern world.

Activity 6

Encourage debate and discussion before students write their essay.

Activity 7

Reflection is an important part of the course, so it is important to allow class time for this kind of activity. It may be useful to use a learning journal. This might allow for some ongoing written dialogue about the issues. It's key here to avoid simple praise or giving a student's thoughts a value – rather, try to engage a student in discussion over time, include questions in your written response which will push the student to the next level, and expect them to respond.

Suggested answers to examination practice

Question 1

a) Issues to do with youth unemployment / mismatch of attitude and expectations between young people seeking employment and older people seeking employees / young people not dressing or behaving appropriately / older people seeing only the appearance and not the person / applying for the right type of job. [3]

b) The teenager's perspective is likely to be one of frustration at constant rejection and lack of understanding why, and perhaps a frustration with the system. This might be combined with a determination to be themselves, to look shocking and a need to be accepted even whilst rejecting the acceptance of the establishment. The employment adviser's perspective is likely to be one of combined desire to help young people meet a complex system after an education that doesn't meet their needs and frustration at young people for not meeting the expectations of the establishment – 'why can't you just take the piercings out and wear a suit?' It might be partly disdain for half-educated youths who don't even know that they shouldn't put their boots on the table. Reward clear explanation using Cambridge's most recent generic mark scheme. [3]

Consider Document 2.

c) 'Try having a wash, turning up on time and doing your fair share of the work' [1] / 'Try having a calm chat with your boss... explaining... ask for advice.' [1] / 'Treat your colleague just exactly the way he treats you' [1] / 'Explain your perspective to your boss' [1]. [3]

d) If there are different perspectives, they would be different personal perspectives. Some of the issue could be explained by the different perceptions and beliefs that each person has. For instance, it may be that John doesn't realise that he is upsetting @sadandunhappy. He may think that he is making jokes or being friendly, or he may be insecure and trying to make himself look better. @sadandunhappy may not realise that their deodorant is failing, and may not realise how much work John actually does do. Or there may be deeper perspectives – @sadandunhappy might be from a minority community or female, and John may be racist or sexist (possibly without even realising it). In this case, his beliefs and perspective would play an important part in this dispute, but it may also be that John is unpleasant, or that @sadandunhappy is lazy. In this case, the dispute would be less about perspectives and more about sorting out difficult behaviour. [3]

Question 2

a) The boss's opinion in their own words / reports written by the boss about @sadandunhappy / possibly accept second-hand evidence from a reliable witness who has overheard the boss talking about @sadandunhappy (but this could be troublemaking) / evidence about John getting the next promotion. (For four marks look for directly relevant information. Be wary of 'we need to know whether @sadandunhappy is lazy' – because people have different perceptions, the boss might believe that @sadandunhappy was lazy even if s/he isn't.) [4]

b) Ask the boss / ask for written reports / talk to people the boss talks to / spend a week in the office observing John, the boss and @sadandunhappy. [2]

Consider Document 3

c) It is reasonable to suggest that date collection in very poor countries is ineffective, and that this would mean that our data / evidence on youth unemployment is underestimated because it does not include missing data from these very poor countries. However, it is less reasonable to conflate underemployment and unemployment. If people are underemployed, it is a problem, but this is not the same as being unemployed.

How effective is the use of evidence in Document 3 to support the claim that youth unemployment is significantly underestimated? [8]

Question 3

a) The ILO is a reliable source of information on labour and employment. It has experts who use sophisticated statistical techniques, and access to statistics collected by governments around the world. It probably has an agenda or bias regarding what it wants to achieve, but this is unlikely to make it misreport data. It may be that their estimate is conservative (in this case too small), because they would only use reliable information.

b) @teeniusgenius is only young (presumably, on the basis of the name and the references to school and summer jobs) and doesn't have much experience in work. But what they say about teachers can be crosschecked with our own experiences of teachers, and otherwise they are giving opinions, and they do have relevant experience to base the opinions on. So @teeniusgenius is reliable enough here. [3]

c) Use Cambridge's most recent generic mark scheme. Suggested answers include: @juniperberry's reasoning is very bad. S/he assumes that John is right about @sadandunhappy being lazy without any evidence, and jumps from this to layabouts and a decline in productivity with no logic.

The reasoning is emotive, jumps from one consequence to further, unrelated or extreme consequences without justification (slippery slope or disaster reasoning) - even if there are a few people who don't do enough work, that isn't enough to lead to recession and a huge rise in the crime rate. It might be true to say that 'if you were actually doing your share of work your boss would notice,' - however, it may be that @sadandunhappy's boss has noticed, and that @sadandunhappy is mistaken. Or it may be that the boss does accept John's view (because he is loud, because he is friends with the boss, because he is the same type of person as the boss...) so there are alternative possibilities that shouldn't be ignored. Doing some work might help @sadandunhappy, but if s/he actually already does too much work, that might not be the right solution. The real issue here is that @juniperberry is forming fairly extreme (and offensive) opinions without facts. [6]

d) Use Cambridge's most recent generic mark schemes. Indicative content includes: @juniperberry predicts the consequence that a decline in productivity 'is going to lead to economic recession and unemployment.' This is possible. But together with the belief that the cause is 'layabouts', it becomes less likely. It seems as if @juniperberry is just using scare tactics and sensationalism. They also predict the consequence that recession and unemployment 'will cause a huge rise in the crime rate.' It is plausible that an increase in unemployment will lead to an increase in theft and robbery, as people steal to get things they used to earn, but a 'huge' rise seems extreme, and you'd need to look at crime rate statistics from past recessions to see if there was a significant effect on other kinds of crime.

@teeniusgenius predicts the consequence that asking for advice rather than getting personal is more likely to get results. This seems to be a likely consequence because it's not confrontational. It can defuse the situation, clarify perspectives and make sure that people are paying attention to the facts. @hairyjumper predicts the consequence that stopping doing John's work will make him and the boss realise how much @sadandunhappy is actually doing. This depends on the psychology of the case. It may be that John would point to the things that @sadandunhappy has stopped doing as evidence that @sadandunhappy really is lazy. Or it may really become evident that @sadandunhappy is working hard. @hairyjumper implies the consequence that being rude to John and telling the boss what a loser John is will help the situation. This seems less likely -

they might decide s/he was lazy *and* rude How likely are the consequences suggested by @juniperberry, @teeniusgenius and @hairyjumper? [9]

Question 4

Use Cambridge's most recent generic mark scheme.

4 Fuel and energy

Introduction

There are many different approaches to discussing fuel and energy. The Student Book provides one possible approach. Teachers should feel free to take a different approach if it will suit their class better, but the focus of any teaching should always be the Global Perspectives skills. The written examination will test skills, rather than subject knowledge.

Fuel and energy are important because of the significant roles they play in our economy, our security, our current wellbeing and our wellbeing in the future. We need to make decisions about our fuel and energy use now – should we use the most environmentally friendly fuels even though they are not yet productive enough? Should we get cheap fuel from countries we may find ourselves at war with? Should we invest in any kind of energy we can make in our own countries, even if it is extremely bad for the environment?

Suggested resources

http://www.iea.org/topics/renewables/	International energy agency, information about renewable energy.
http://www.sciencedaily.com/releases/2015/12/151207113733.htm	Article predicting a decline in fossil fuel emissions. Could be contrasted with the predictions in Source 1 of the examination practice in this chapter.
http://www.biomassenergycentre.org.uk/portal/page?_pageid=76,539186&_dad=portal&_schema=PORTAL	Information on climate change and biomass.
http://uk.reuters.com/article/uk-climatechange-summit-extended-idUKKBN0TU0H020151212	Early report on agreements at the Paris summit 2015, which might turn the tide on global warming.
http://www.globalfueleconomy.org/	Supranational organisation, links to lots of information, includes accessible summaries.

Suggested answers to the key vocabulary and language activities

Activity 1

1. Accept any answer which can be justified.
   (a) Sustainability
   (b) Energy security
   (c) Access to energy, energy poverty, energy as a right
   (d) Climate change
   (e) Energy poverty, energy as a right, inequity.

2. Accept any answer which can be justified.
   (a) A, E (expressed as a personal issue)
   (b) B (includes issues relating to individual nations), E (relating to nations)
   (c) B, C, D

3. Encourage students to apply their skills, to research and to discuss and debate.

Activity 2

It cannot be emphasised enough that dictionary skills – whether online or in print – are valuable, and that online translation tools de-skill students and generally provide poor translations. Suggestions are provided, but encourage students to consider various definitions.

Activity 3

1. Even if we reduce carbon emissions now, it will be too late to save the planet.

2. If the government provided incentives for companies to reduce energy use, companies would be more likely to adopt energy efficient practices.

3. If we had actually changed our energy use in the 1980s, we would not have such a big problem now.

Skills practice exercises

Activity 4

1. $9.64

2. $5.80

3. Encourage students to think about this. Suggested answer: It seems that advanced economies are transforming fuel into economic growth more efficiently than BRIC countries – possibly because they have better technologies.

4. 67%

5. Encourage students to really think about this. Suggested answers include: Importing energy is expensive, which has economic consequences. There are also significant risks – what if the energy supplier refuses to supply you? What if there is a war? Many of the energy supplying countries are somewhat politically unstable, and we would want our energy to come from a stable source.

6. The WEF says of itself that it: 'is the International Organization for Public-Private Cooperation. The Forum engages the foremost political, business and other leaders of society to shape global, regional and industry agendas. It was established in 1971 as a not-for-profit foundation and is headquartered in Geneva, Switzerland. It is independent, impartial and not tied to any special interests, working in close cooperation with all major international organisations' – **http://www. weforum.org/world-economic-forum.** This organisation is likely to have access to relevant and reliable information and sufficient expertise to assemble and interpret it. From this perspective, it seems highly reliable. It claims that it is independent and lacking bias – although it also claims that it wants to shape agendas, so it is probably not totally lacking bias. On the whole, a reliable source of the kind of information in the chart.

Activity 5

1. Look up http://www.redpepper.org.uk. How reliable is this as a source of information? Explain your answer. Redpepper.org.uk is a left wing online magazine which aims to fundamentally challenge our economic system. It clearly has a political bias and an agenda to further, but this does not mean that its facts are incorrect – simply that we need to bear their perspective in mind. It is unclear how much expertise or information it has access to – again, this does not mean that it has none, simply that we do not know. So this organisation is not as obviously reliable as the WEF in terms of access to information – and the opinions should be judged on their own merits.

2. If the five power stations mentioned will burn five times the UK's wood production, it seems likely that a significant proportion of the wood will need to be imported. The figure of 80% seems realistic, but you'd have to find out more about how much wood is needed, and whether the UK could produce more wood rather than importing it. Trees do take quite a while to grow, so a fast change is unlikely.

3. The article concludes that, 'the government's renewable energy strategy will continue to make climate change, deforestation and air pollution ever worse.'

   (a) It seems likely on the basis of this article that biomass energy will have negative effects regarding deforestation and air pollution. It's not at all clear that it will make climate change worse than burning coal, or mining uranium. Biomass energy is also only one part of the government's strategy, so it might be unfair to say that the whole strategy will make things worse. You'd need to read more about it.

   (b) Encourage students to think carefully about what they read – does this look like a list of proper scientific studies? Is it a representative sample or have they just picked those which support their view and ignored more which would oppose them? The reasons and evidence do seem to give us good reasons to oppose biomass power plants. In particular the idea that biomass means cutting down trees in vulnerable areas – if it were left over wood from other businesses, or pine trees grown locally it would be a different matter.

4. Some options are solar energy, wind energy, tidal energy . . . encourage students to think carefully about the possible consequences.

Activity 6

1. Suggested answers:

Predicted consequences:

- Humans could be extinct in 100 years because of overcrowding, over-used resources and climate change.

- A serious increase in average global temperatures could lead to flooding, famine, drought, sea level rises, mass extinction and the passing of a tipping point.

Possible solutions:

- Reduce carbon emissions as soon as possible.

- Move to cleaner energy sources.

- Find the technologies to undo the damage we have already done.
- Coordinate efforts (internationally).

2. Encourage students to apply their skills and justify their answers with specific references to the text. Accept any reasonable answer. Suggested answers:

   (a) There is very little evidence. This passage is mostly opinion. Where evidence is given, such as specific temperature rises, these are not examined closely. It is assumed that the highest temperature rise will occur, and the worst possible consequences.

   (b) Serious and extreme consequences are likely to follow from climate change. However, this author takes the most serious possible consequences as the most likely.

   (c) There is also quite a lot of emotive exaggeration – talking about the 'climate apocalypse that has already begun', for example.

Discussion

Encourage debate and discussion, with research as necessary.

Reflection

Reflection is an important part of the course, so it is important to allow class time for this kind of activity. It may be useful to use a learning journal. This might allow for some ongoing written dialogue about the issues. It's key here to avoid simple praise or giving a student's thoughts a value – rather, try to engage a student in discussion over time, include questions in your written response which will push the student to the next level, and expect them to respond.

Suggested answers to examination practice

Question 1

a) World energy use was increasing until 2010, and projections indicate that it is likely to continue to increase significantly until 2040. Apart from in nuclear power, there was a dip in world energy consumption in 2008/9 to correspond to the economic crisis. Consumption of liquid biofuels was increasing steadily until 2010 and is predicted to increase at the same rate. Coal consumption rose particularly steeply until 2010, and is predicted to continue to rise fairly steeply before levelling off towards 2040. Natural gas consumption increased fairly steadily, and is predicted to continue to do so.

Renewable energy use increased quite slowly up to 2010, but is predicted to increase more rapidly. Nuclear energy consumption remained fairly steady at around 5% until 2010 and is predicted to rise slowly to 7% by 2040.   [6]

b) Reward thoughtful exploration. Use Cambridge's latest generic mark scheme. Accept any reasonable answer. Suggested answers include:

It is highly personal for those who lost their homes and may wish to return, or for those who may be forced to return but do not wish to – possibly because they do not believe that it is really safe. The loss of a home is extremely emotional and personally important – and any decision relating to that will be of personal significance.

This is a national issue because it signals the overcoming of a national crisis which is important to national identity. Decisions also have to be made on a national level.

This is a global issue because it gives a signal to the rest of the world about the scale of the Fukushima disaster and sends messages about how dangerous nuclear power is.   [6]

Question 2

Reward thoughtful questions which really would help with decision making, using Cambridge's latest generic mark schemes.

a) Suggested answers: Reward focus on safety.
   - What evidence is the government using to make the decision?
   - Does this evidence come from a reliable source?
   - Has it been crosschecked and verified?
   - Does the government have a political reason for wanting to declare Fukushima safe that might override other concerns?
   - Is the water drinkable?
   - What is happening to other animals in the area?
   - Exactly what level is the radiation?   [6]

b) Suggested answers: Reward focus on the decision making process.
   - Fully understanding the evidence the government is using and where it comes from will help Mr Yamauchi to decide whether to move home, because it will help him to fully understand the safety issues and avoid fear. It is also helpful to think about the evidence rather than simply believing what someone tells you.

- If the government has a political reason for wanting to declare Fukushima safe, they may send people back there even if it is not really quite safe anymore. It is important to know this so that Mr Yamauchi can decide whether to believe what the government says, and so that he can make his own, informed decision about whether to return home.

- If the water is drinkable, other animals in the area are healthy and radiation levels are low, then it should be safe to return home.

- However, safety factors are only one element in the decision about returning home. It may not be possible to make a living there now because the community has been destroyed. It may be too difficult emotionally to go back. Mr Yamauchi and others like him may have started to make a life elsewhere, and decide to go forward rather than back. [8]

Question 3

a) Opinion – it cannot be verified and it can be opposed. [2]

b) This seems reliable. It comes from WEF, which has access to information and expertise, and claims to be independent and without bias. There is no good reason to suppose that they are lying or misleading – so we can conclude that it is reliable. [3]

c) Use Cambridge's most recent generic mark scheme. Suggested answers:

Hassan sounds reasonable, but he mostly states facts and states that the situation is unacceptable and no good. He does not use evidence or reasoning to develop an argument. What he says sounds plausible – normally peaceful men fighting, businesses going under because of lack of fuel, ambulances not getting to sick people – these are all reasonably likely consequences of a fuel shortage. Hassan says that the government needs to act – but he does not argue for this, and only assumes that it is the government who needs to act. He does not suggest how they might act – it is more of a desperate cry for someone to sort out the problems than a suggested solution.

Mohammad is rather more extreme. He uses the fuel shortage to argue against democracy and for army rule. But one difficult situation cannot show that a form of government is completely bad. Furthermore, Mohammad says that democracies want to please people – but this is slightly inconsistent, because it would please people very much if there were fuel available. Mohammad's suggestions, reasoning and language are all rather extreme, exaggerated

and illogical. 'There is no other alternative ....' This should invite students to look at other possible alternatives.

Iqbal is also more reasonable. He is calmer, more relaxed and more thoughtful about the situation, and less inclined to jump to desperate conclusions. It is likely that this crisis will pass, like previous crises – but it isn't necessarily the case. As we get closer to running out of fossil fuels, there may come a point when the crisis does not pass. However, Iqbal's point that we should look at alternatives is a good one. He gives an example of his own bicycle purchase – which will be a good alternative if he actually continues to use it after the crisis is over – and gives a reason why solar power would be good for Pakistan. He doesn't say much, and it is not a very strong argument, but there is more of an argument than Hassan provides. [15]

Question 4

Use Cambridge's most recent generic mark scheme. [24]

Globalisation

Introduction

There are many different approaches to discussing globalisation. The Student Book provides one possible approach. Teachers should feel free to take a different approach if it will suit their class better, but the focus of any teaching should always be the Global Perspectives skills. The written examination will test skills, rather than subject knowledge.

Globalisation is important because of the many different ways it affects individuals, nations and the world, on economic, political, cultural and social levels. On a personal level, globalisation can seem very frightening – the ever-present *Other* can seem to overwhelm our personal and cultural identities, and this can fuel nationalistic, populistic backlashes. On the other hand, globalisation does seem to increase prosperity for the majority, and can lead to fulfilling cross-cultural and international friendships.

Suggested resources

https://netivist.org/debate/globalization-pros-and-cons-economic-cultural-and-political	Pros and cons of globalisation.
http://www.economicshelp.org/trade/globalisation/	Accessible information on the economics of globalisation.
http://www.who.int/trade/glossary/story012/en/	World Health Organisation on cultural globalisation.
http://www.bbc.com/future/story/20120522-one-world-order	Interesting but challenging article on whether globalisation means we will become one culture. With help, many students should be able to grasp the key ideas.
http://www.sciencedirect.com/science/article/pii/S0277953615001744	Challenging but interesting paper on the link between globalisation and obesity. The key ideas are clearly summarised, and there are some useful graphs and charts. Parts of this would make the beginning of interesting discussions on how and why globalisation might cause or contribute to obesity. Food for thought.
http://www.ted.com/search?q=globalization	Links to a variety of ted talks on themes relating to globalisation.
http://www.bbc.co.uk/news/magazine-35075439	Comparison of the views of Donald Trump and Marie le Pen, both extreme right wing politicians, which can be seen as a reaction against globalisation.
http://www.abc.net.au/radionational/programs/betweenthelines/pat-buchanan-on-donald-trump/6712594	Australian article looking at Trump as part of a global wave of nationalism in response to globalisation. Includes audio. Part of the Between the Lines series – 'Making sense of Australia's place in the world, Between the Lines puts contemporary international issues and events into a broader historical context, seeking out original perspectives and challenging accepted wisdoms.'
https://www.youtube.com/watch?v=12YDLZq8rT4	A documentary by Swedish writer Johan Norberg arguing that Globalisation is beneficial.

Suggested answers to the activities

Activity 1

1. Accept any answer which can be justified.
   - (a) Economic and cultural globalisation
   - (b) Globalisation vs. nationalism
   - (c) Globalisation and inequality
   - (d) Social globalization, human impact of globalisation
   - (e) Global and national governance.
2. Suggested answers:
   - (a) A
   - (b) (B), E
   - (c) B, C, D
3. Encourage debate, research and discussion.

Activity 2

It cannot be emphasised enough that dictionary skills – whether online or in print – are valuable, and that online translation tools de-skill students and generally provide poor translations. Suggestions are provided, but encourage students to consider various definitions.

1.

Social globalisation	The impact of globalisation on people, including their lives, their work, their families and their societies. It includes the idea that social relationships are much more international than they used to be, so events that affect people in one part of the world will also affect their friends and colleagues in other parts of the world.
Political globalisation	The tendency for governance and government action to be international and global. Organisations such as the UN are playing a greater role, and individual countries are grouping together to find political and governmental solutions to international problems.
Cultural globalisation	The swift international movement of ideas, attitudes, values and cultural products such as music, film, literature, etc.
Economic globalisation	The increasing interdependence of economies on the economies of other countries. This is caused by the cross-border movement of goods, services, capital and technology.
Localisation	The adaptation of a product to meet the needs of a particular country or culture.
Nationalism	The belief that your own country is better than all other countries. Also the process of nations working independently for their own interests rather than working together.
National sovereignty	The right to self-government by a state.
Governance	The act of governing or ruling; the establishment and implementation of policies which will enable effective government.
Outsource	To purchase goods or services from independent, outside suppliers. Is often used to refer to international outsourcing, for example, British companies outsourcing telephone query services to Indian companies.
Exploit	Make full use of a resource and benefit from it; make use of a situation, resource or people in an unfair way.
Core	Dominant capitalist countries which exploit less wealthy countries for labour and resources. These are seen as the core, or centre of the system, with most power. These countries benefit most, and gain wealth.
Periphery	Less wealthy countries seen as on the edge of the system, depending on core countries and supplying them with labour and resources, often to their own disadvantage. These countries are seen as not being powerful.

Activity 3

No specific answers.

Activity 4

1. Suggested answer: People are insecure about changes so they are becoming more nationalistic to protect themselves. Many European countries are showing increasing support for nationalist parties. The most important solutions are:

   - Partnerships and cooperation
   - Issue awareness
   - Education for citizens

2. Encourage thoughtful debate and discussion.

3. One possibility is that these possible solutions will have no effect at all, because people's fear overrides their understanding, or because the people who are likely to take notice of these measures are in any case the people who are already thinking about the issues and wanting to combat the increase of nationalism. Another possibility is that, if effectively done, these measures could reduce people's fear for their livelihoods, and that this will either slow the rise of nationalism or somewhat reduce it. Encourage debate and discussion, with a real focus on what is likely or probable.

4. Different solutions are likely to be needed for the specific needs of different regions.

5. Encourage debate and discussion.

Activity 5

1. (a) Steam engine.

   (b) Encourage students to apply their skills and to think carefully. It is likely that most students will argue for either petrochemicals allowing for physical global contact or communications technology allowing for digital global contact, but encourage justification and discussion.

   (c) Encourage research, debate and discussion.

Activity 6

Encourage debate and discussion, with research as necessary.

(a) Likely to make money, may have to travel a lot.

(b) Likely to benefit – without globalisation, this farmer would not have been able to sell flowers to the European market. However, vulnerable to economic fluctuations in Europe.

(c) Globalisation has made it possible for the American tourist to travel to Kenya easily. They will probably find that many people speak English, that there are ATMs they can use, and that many facilities are laid on so that their tourism is fairly close to being at home – this is very different from tourism 30–40 years ago.

(d) May have international exchanges with a variety of countries, may Skype and talk with other students from around the world, can expect to work in a globalised industry.

(e) More work!

Reflection

Reflection is an important part of the course, so it is important to allow class time for this kind of activity. It may be useful to use a learning journal. This might allow for some ongoing written dialogue about the issues. It's key here to avoid simple praise or giving a student's thoughts a value – rather, try to engage a student in discussion over time, include questions in your written response which will push the student to the next level, and expect them to respond.

Suggested answers to examination practice

Question 1

a) Ireland, according to the Index of Globalization. [1]

b) Generally speaking, there is a correlation between a country's degrees of economic, political and social globalisation. This could be because economic interaction with other countries leads to social interaction – if you are trading with another country, individuals will develop social contacts, for example. And interconnected economic and social affairs mean that governments have to cooperate to find joint political solutions to their joint problems. [3]

c) Reward thoughtful discussion using Cambridge's most recent generic mark schemes. Suggested answers:

   Cartoon 1 raises issues of the definition of globalisation and inequality. (Require discussion) Cartoon 2 raises issues relating to the different roles different countries have, and the financial organisation. (Require discussion) Cartoon 3 raises issues relating to the contradictions inherent in using global technologies and raising global protest against globalisation. (Require discussion) [4]

d) Reward thoughtful discussion using Cambridge's most recent generic mark schemes. [4]

   Suggested answers include: There are important global effects of globalisation. These include the way that international economies work, international governance and the relationships between countries. This includes who is more powerful. So, many of the effects of globalisation are felt at a global level. You could say that this makes them the most important.

However, these changes affect nations and individuals. The global economy means that many of us now work in virtual international teams. This is a sharp contrast to our great grandparents, who worked in local jobs all their lives. Globalisation also means, for example, that an economic crisis in one part of the world can spread to other parts of the world. So individuals can lose their income because of something happening across the world. This is an important and very personal aspect of globalisation.

Question 2

a) Reward thoughtful discussion using Cambridge's most recent generic mark schemes. Suggested answer:

The extract from the article gives examples of nationalist tendencies, but doesn't really use them or cite evidence. The examples chosen are good examples of powerful nations where nationalism is a big issue, and where there are potential conflicts. It carefully states in each case that there is a question in each case about nationalism versus political cooperation. However, it then concludes that 2015 will be a bad year without giving reasons why nationalism will triumph over cooperation, so there are weaknesses here. Having said that, it does seem likely that nationalist tendencies combined with conflict situations will lead to negative consequences. [6]

b) Reward thoughtful discussion using Cambridge's most recent generic mark schemes. Suggested answer:

Focus should be on research methods rather than on giving information about what sort of year 2015 was. Use a variety of news sources, looking for 'conflict', 'nationalism', 'international cooperation.' Compare with previous years.
Think about wars, political disagreements, political tension, and so on. Consider the political importance of the nations disagreeing – Russia and the USA disagreeing will probably have a greater effect on the whole world than two smaller nations disagreeing, especially if it looks likely that they will resort to armed conflict.
Statistical information, anecdotal information, opinion and analysis pieces would be useful. Rely on well-regarded sources such as the UN, or magazines with a reputation for high quality journalism. [8]

Question 3

a) The biggest security question facing Europe – and perhaps the world – will be whether President Putin rides the nationalist wave he has helped to create / the relationship between nationalist rhetoric and territorial disputes will also be critical to the future of Asia / political leaders are likely to try to manage their differences without conceding on basic issues of principle. [1]

b) Fact – it can be verified and measured. Or falsified if it is untrue. [3]

c) Irina seems to belong to a rich nation, or at least to belong to a group which has become richer because of globalisation, so this will bias her in favour of seeing the benefits of globalisation overall. [1]

d) Reward thoughtful discussion using Cambridge's most recent generic mark schemes. Suggested answer:

Overall, Irina's reasoning is probably the most effective, even though it contains significant weaknesses. Irina is measured and mostly thoughtful, uses sensible language, and she does give a conclusion supported by reasons, mini-conclusions and some examples. Some of these are good reasons, and she does show that there are benefits to globalisation. However, she does not show that everyone benefits, or that it is a win-win situation, because she is far too selective, only seeing the good side. For example, a Kenyan coffee farmer might be better off if they were not entirely dependent on a market that wants to pay less and less for coffee. It is true that companies benefit from outsourcing in a global economy, and that workers in other countries benefit, but that does not mean that the situation is only beneficial – the workers who used to do the jobs may be unable to get alternative work. So, overall this is quite good but not perfect.

Some of what Kwame says is reasonable – there is good evidence out there to show that the poor are exploited by the rich in a global economy and that this does exaggerate income inequality – but there are also alternative perspectives on this. However, Kwame has not quoted or used any of this evidence, merely stated the conclusion as a fact, and repeated it. This repetition does not make it stronger. He offers no reasons to support his view. Calling the World Bank and IMF 'evil' is extreme.

Rennick's views are entirely opinion based and to some extent counter factual. Evidence does generally support the view (against Rennick) that rich countries are, overall, better off because of globalisation. There are clearly segments of society which are not better off, so there is a kernel of truth to Rennick's rant, but he exaggerates and plays on people's fears rather than arguing. [15]

Question 4

Reward thoughtful discussion using Cambridge's most recent generic mark schemes. [24]

6 Law and criminality

Introduction

There are many different approaches to discussing law and criminality. The Student Book provides one possible approach. Teachers should feel free to take a different approach if it will suit their class better, but the focus of any teaching should always be the Global Perspectives skills. The written examination will test skills, rather than subject knowledge.

Law and criminality affect everyone's life. Without the rule of law, our lives are insecure and economic prosperity is almost impossible. One of the biggest differences between the global rich and poor is access to effective security measures and legal redress. It is a fundamental principle of democracies that all are equal before the law – but even in wealthy, democratic countries, some are more equal than others. Even where corruption is limited, money still buys better lawyers. A further issue is that criminal activity is increasingly international, cross-border and globalised, whereas laws remain national, and most law enforcement agencies are regional or national. Efforts are being made to internationalise law enforcement, but these are progressing much more slowly than the internationalisation of crime.

Suggested resources

http://www.interpol.int/	Website of the international police agency.
https://www.hrw.org/topic/international-justice/international-criminal-court	Information on the international criminal court from Human Rights Watch, with links to other relevant issues.
https://www.globalpolicy.org/international-justice/international-criminal-tribunals-and-special-courts.html	Information on international criminal tribunals for specific areas of the world from Global Policy, with links to other relevant issues.
https://www.unodc.org/unodc/en/data-and-analysis/statistics/crime.html	Links to a variety of statistics on crime from the United Nations Office for Drugs and Crime.

Suggested answers to the activities

Activity 1

1. Accept any answer which can be justified.
   (a) Preventing crime, surveillance
   (b) Justice and development
   (c) Preventing crime, funding the criminal justice system
   (d) Crime prevention and causes of crime.
2. Suggested answers:
   (a) C, D   (b) A   (c) B, D
3. Encourage debate, research and discussion.

Activity 2

It cannot be emphasised enough that dictionary skills – whether online or in print – are valuable, and that online translation tools de-skill students and generally provide poor translations. Suggestions are provided, but encourage students to consider various definitions.

No specific answers.

Activity 3

1. If we cooperate with Interpol, we will be able to track international criminals more closely.
2. If the government provided enough jobs, there would be less crime.
3. If Daria had not paid the people smugglers, she would be in prison for expressing her opinion.

Activity 4

1. Encourage students to think carefully and to explain and justify their views. Suggested answer:

   Darius is slightly but not significantly wrong about the time he left work – this is within a normal margin of error, so it is plausible. If Darius were lying to cover up his bank robbing activities, he would probably say he had left at a completely different time so that it looked as if he were not in the area.

   His reason for wrapping himself in a scarf is plausible – many people do wrap up in scarves when it is cold. We would need to check how cold it actually was that evening.

It is plausible that Darius took a long time getting ready before asking his girlfriend to marry him, but he would have a reason to lie about this if he were the jewel thief, so we would need corroboration – did his neighbours see or hear him?

Darius should have a receipt to corroborate his purchase of the ring last week, and it is plausible that he did buy the ring last week if he was planning to ask his girlfriend to marry him.

We can't simply trust his claim that he didn't go into the store today, because he would have a strong reason to lie if he did rob the shop, but the claim is plausible.

Overall, everything Darius says is plausible, but he would have such a strong reason to lie if he were the robber that his statement is unreliable and needs to be corroborated.

2. Encourage students to think carefully and to explain and justify their views. Suggested answer:

You need to know whether the weather was very cold, whether Darius was seen on any other CCTV cameras and what he was doing, whether he was seen or heard at home by neighbours, whether he does in fact have a receipt for the ring he says he bought last Tuesday. All of these could corroborate his story – or not. You need to know whether any other possible robbers were seen in the area. This could provide an alternative thief.

3. Encourage students to think carefully and to explain and justify their views.

Activity 5

1. Encourage students to research carefully, using their skills.

2. Use the article to complete the table:

Arguments in favour of death penalty for corruption	Arguments against the death penalty for corruption
Fight corruption act as a deterrent	It doesn't work.
It would go against the will of the people to abolish it. Proponents of the death penalty are also convinced that it would play a crucial role in repairing the shattered trust of foreign investors.	Variants of: the death penalty is a poor alternative to sorting out the real problems with corruption. The death penalty cannot be used in place of larger, more comprehensive long-term moves to weed out corruption.

3. Encourage debate and discussion. Suggested answer:

The death penalty is a personal issue to the extent that each individual should think about it and form their own opinion, based on evidence and reflection. It is highly personal to those who face the death penalty, or who have family or friends facing the death penalty, and especially if these people are innocent and wrongly convicted. Some victims of crimes also become personally involved in seeking justice or revenge through the death penalty.

The death penalty is a national issue because laws regarding punishment for criminal offences are usually made at a national level. The debate about capital punishment needs to be held at a national level, in the press and in parliament.

The death penalty is a global issue to the extent that there are global campaigns against it and there are various human rights issues involved. It is debatable whether global organisations should be able to intervene in a national criminal justice system.

4. Encourage research and debate. Students should justify their views.

Activity 6

1. Suggested answer:

   i) People who are charged under PoTA cannot appeal via the courts.

   ii) It is important that people can appeal via the courts to ensure that the government does not abuse its power or violate individuals' rights.

   iii) So PoTA is against democracy and the rule of law.

2. Encourage students to think carefully, to relate their views to the quotations and to justify their views. Key issues include the weakening of the assumption of innocence and the use of sensitive or complex information in court.

3. Encourage research.

4. Encourage students to apply their skills, to debate and to justify their views.

Practice examination paper

Question 1

Consider Document 1.

a) USA [1]

b) Japan [1]

c) Guns are legal or available where the rates are high and illegal or not available where the rates are low/ most high gun crime countries are LEDC or MEDC, most low gun crime countries are HEDC [1]

Consider Document 2.

d) Reward thoughtful discussion using Cambridge's most recent generic mark schemes. Suggested answers:

The sentences have caused outrage because the punishments do not seem to fit the crimes. The wealthy banker who stole $10 million seems to have a very short sentence, whereas the migrant agricultural worker who stole a much smaller amount has a very long sentence. You might question whether it is so much worse to break into someone's house than to sit in your office and steal using a computer – or whether the rich man gets less punishment than the poor man. People might also be outraged by the farmer who was defending his property getting such a high sentence. He didn't go out intending to murder someone, just shot someone who had already broken the law and was a threat to him. (Note that it is possible to defend these sentences – killing is killing, for example, and therefore worse than any kind of theft...) [6]

e) The punishment (for fraud and burglary) should reflect the amount of money stolen / we should pay bankers and agricultural workers the same amount of money (so there would be less greed) / I think the criminal, irresponsible few (bankers) should be punished more harshly. [3]

Question 2

Reward thoughtful discussion using Cambridge's most recent generic mark schemes. Suggested answers: [14]

1. The migrant worker's sister / wife / daughter / brother is a domestic servant at the millionaire's house / The migrant worker had done some maintenance work for the millionaire.

2. The migrant worker was captured clearly on CCTV in a different city at the time of the burglary / the migrant worker has visa stamps in his passport showing that he was in a different country at the time.

   The pieces of evidence suggested in 1) are not direct evidence that the migrant worker did not commit the crime, but they do offer good reasons why his hair might be at the crime scene, even if he didn't commit the burglary. He was convicted because one of his hairs was there, so if he can show an innocent reason why his hair was at the scene, there is reasonable doubt.

   The pieces of evidence suggested in 2) are hard evidence showing that the migrant worker could not have committed the crime (unless he had an identical twin). If he was in a different city or a different country, he could not have committed the burglary.

   If you can show that he could not have committed the burglary, and that there is an innocent reason for his hair to be on the scene, you have shown his innocence.

Question 3

a) This is a value judgement (which is a form of opinion) because it is placing a value on defending your home / on life. It is expressing a moral opinion about what you should or should not do, which is a value. [2]

b) Reward thoughtful discussion using Cambridge's most recent generic mark schemes. Suggested answers:

@hope for the future suggests two consequences: that punishing people according to the amount they have stolen would lead to a fairer criminal justice system, and that paying bankers and agricultural workers would lead to less greed, a happier society and less crime. These consequences (especially the second) are both rather idealistic and unrealistic – wishful thinking. Punishing people according to the amount they have stolen might be fair in one way – but it doesn't take into consideration how unpleasant it is having an intruder in your home – is it fair to punish people for that kind of distress? Paying bankers and agricultural workers the same might lead to a somewhat happier society, with less resentment and fewer problems arising from inequality. But the consequences suggested here are too good to be true – too extreme. [3]

c) Suggested answers: Yes, having someone invade your private space makes a theft worse / no, this value judgement falls down because the money in bank accounts might really exist, and be people's savings. [3]

d) Reward thoughtful discussion using Cambridge's most recent generic mark schemes. Suggested answers: [12]

@innocentbanker's reasoning is better than @amazinggrace's. This is because @innocentbanker gives reasons and explanations which are quite logical, and because it makes a difference between criminal bankers, greedy bankers and other bankers – it doesn't treat them as if they're all the same. It predicts a reasonable consequence – harsh punishment might make other bankers realise they can't get away with crime. On the other hand, @amazinggrace is ranting, being emotional and jumping about from one grievance to another without giving reasons or being logical. 'You can't even defend your home any more' doesn't take into account that the farmer killed the burglar – killing is an extreme form of defending your home. There is also no evidence to support the opinion that 'it's being soft on kids that leads to all this crime' – it's just an opinion and there is no reason to accept it.

Question 4

Reward thoughtful discussion using Cambridge's most recent generic mark schemes. [24]

⑦ Migration

Introduction

There are many different approaches to discussing migration. The Student Book provides one possible approach. Teachers should feel free to take a different approach if it will suit their class better, but the focus of any teaching should always be the Global Perspectives skills. The written examination will test skills, rather than subject knowledge.

Dealing with migration is possibly one of the greatest challenges of our time. The scale of migration at present is staggering. Around the world people are migrating in huge numbers to escape poverty, oppression, war and privation. People from the Middle East and parts of Africa are travelling to Europe; people from Indonesia are travelling to Australia; people from Central America are travelling to North America. Wealthy countries are feeling overwhelmed by the sheer numbers of migrants, and fearful of the consequences of accepting them. Yet there are also good reasons to welcome migrants – legal obligations under the Geneva Convention, moral obligations of human decency, and self-interest: Steve Jobs, the founder of Apple, was the son of a migrant from Syria.

Suggested resources

http://www.nytimes.com/ interactive/2015/04/20/ world/europe/surge-in-refugees-crossing-the-mediterranean-sea-maps. html?_r=1	Graphics from the New York Times showing information relating to refugees arriving in Europe.
http://www.nytimes.com/ interactive/2015/06/09/ world/migrants-global-refugee-crisis-mediterranean-ukraine-syria-rohingya-malaysia-iraq.html	Another set of graphics from the New York Times showing information relating to refugees.
http://www.theguardian. com/artanddesign/2015/ dec/11/banksy-uses-steve-jobs-artwork-to-highlight-refugee-crisis	UK newspaper the Guardian reports on Banksy's street art relating to refugees.
http://www.global-migration.info/	Useful graphic from Global Migration.
http://www.theatlantic. com/photo/2015/06/ fleeing-by-the-millions-migration-crises-around-the-world/394805/	Article on migration with moving photographs, from the Atlantic

Suggested answers to the activities

Activity 1

1. Accept any answer which can be justified.
   (a) Managing migration, duty of care to migrants.
   (b) Anti-migration sentiment
   (c) Managing migration
   (d) Effects on country of departure, migration and development
   (e) Anti-migration sentiment, effects on host country.
2. Suggested answers:
   (a) B, C
   (b) (B), D, E
   (c) A
3. Encourage research, debate and discussion.

Activity 2

It cannot be emphasised enough that dictionary skills – whether online or in print – are valuable, and that online translation tools de-skill students and generally provide poor translations. Suggestions are provided, but encourage students to consider various definitions.

No specific answers.

Activity 3

1. If we welcome migrants now, we will reduce the risk of terror attacks.
2. If the government provided incentives for educated migrants to come, we would develop thriving economic communities.
3. If I had stayed in the town where I was born, I would not have a good job in the bank.

Activity 4

Refer to Documents 1 and 2.

1. The staggering number of migrants, which can cause problems and can be frightening, but which also reflects the huge problems and inequalities in the world. Also the issue that we are all human and all share one Earth, and those of us lucky enough to be in rich countries should remember this.

Activity 5

Refer to Document 3.

1. Conflict in Syria
2. National
3. Encourage students to apply their research skills.
4. Encourage students to think and to justify their views.

Activity 6

Refer to Document 4.

1. Make safe and legal routes available to asylum seekers / share responsibility for refugees amongst European countries / provide more resettlement places in European countries.
2. Encourage students to think about what is really likely
3. Encourage student to apply their research skills.
4. Encourage students to reflect and to justify their views.

Activity 7

Encourage students to justify their views.

Reflection

Reflection is an important part of the course, so it is important to allow class time for this kind of activity. It may be useful to use a learning journal. This might allow for some ongoing written dialogue about the issues. It's key here to avoid simple praise or giving a student's thoughts a value – rather, try to engage a student in discussion over time, include questions in your written response which will push the student to the next level, and expect them to respond.

Question 1

Refer to Document 1.

a) Human trafficking is buying and selling human beings as slaves. People smuggling is taking people's money to help them get to another place. [3]

Refer to Document 2.

b) Poverty, unemployment, discrimination, a lack of social and economic opportunities, and global financial crises (any three). [1]

c) Reward thoughtful and focused explanation. [4]

Refer to Document 4.

d) There is no clear fleet of smuggling boats to target with air strikes – smugglers use any boat, such as fishing boats, and they buy them from fisherman at any time. So if the smugglers' current boats were destroyed, they would simply buy some more fishing boats. In addition, it is easy for anyone to become a people smuggler with very little effort. [4]

Question 2

a) Reward thoughtful, focused questions with clear explanations of how they would help to decide whether the woman is a legal migrant. Accept any reasonable response. Suggested answers:

Ask for her personal details and anything that would help to check with legal records which would show whether she was legal – for example, her name, date and place of birth and the place where her visa was issued, when and where she entered the country, any details she remembers from her passport – number, expiry date, place of issue.

Ask her for details of how she came to be working for the couple and treated so badly – her story may have inconsistencies which would help the police to decide that she was lying, or details which are likely to only be true if she is in fact a legal migrant. [6]

b) Reward thoughtful discussion using Cambridge's most recent generic mark schemes. Accept any reasonable response. Suggested answers:

The evidence from conversations with smugglers and coastguards shows that there is no easy way to stop smugglers, and no shortage of smugglers. The amount of money people are prepared to pay, combined with the numbers of people who seem to keep coming indicates that there is a steady supply of people wishing to be smuggled. The references to the continuing conflicts show that people are likely to continue to have a reason to try to get to Europe. So the author has shown that there is no reason for people smuggling to stop, and it is an easy inference to the claim that people smuggling will continue. Although the evidence is mostly based on conversations, it seems to be fairly thorough journalistic evidence. Of course the prediction that people smuggling will continue has not been proven, but it has been shown that it is highly likely. [8]

Question 3

Refer to Document 3.

a) As an international police agency, Interpol is reliable in giving definitions – they have sufficient expertise and access to information. It would also be reliable in giving statistics relating to the work that they do. Interpol may have certain biases and specific perspectives, but these will not make a definition unreliable. [3]

b) Reward thoughtful discussion using Cambridge's most recent generic mark schemes. Accept any reasonable answer.

Suggested answers:

This is a second hand account, which is based on someone else's story, so its reliability depends on how well the migrant domestic worker knew her friend, how trustworthy her friend was, and how much the worker really knew about her friend's situation. The worker may be totally honest, but have been misled by her friend, for example. It might be possible, for example, that her friend was bruised in a fight or by a boyfriend and lied about it.

The migrant domestic worker may have a bias in favour of her friend, and may lie about her status as legal to protect her, which would make her evidence a little less reliable if she were talking to the police. However, she is telling her story to an anti-slavery charity, so she has no obvious reason to lie.

We have no clear reason to believe that the worker is dishonest or unreliable, but her story depends on the reliability of her friend. [6]

c) Reward thoughtful discussion using Cambridge's most recent generic mark schemes. Accept any reasonable answer. Suggested answer:

This appears to be good quality investigative journalism, so it is likely that the journalist found the most reliable source they could, but this is not saying much. Hajj is not the man's real name, and he is a criminal talking to a journalist, so he is likely to tell only part of the story, and likely to tell the story in a way that makes himself sound better – anything he says about himself is likely to be fairly unreliable. However, Hajj does appear to have some expertise and information, which makes him reliable in terms of the methods that smugglers use and the prices they charge. [6]

d) Reward thoughtful discussion using Cambridge's most recent generic mark schemes. Accept any reasonable answer. Suggested answer:

There is no clear conclusion to this reasoning – it is not clear whether it is arguing that Europe has already done enough or that Europe should do more but in a realistic way. The claim that Europe cannot help all the refugees in the world is reasonable, and the reasons offered to support it – Europe isn't big enough or rich enough – do give some support. But there is a problem here – this is arguing against a straw man, against an argument that no one would ever offer. No one is claiming that Europe should help all the refugees in the world, or that Europe should solve all the world's problems. The claim that we want to help people in need sounds reasonable, but it is followed by two claims which significantly undermine it. The idea that 'we are drowning in other people's problems' is emotive, appealing to fear, and somewhat exaggerated. Furthermore, 'we have enough problems of our own' seems rather churlish – to compare Europe's problems to the problems of Syria or Eritrea seems unreasonable. [5]

Question 4

Reward thoughtful discussion using Cambridge's most recent generic mark schemes.

8 Transport systems

Introduction

There are many different approaches to discussing transport systems. The Student Book provides one possible approach. Teachers should feel free to take a different approach if it will suit their class better, but the focus of any teaching should always be the Global Perspectives skills. The written examination will test skills, rather than subject knowledge.

Transport systems are a key feature of our lives. We are all aware of their effects on our personal lives. Good roads and good bus services make the journey to school or work much more bearable, whilst a lack of good transport systems cannot only make our daily journeys a misery, they can significantly limit our personal options. A child can only go to a good school if they can get there. An adult can only take a good job if they can get to it on time and reliably. On a national level, effective and efficient transport systems are essential to economic growth and to development. A great deal of global commerce also depends on transport systems.

Suggested resources

http://www.uitp.org/statistics	UITP – a passionate champion of sustainable urban mobility – has collections of statistics and information, including a variety of graphics.
http://www.worldbank.org/en/topic/transport	Information and links from the World Bank relating to transport.
http://www.citymetric.com/transport/high-speed-rail-popping-all-over-world-heres-why-thats-good-thing-1282	Article on high speed rail.
http://www.theatlantic.com/business/archive/2015/01/why-cant-public-transit-be-free/384929/	Article from the Atlantic looking at the possibilities and limitations of free public transport and other possible solutions. Includes examples from around the world.
https://www.ted.com/topics/transportation	TED talks on transportation.

Suggested answers to the activities:

Activity 1

1. Accept any answer which can be justified.
    (a) Who should fund transport systems, environmental issues.
    (b) Comfort and convenience, environmental issues
    (c) Aging transport systems, environmental issues, who should fund transport systems.
    (d) Efficiency of transport systems.
    (e) Transport and development.
2. Suggested answers:
    (a) B
    (b) A
    (c) (B), C, D, E
3. Encourage research, debate and discussion.

Activity 2

It cannot be emphasised enough that dictionary skills – whether online or in print – are valuable, and that online translation tools de-skill students and as generally provide poor translations. Suggestions are provided, but encourage students to consider various definitions.

No specific answers.

Activity 3

1. If we go by car instead of by train, we will arrive much sooner.
2. If the government provided incentives people to use public transport, fewer people would drive their own cars.
3. If the government had started to plan the public transport system earlier, it would not be so inefficient.

Activity 4

Refer to Document 1

1. Fact: The infrastructure is new and growing fast / my parents don't have electricity
    Opinion: The pace of change is too fast
    Prediction: This (pollution) is going to get worse

2. This could be either fact or exaggeration. If it can be verified, it's a fact. But *hardly breathe* does sound like an exaggeration. Pollution in Chinese cities certainly has been bad, and can be thick like smog, which makes it harder to see and affects breathing.

3. Encourage students to think about search terms, what sort of site would be useful, using images.

4. This is an opinion because it can't be verified – certainly not for the whole infrastructure system of the UK. But it can be supported by looking at which bits of infrastructure are breaking, or are not meeting demands. It's not an unreasonable opinion, but it is a bit too generalised.

5. Encourage students to think about search terms, what sort of site would be useful, skim reading, etc.

6. Allow students to discuss and expect them to support and justify their opinions with evidence and arguments.

7. It may be a fact that a lot of the speaker's things do not arrive at their destination. Half is likely to be an exaggeration, and if you checked, you would find it was less than this. It may be a fact that the postman is dishonest and gives some things he should post to his family. But unless the speaker has actually checked that the missing items go to the postman, it is an opinion.

8. Encourage students to think of what sort of information would be useful to check this – could include Alina's records, an interview with the postman, an investigation of what jewellery the postman's family has, whether any of it was made by Alina, and if so, whether they have receipts to show that they purchased it, and whether it matches items that were sent out and lost.

9. It is not clear from the context. Everything Alina says could apply to high, medium or low economic development countries. There are areas in all countries where the internet connection is unreliable (in MEDCs mainly rural areas), there are dishonest postmen in all countries, our demands on infrastructure are so great that all countries need to invest in it, and the question of who pays is valid in all countries. So, while it might be more likely that she is in a LEDC, a MEDC is possible.

Activity 5

1. Suggested answers:

   (a) Kedah Chief Minister dreams of being the driving force of economic development in his state / wants to be like his father /Kedah is ruled by the governing party of Malaysia, whereas the main rival Penang is ruled by the opposing party.

   (b) It could turn Kedah into a tourist destination / it could drive economic development

   (c) It is likely to cost US$700 million, which would be wasted if no one wanted to go there because it was 'the middle of nowhere.'

2. Mainly personal, regional and national.

3. Suggested answers:

   (a) Expand Penang International Airport – because it is the third busiest airport in Malaysia with fast growing passenger numbers and receives a lot of foreign investment.

   (b) There is allegedly no space to expand Penang International Airport – land would have to be reclaimed. Furthermore, a political reason against this is that the government would want to fund development in areas which are controlled by its party, not the opposition.

4. Encourage students to apply their skills.

5. Encourage students to apply their research, discussion and reflection skills.

6. Encourage students to apply their skills.

Activity 6

1. Accept any reasonable answers.

   (a) Very little infrastructure – although irrigation and roads to market would help

   (b) Irrigation, electricity, refrigerated transport, a local airport, good roads, hotels for business partners, telecommunications . . .

   (c) Hotels with websites and WiFi, restaurants, ATMs, transport to and from the airport, electricity, telecommunications. Possibly swimming pools, saunas, spas.

   (d) Books, pens, IT, transport to school. Food, toilets.

   (e) IT, transport, electricity, sanitation.

2. and 3. Encourage research, debate and discussion.

Suggested answers to examination practice

Question 1

a) London and Tokyo. [2]

b) London has the most in terms of miles, but Delhi has a higher proportion. [1]

c) Bogota. [1]

d) Reward thoughtful discussion using Cambridge's most recent generic mark schemes. Accept any reasonable response. Suggested answer:

London and Tokyo have the most developed transport systems with the most connections and most lines, so you would expect them to be more equal to the needs of the large populations that the very simple transport systems in Delhi and Bogotá. However, London's transport system is rather old. If you do know this, you would expect its age to lead to maintenance needs and inefficiency. The Japanese have a reputation for technical excellence, so on that basis you might expect them to have the most efficient public transport system. [4]

e) Reward thoughtful discussion using Cambridge's most recent generic mark schemes. Accept any reasonable response. Suggested answer:

Personal because it affects each individual's quality of life and ability to get to work /school and the comfort of the journey. It might affect our decisions about whether to use public transport rather than driving.

Local because transport systems are often local to particular towns, cities or regions, and may be funded at a local level. Local economies depend on good transport links.

National because it is linked to economic growth and development. It may be funded nationally. [4]

Question 2

Suggested answer:

Overall, a survey is likely to generate a more accurate image, but visiting each place would give you a better personal feel for the efficiency of each system.

Trying them out yourself would be time consuming and expensive. By definition you cannot test them all at the same time, so you would be unsure whether variations you observed were due to different times of the year. Trying them out yourself would give you a very personal, subjective experience, but it would still be limited. How long would you need to try them out for to be sure? It could be that you tried Delhi on the one day that it was inefficient and Bogota on the one day that it was efficient – that is, there is a danger of generalising too much from insufficient data.

Conducting surveys could be done online or by phone. This would be more cost effective than visiting each place and it would also allow for the collection of more data – lots of people's experiences on many days would be likely to generate an accurate statistical image of how efficient each transport system is. It would still be a report of subjective experiences and perceptions, however. It may be that people would only respond to the survey if they were annoyed about a specific delay, so such a survey might generate an overly negative image. A well-constructed survey would select representative samples, which would improve accuracy. [14]

Question 3

a) Opinion – it cannot be verified and it can be argued against. For instance, if the transport system were really a disaster, there would not be a bus to replace the train. This person is describing a mildly delayed and uncomfortable journey – not a total disaster. [3]

b) @frustrated and angry has had a difficult and uncomfortable journey, which will make them emotional, and it is hard to keep an objective head in those circumstances. So @frustrated and angry is probably seeing one bad journey is a biased light. [2]

c) Reward thoughtful discussion using Cambridge's most recent generic mark schemes. Accept any reasonable response. Suggested answer:

@frustated and angry gives narrative not reasoning. It exaggerates the discomfort – and generalises from one instance, as is made clear by the contrasting comment from @impressed tourist.

@frequent traveller provides supposition and surmise with no supporting evidence. Also generalises from something happening in one small part of the train network. However, the explanation they give is plausible – companies do like to make money by making cuts.

@business realist makes a reasonable point about buses being cheaper than trains, but makes a large and unfounded leap to the stupidity of heavily subsided rail systems. We have to assume that this particular rail system is heavily subsidised. There is also a totally unfounded claim about train companies deliberately claiming subsidies without bothering to run trains. All of this is unwarranted generalisation from a single example in a large transport system. The language is emotive and extreme.

The response to @business realist provides the strongest reasoning, although it is not very strong. It is reasonable to make a distinction between a train service and a for-profit company, although it is also reasonable to argue which one of these train services / companies should be. It is also reasonable to comment on the fluctuating levels of passengers at different times, and this provides some support for the claim that 'it evens out.' If you believe that it should be a train 'service' this will seem a reasonable, logical argument. If you believe that train companies should be making as much money as possible, it will not. It is measured, calm and thoughtful.

@impressed tourist simply makes a comment – but this comment does help to set the complaints in perspective. [15]

Question 4

Reward thoughtful discussion using Cambridge's most recent generic mark schemes. Accept any reasonable response. [24]

Skills development activities
Worksheet: 1.1 Searching for information

Activity 1

Match the words below to the definitions in the table.

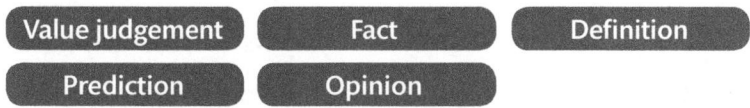

	Word	Definition
1		The exact meaning of a word.
2		Information or an idea that can be proved to be true (can be verified).
3		A personal belief that may or may not be based on facts and knowledge.
4		An assessment or personal belief about how good or bad something is.
5		A statement about what might happen in the future, or what the consequences of an act might be.

Activity 2

Use the search skills you have developed to help you answer the following questions:

(a) Which team won the Football World Cup in 1970?

(b) What is the capital city of Morocco?

(c) What did people do before social media sites became so popular?

(d) Why did the UN produce the Declaration of Human Rights?

(e) How does ecosystem loss affect individuals in your country?

Activity 3

Find information about the following topics. Think about your search terms.
Think about what type of information you need to find.

(a) Crime rates for different crimes in different countries.

(b) The most efficient public transport system.

(c) The best ways to reduce fuel use in schools.

(d) The effects of unemployment.

Skills development activities
Worksheet: 1.2 Reading and recording

Activity 1

1. Find the following words in the word cloud:

   (a) enterprise

   (b) Alliance's

   (c) verified

   (d) resources

   (e) Rainforest.

2. Use online tools such as http://www.wordle.net/ create and http://www.puzzle-maker.com/WS/ to make word clouds and word searches using key words from your research. Give the puzzles to your friends to complete.

Activity 2

1. Find the following words in Document 1 on the right:

   (a) emigration

   (b) immigration

   (c) population growth

   (d) fertility decline.

Document 1

In the 1990s, Hong Kong saw a massive wave of migration. Much media attention was focused on the surge in emigration, yet little attention was paid to the equally high levels of immigration. In fact, the population of Hong Kong has increased by approximately 2% every year in recent times. At the same time, Hong Kong has seen a rapid fertility decline (in fact, its birth rate is one of the lowest in the world), and so we can only attribute this rate of population growth to an influx of people.

Skills development activities
Worksheet: 1.3 Setting up research

My research

Complete the following table to help you plan your research.

Overall topic	
Key issues	
Aspects that interest me	
MY GLOBAL QUESTION	
Sub-questions to ask to help me answer my global question	
Causes and consequences	
Perspectives	
Possible solutions	
Things I still need to do	
My personal perspective and the reasons for it	

Skills development activities
Worksheet: 2.1 Identifying information and trends

Document 1

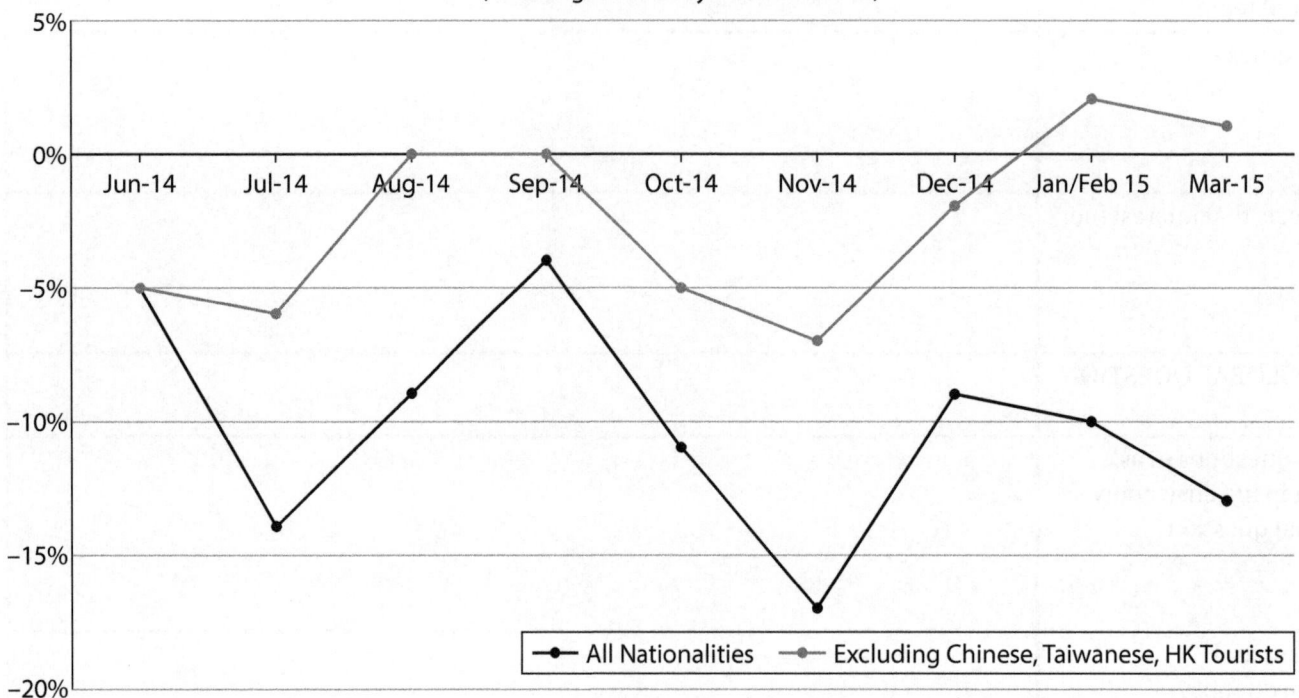

Vietnam Tourism: Is the Decline Only Caused By Chinese Tourists?
(% Change Month by Month Arrivals)

Activity 1

1. Describe the trends in the graph in Document 1.
2. Consider this question: Why did tourism in Vietnam decline during this period?
   (a) Generally speaking, what sort of things could cause tourism to decline?
   (b) What sort of information will you need to answer this question?
   (c) What search terms will you use?
   (d) Now reseach the question.
   (e) Did your findings match your expectations?

Activity 2

1. Look at the statements below. What else do you need to know in each case?
   (a) Vietnam is quite cheap. We should go there for our holiday.
   (b) Lots of people die in gun fights. The government should make guns illegal.
   (c) We are losing the rainforest. We should use less paper.
   (d) Communications technology is vital to economic development. Remote tribes should get mobile phones.
   (e) Biodiversity is declining. We should campaign to get investment in schemes to protect wildlife.

Skills development activities
Worksheet: 2.2 Understanding key issues

Activity 1

1. Choose names for the people in the dialogue below. Write the names in the spaces provided.

2. What are the key issues for each of these people?

3. What are the cultural and national perspectives that underlie these issues?

Person 1 –   : I wasn't born here, but I can't go home. My home has been destroyed. The country I was born in no longer exists. It has been taken from us by foreign invaders who will not let us practise our religion. They tortured and killed my husband. They tortured and abused me. I will not let them torture, abuse or kill my children. I just want my children to be safe, to live in peace, and to get a good education.

Person 2 –   : We all want that, but there are gangs here that are after all our children. You've had a tough time, tougher than most, but life is tough for all of us. I don't know how to make my wages stretch to everything my family needs. I'm working every day, but I can't buy coats for my kids, or pay for the car I need to get to work. If people are coming over here and getting free housing and free food, it's not right. You should be working.

Person 1 –   : I would love to, but I'm not allowed to work.

Person 3 –   : There isn't enough work to go round either. We're happy to help, but if you take our jobs, we're as badly off as you. There are too many local workers – builders, plumbers, restaurant owners and the like – who can't get work. We just can't deal with more people around here.

Person 1 –   : I am a doctor. I am not a threat to builders or plumbers – in fact, I could help you. There are not enough doctors here.

Person 4 –   : My problem is that there are already too many people here already, using all the resources. We waste too much water, eat too much food, use too much electricity, burn too much fuel and make too much waste. The problem is not how our taxes are used or the demands on our police forces or our hospitals, as some people say. The problem is that each piece of land can only sustain so many people. And this land is overstretched with too many people. The more people who come here, the worse it is going to get.

Person 5 –   : We should keep our country's scarce resources for people who were born here.

Person 6 –   : Why should *we* keep everything from this land? Why does being born here give us any more right to the land's resources? What if I said that my part of the country didn't want to share resources with your part of the country? What does it mean for us to be a nation anyway? Fifty years ago, this country didn't even exist. We were invented by some politicians with an agenda. I'm just hoping that we aren't torn apart by some more politicians with an agenda.

Skills development activities
Worksheet: 2.3 Identifying causes and consequences

Activity 1

1. Draw diagrams showing the causes and consequences in the following situations.

> **1**
>
> People burn fossil fuels, which leads to the production of greenhouse gases. These gases linger in the atmosphere and trap heat in the Earth's atmosphere, resulting in climate change. Because of this there are more extreme weather events.

> **2**
>
> As a result of the long drought, livestock herds are dying because of lack of water, crops are withering in the fields, and farmers are worrying about how they will survive the next year. Some of these farmers own their land, and are rooted in the land, almost as if they themselves are part of the landscape. These farmers will continue to farm for as long as they can. But others are attracted by the easy wealth apparently on offer in the city. These farmers and farm workers will leave the land. Arriving in the city with very little, they will probably end up in the poor parts of the city that have poor sanitation and limited opportunities.

Activity 2

1. For each of the following, decide whether it is a case of cause and consequence or simply a sequence of events.

> Think about *how* you will know whether or not it is a case of cause and consequence. Because you have been told? Because you can work it out? Because you have studied the evidence? What else might you need to know?

(a) The sun rises. The sun sets.

(b) The dog barks. The postman walks away.

(c) People burn fossil fuels. The earth's climate changes.

(d) It doesn't rain for 26 months. The crops fail.

(e) Dinesh is standing next to Amir holding a pistol. Amir has a serious gunshot wound.

(f) There is an earthquake. Buildings collapse.

(g) The spacewoman sends compressed gas out of the fuel canisters beneath her. She moves upwards.

(h) A car hits a child. The child has broken bones.

Skills development activities
Worksheet: 2.4 Identifying and evaluating possible courses of action

Exploding rockets and starving astronauts!

Questions over future of space station

A rocket delivering supplies to the International Space Station has exploded just seconds after take-off, shocking observers and leaving astronauts in a perilous position. As this second supply mission in two months fails, there are bound to be questions about the viability of the space station.

Our own astronaut, Dr Jo Imam, is on the ISS, as part of a year-long research mission. Five other astronauts – from the USA, Canada, Russia and Europe – are also on the space station. The unmanned cargo craft was carrying water, food, fuel, spare parts, scientific equipment and medication. Dr Smith reports that all astronauts are in good spirits, but adds that food is in short supply. 'We also needed the spare parts to fix an ongoing electrical fault, which could have serious consequences if it affects our communications with Earth,' she says.

Here on Earth, people are questioning the value and viability of the International Space Station. Hundreds of millions of dollars' worth of scientific equipment was lost today, as one aging Russian rocket failed. Is it really worth leaving people stranded in space? What benefits could there possibly be that make the human and financial cost worth it?

Activity 1

1. Work in teams of 3 to 4 people. Your tasks are:

   (a) To come up with a short-term plan to ensure the survival of the astronauts

   (b) To decide on the best long-term course of action regarding the future of the space station.

In order to help you, you should:

- Conduct research to find out details about how the space station is supplied, the costs and possible benefits of the space station, and the possible risks of the space station

- Consider the positive and negative consequences of a range of possible courses of action

- Weigh up these consequences

- Debate the best short-term and long-term courses of action.

2. Working individually, write a reasoned case to support your chosen courses of action.

Skills development activities
Worksheet: 2.5 Identifying different perspectives

Document 1

Chinese President Xi Jinping will speak at the headquarters of the Arab League in Cairo during his visit to Egypt, Saudi Arabia, and Iran, said Zhang Ming, Vice Minister of Foreign Affairs, on Monday.

The President will discuss the situation in the Middle East and elaborate on China's plans to cooperate with other global powers in the region. These may include discussions on infrastructure, trade, technology, energy, and investment, Zhang said.

Source: Chinese newspaper

Document 2

The CSIS Middle East program is studying the implications of China's increasing role in the Middle East. As China becomes a global power and many Middle Eastern countries look for a counterweight to the United States, Chinese approaches to energy security, export markets and military ties have an important impact on global diplomacy. At the same time, the Chinese experience of economic growth without significant political liberalization remains an interesting, if not outright attractive, example for some Middle Eastern regimes. Through seminars in China, the Middle East and the United States, the Middle East Program will evaluate emerging trends and opportunities in China's evolving relations with the Middle East.

Source: http://csis.org/program/china-middle-east

Document 3

The delicate balance of power in the Middle East has already suffered one dramatic upheaval this year, after Moscow's decision to launch its military intervention in support of Syrian dictator Bashar al-Assad. Now there are mounting concerns that the region could suffer further instability following China's decision to establish its first overseas military outpost in one of the world's most troubled hotshots.

Ever since President Obama decided to scale down American involvement in a region that has for decades been regarded as Washington's sphere of influence, policymakers have been warning that the power vacuum would be filled by regimes that did not have Western interests at heart.

Source: http://www.telegraph.co.uk/news/worldnews/middleeast/syria/12055805/China-is-moving-intyo-Syria-why-is-no-one-worried.html

Activity 1

Identify the different perspectives in each of the documents above. Think about the sources, about the beliefs they hold, and the issues that they consider to be important.

Skills development activities
Worksheet: 3.1 Questioning knowledge claims

Document 1

The Ethiopians want to build a dam on the Nile. They're stealing our water. We should explode the ships bringing materials for the dam so they can't build it.

Document 2

We're running out of oil. If we keep using oil like this, there will be no oil left by 2025. So the government should ban us from using cars.

Document 3

> Tiger parents are strict, demanding parents who push their children for excellence.

Tiger mothers are in the headlines, with the Prime Minister heaping praise on their pushy, proactive approach to parenting.

But I do not like tiger parenting. In fact, I think it's counter-productive, producing intolerable, precocious children and smug, arrogant adults. I'm also convinced it leads to anxiety and dysfunctional behaviour in later life.

Most of all, though, I dislike the principles of tiger parenting — 'work, try hard, believe you can succeed, get up and try again', as the Prime Minister put it — because it seems to me that they are not so much designed to equip the child for life as to glorify the efforts of the parent.

Tiger parenting is vanity parenting, espoused by people who see their children not as individuals with independent hearts and minds, but vessels for their own, perhaps thwarted, ambitions — and vehicles for their own self-aggrandisement.

That's where tiger parenting goes wrong. You kid yourself you're doing your child a favour by turning them into a chess/tennis/maths champion; in fact, you're just being an awful bully. Bullying can toughen up a child, but it can also destroy their confidence and tie their egos in lasting psychological knots that can take years to unravel.

> Read more: http://www.dailymail.co.uk/femail/article-3396713/SARAH-VINE-Grrr-Tiger-Mums-drive-kids-crackers.html#ixzz3xobzldhM.

Activity 1

Evaluate the reasoning in Documents 1, 2 and 3 above.

Activity 2

Debate: Does tiger parenting count as an abuse of children's human rights?

Hold a class debate. One group should concentrate on the quality of arguments and evidence used by the teams who are debating.

Skills development activities
Worksheet: 3.2 Questioning the reliability of information

Document 1

Last Thursday, there were a number of thefts at St Rufus School. St Rufus is a fee-paying school with many wealthy pupils. It also takes a small number of exceptionally intelligent students from challenging backgrounds. The head teacher is trying to find out who is responsible for the thefts. The thefts were mainly personal items taken from girls' bags and lockers in the changing rooms, but Miss Hiddlestone's phone has also disappeared. The head teacher has been conducting interviews and the following statements were taken.

Miss Hiddlestone: Well, I'm not sure really. I had my phone in the morning, and I would have put it in my bag. When I wanted to use it after school, it was not there. I blame Sukie Jones. She comes from a family of thieves and we all know that children are like their parents.

Sukie Jones: I didn't take anything from anyone. I am not like my family; I want a different life. I work hard, I get good grades, I behave better than the other girls, but everyone still judges me because of my family. It's not right. Why don't you look at the facts? Last Thursday, I was doing exams all day, and in the lunch break I was doing science revision with Mrs Smith.

Mrs Smith: Sukie Jones was in exams all day on Thursday, and during the lunch hour she was doing revision with me, although she did leave to go to the toilet. She was gone for about five minutes. As regards Miss Hiddlestone, I don't really want to be rude about a colleague, but she leaves her phone all over the place. Only last Tuesday, I found it in the science labs, and goodness knows what she was doing in the science labs. She's a PE teacher.

Eloise Charborough: I had an expensive pen taken, and a diamond bracelet that was a gift from my father. I expect it was Sukie Jones. My older sister Amarantha says that Sukie is always looking at her things. She's been expecting her to steal something.

Mrs Betteridge, the Gardener: Last Thursday, I was pruning the roses down by the school gates from lunchtime until about 3.30. Miss Hiddlestone was there at lunchtime, fiddling with her phone. I saw Eloise Charborough talking to a boy through the gates; this was at about 2pm, when she should have been in lessons. It looked like they were having an argument. I didn't really hear what they were saying, except I'm sure the young man said, 'You owe me!'.

Activity 1

1. Read the scenario in Document 1 above, then answer the following questions.

   (a) How reliable are the claims that Sukie Jones must have taken the items?

   (b) How reliable is Miss Hiddlestone's statement about her phone?

   (c) How reliable is Sukie Jones's statement?

   (d) What do you think happened to Miss Hiddlestone's phone? Justify your answer.

   (e) Who do you think could have taken the items from girls' bags and lockers? Justify your answer.

Skills development activities
Worksheet: 3.3 Evaluating causes and consequences

Activity 1

1. Listen to this TED talk by Jon Gosier: https://www.ted.com/talks/jon_gosier_the_problem_with_trickle_down_techonomics?language=en.

2. Now read this After TED talk with Jon Gosier: http://www.aftertedtalks.com/jon-gosier/.

3. Discuss the issues that Jon Gosier raises.

Activity 2

1. Work in teams. Collect examples of unintended consequences that have occurred throughout history. Make a display.

2. Discuss whether or not people are responsible for consequences they have not intended. Do the following make a difference:

   - How carefully they have thought through the consequences?

   - How likely the consequences are?

Worksheet: 3.4 Questioning underlying beliefs

Activity 1

1. Listen to this TED talk: https://www.ted.com/talks/derek_sivers_weird_or_just_different/transcript?language=en. Write your response in your reflective journal.

Activity 2

1. Listen to this TED talk: http://www.ted.com/talks/chimamanda_adichie_the_danger_of_a_single_story#t-25497. In the talk, Chimamanda Ngozi Adichie gives examples of how a single story can give people a limited perspective.

2. Think of examples of when other people seem to have judged you or your country by a single story. How could you help them to broaden their perspective?

3. Think of examples of when you have judged other people or other countries by a single story. How could you broaden your perspective?

Activity 3
Document 1

1. Choose one of the images in Document 1 and write the story of the person or people shown. Are these people brave adventurers or desperate migrants? How does that change your perspective of their story? Think about the people's perspectives, their beliefs and their values. Think about the perspectives, beliefs and values of those they encounter on their journey.

Skills development activities
Worksheet: 4 Developing a line of reasoning

Activity 1

Three students have answered this question: 'Is globalisation making the world a better place?'. Their answers are below.

(a) Use Cambridge mark schemes to mark the students' answers.

(b) Improve the answers so that they meet the criteria.

Answer A

Globalisation has advantages and disadvantages. The advantages are that we are all richer because of globalisation. Also, everyone speaks English so we can all communicate. The disadvantages are that some people are poorer because of globalisation, and some local communities are losing their languages. Overall, globalisation is making the world a better place.

Answer B

Globalisation increases the movement of traded goods and money around the world. Different countries have different resources. In a globalised world, the countries can specialise and use their resources efficiently. Companies get access to wider markets for their products and this promotes understanding and goodwill between countries.

Globalisation can mean the hegemony of one culture. So one dominant culture is popular and everyone in the world wants to be like that, so countries lose their traditional dress and their customs. Everyone wears jeans these days.

Answer C

Globalisation does make people better off for several reasons. In a globalised world, countries can export their goods and services around the world, and import from the best provider. This increases the movement of goods and money around the world so there is more money going around. This means that most people are financially better off. But the poorest people might be worse off. Globalisation means that customers get the products they want for less money. This is a good thing from an individual perspective but from a global perspective it means that people are probably buying more things, which are being transported around the world. This is bad for the environment. So globalisation makes individuals better off but it harms the world overall.

Skills development activities
Worksheet: 5.1 Reflecting on issues and perspectives

Activity 1

Discuss the dilemmas below. What do you think in each case and why? Does everyone in the class agree?

Dilemma 1

You are a doctor. You are caring for five patients who are waiting for organ transplants. A person has been involved in a car accident. By chance, this one person could provide all the organs you need to save all five other patients. Should you provide medical help to this person, knowing that the five other patients will certainly die? Or should you withhold medical help, knowing that the five other patients will live?

Dilemma 2

A bomber has planted several bombs in busy parts of town. She has been caught by the police planting the final bomb, and she is certainly the bomber. She refuses to say where the other bombs are. Are the police justified in torturing her to gain the information that will save the lives of many innocent people?

Dilemma 3

In January 2015, Corrine Rey returned to work after collecting her daughter from Kindergarten. She was a cartoonist at Charlie Hebdo, a French satirical magazine. Two gunmen threatened to shoot Corrine's daughter unless she entered the code to open the door of the magazine's offices. It was clear that they intended to shoot and kill the people inside the magazine's offices. What should Corrine have done?

Dilemma 4

If you could make all humans happy, peaceful and profitable by torturing one little girl, would you do it?

Dilemma 5

A ship has sunk, and the captain and twenty others are rowing the small, overcrowded lifeboat. It is hard work, you have no idea whether you will be rescued, and your chances of survival don't look good. The captain says that the best thing to do is to set nine people overboard. This will give the remaining 12 people the opportunity to survive. He says that if you don't set the nine people overboard, then everybody will die, so it is not wrong. What do you think?

Skills development activities
Worksheet: 5.2 Reflection on teamwork, outcomes and own performance

Activity 1

1. Read the reflections on teamwork below.
   - How effectively are the students reflecting on their own performance?
   - How effectively are the students reflecting on their teamwork?
   - Can you improve their reflections?

Student 1

In our team, we argued today. Samara kept telling me I was wrong, and wouldn't accept that she was the one who was wrong. Tomorrow, I will work harder to persuade her.

Student 2

In our team, we have been having difficulty with our time planning. Everything takes so much longer than we had initially thought, and we all have busy schedules. We are all doing lots of homework and coursework, and several of us have music lessons and sports activities. I think that if we planned better exactly who has to do what, and thought about what it involved, it might not take so long. I have been struggling with time because I have been spending too long reading articles that aren't relevant. So I can improve by skim reading and ignoring irrelevant things.

Student 3

Things didn't go well today. The internet connection broke, then Paul yelled at me because I hadn't done my share of the research, but it wasn't my fault because I needed the internet. Zakia told me it was my fault because I shouldn't have left my research until the last minute. She is not a helpful team member. She needs to work on her teamwork skills. She should try being empathetic when other people are struggling. Tomorrow we will do better.

Student 4

We had a crisis in the team today. Jez and Dem were stressed and struggling. They were ready to give up because they had spent a long time preparing a poster and the computer crashed before they had saved it. We needed to get the poster printed and around school to raise awareness of our concert and our charity, and Jez had to go to a meeting with one of the bands who was supposed to be playing. I had to spend quite a long time talking to them to cheer them up. In the end, I helped Dem to reproduce the poster while Jez went to talk to the band. I phoned the printing company and they have agreed to print the poster even though we will be delivering it a bit late. I think we worked well together to save the situation, and I was quite pleased with my role in finding solutions and helping the others to cheer up.

Skills development activities
Worksheet: 5.3 Reflect on personal learning

Activity 1

1. What is learning? Work together to make a list of all the types of learning you can think of.

Activity 2

1. Look at the classroom activities listed in the table below.

    (a) In the 'Fun' column, rank the activities according to how much fun they are.

    (b) Can you agree on the ranking as a class? Why or why not?

    (c) In the 'Useful' column, rank the activities according to how useful they are in helping you to learn. Think about what they are useful *for*.

    (d) Can you agree on the ranking as a class? Why or why not?

    (e) Are the most fun activities always the most useful?

    (f) What other classroom activities would you add to the list? How fun and/or useful are these?

Ranking: 1 = the most fun/useful; 10 = the least fun/useful.

	Fun	Useful
Listening to the teacher		
Reading information		
Finding information		
Playing games		
Class discussions		
Watching documentaries		
Filling in forms		
Working in teams		
Giving presentations		
Doing old exam questions		

Activity 3

1. Read the entry from Emmeline's learning log below.

    (a) How effective is Emmeline's reflection?

    (b) What could Emmeline do to improve her reflection?

    (c) What could Emmeline do to improve her teamwork?

Emmeline's learning log:

I enjoyed the class discussion about migration. I had never thought before about why people migrate or about what they are leaving. I suppose I had always thought about how it might affect me. I don't like having to work in teams. I would rather just do my own work. It is unfair because some people in teams work harder than others. So I end up doing more work.

Skills development activities
Worksheet: 6.1 Planning a project

Your group is doing a project on the environment. Your aim is to explore possible solutions to two local environmental problems. Your outcome is interviews with local politicians and business people. You want to design and conduct a survey to find out what local people care about and what they think about these two environmental problems, and use the survey results to inform the questions you ask the local politicians and business people.

1. Fit the tasks into this diagram, to show which tasks have to be done in which order.

   (a) Set interview questions
   (b) List possible people to interview
   (c) Research the issues
   (d) Review the survey
   (e) Arrange meetings with people to interview them
   (f) Design the survey
   (g) Contact the people you hope to interview to ask if they are willing
   (h) Analyse survey results
   (i) Conduct the survey
   (j) Research survey design
   (k) Set final survey following review

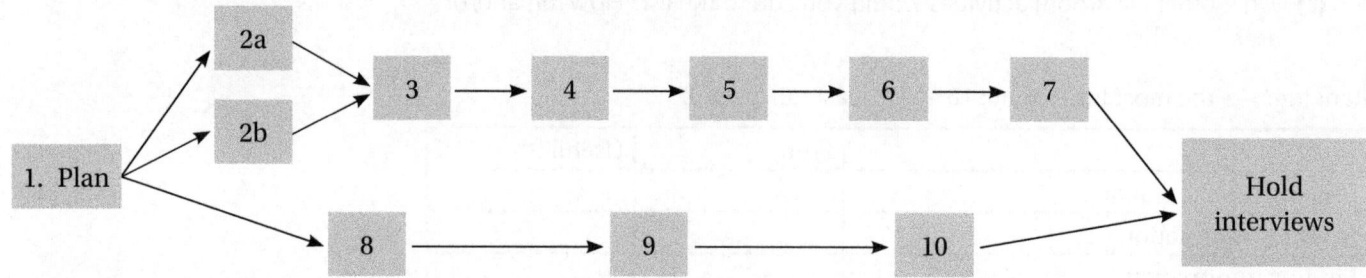

2. You need to submit your project in the middle of May. You decide to hold the interviews in late April and early May. It is now 21 February.

   (a) Decide how long each task will take
   (b) Set a deadline for each task.
   (c) Produce a chart that shows when each task will take place.

3. There are two weeks' school holiday in early April. How does this affect your plan? What changes do you need to make? How will you record the changes?

4. The person responsible for writing the survey is going abroad during the school holiday. How does this affect your plan?

5. You decide you want to video the interviews. What additional tasks will you need to do and when will they need to be done? How will you need to revise your plan?

Skills development activities
Worksheet: 6.2 Teamwork and individual effort

Activity 1

1. Listed below are some characteristics of teams.

   (a) Sort the characteristics into two lists: characteristics of effective teams and characteristics of ineffective teams.

   (b) Which of the characteristics best describe your team?

Some people talk all the time and some people don't say anything.

There are different people who contribute in different ways.

Team members do not keep to the point in discussions.

There are clear goals that everyone understands and has agreed on.

There are unpleasant arguments.

The group can overcome differences in opinion.

Team members are comfortable expressing their opinions.

Some people's ideas are ignored or even mocked.

Group members listen to one another.

Team members provide criticism in a positive way.

Decisions are vague and unclear, and people aren't sure what they have to do.

People talk more than they listen.

One or two people make all the decisions.

The group learns from experience. It reviews and improves performance.

Some people complain about decisions but do not do anything about them.

Everyone understands the tasks they have to do and helps one another.

Team members ignore deadlines.

Activity 2

2. In groups, you will complete a team building game given to you by your teacher.

Your teacher will nominate some people to be observers. The task of an observer is to identify the different skills that team members have using the table below.

As observer, every time you notice someone displaying a skill, write their name in the column next to it.

Group:		
Quality	**Description**	**Names**
Open-mindedness	• Listens • Is tactful • Uses others' ideas	
Participation	• Engages in discussion • Influences the discussion rather than just accepting it • Is active not passive	
Influence on others	• Is persuasive but not bullying	
Spoken Expression	• Is clear and coherent	
Original ideas	• Introduces new ideas • Builds on other people's ideas • Looks at things from a different perspective	
Thinking skills	• Analyses, getting to the heart of the problem • Understands what is important or not important • Is logical • Makes thoughtful judgements	

Skills development activities
Worksheet: 7 Select evidence and present research

Activity 1

1. Which of the following count as plagiarism? There may be more than one answer.

   (a) Buying an essay online.

   (b) Copying another student's essay or Individual Report.

   (c) Copying your work from a single internet source.

   (d) Cutting and pasting large chunks of work without using your own thinking or your own language.

   (e) Including short quotations without admitting that they are quotations.

2. Why do you think that plagiarism is not allowed?

3. Do some research to find out why plagiarism is considered to be wrong.

Activity 2

1. Read the article here: http://blogs.discovermagazine. com/neuroskeptic/2016/01/26/plagiarism-is-theft, then answer the following questions.

   (a) The author of this article identifies different types of theft. What are they?

   (b) Which of these types of theft does the author of the article think that plagiarism actually is? Why?

   (c) What do you think? Why?

Worksheet: 1 Conflict and peace

Activity 1

Document 1

1. Write a story based on image in Document 1.

Activity 2

1. Watch this video clip of an argument from the 1993 film *Mrs. Doubtfire*: http://www.criticalcommons.org/Members/duboisad/ clips/doubtfir-12-1.avi/view.

2. Answer these questions about the video clip.

   (a) What are the couple arguing about?

   (b) How effectively do they resolve their conflict?

   (c) Who do you most agree with? Why?

Activity 3

1. Watch this video clip: https://www.ted.com/talks/ william_ury.

2. Explain the main ideas Willian Ury has about conflict resolution.

3. Watch this video clip: https://www.ted.com/talks/ margaret_heffernan_dare_to_disagree?language=en.

4. Explain the main ideas Margaret Heffernan has about the uses of conflict.

5. Whose views do you most agree with? Why?

Team project
Worksheet: 2 Disease and health

Activity 1

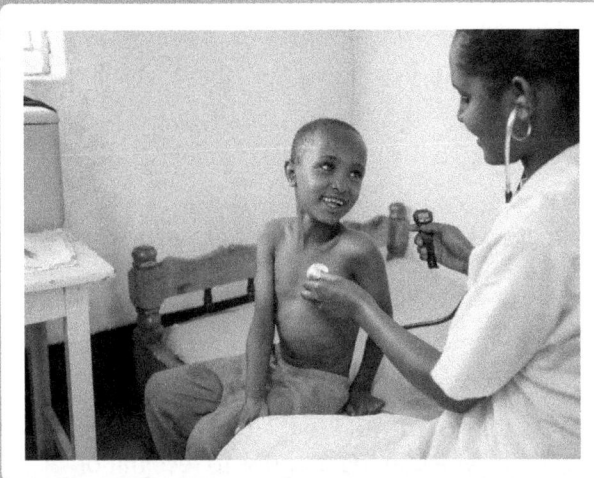

1. Write down all the words relating to disease and health that occur to you when you examine the images above.

2. What qualities do you think a doctor needs?

3. What qualities do you think a nurse needs?

4. How can we make sure that every child has access to clean drinking water?

5. How do you think that we can make sure that every child has access to good healthcare?

Activity 2

1. Watch this video: http://video.mit.edu/watch/how-a-vaccine-works-10952/.

2. In your own words, briefly explain how a vaccine works.

3. Now watch this video: http://science.howstuffworks.com/life/30004-100-greatest-discoveries-the-beginning-of-vaccinations-video.htm.

4. Briefly explain how vaccination was discovered.

Activity 3

1. Research medical breakthroughs from 1850 to the present day.

2. Make a timeline in class of these medical breakthroughs.

3. Add the consequences of these breakthroughs to your timeline.

4. In your opinion, which is the most important medical breakthrough? Why?

5. Hold a group debate. Each group member is given a medical breakthrough, and has to argue why their medical breakthrough is the most important.

Team project
Worksheet: 3 Human rights

Activity 1

1.

> **Infringe:** to break, limit, undermine or go against a right.
>
> **Violate:** to fail to respect, to break, to fail to comply – often used for rights or international agreements.

Infringe and *violate* are synonyms meaning 'to go against someone's rights'. Find more synonyms for these words.

2.

> **Duty:** a moral or legal obligation – something you have to do because it is right or because it is the law.
>
> **Responsibility:** the authority to do something, or something that you are required to do as part of your job, because the law says so or because it's morally right.

Duty and *responsibility* are synonyms meaning 'things you have to do'. Find more synonyms for these words.

3. What duties do you have? What are your responsibilities?

Activity 2

1. Watch this video: http://www.youthforhumanrights.org/what-are-human-rights.html.
2. Give three key events in the progress to recognition of universal human rights.
3. Give three key human rights issues that still need to be addressed.
4. According to the video, what responsibilities do we have?
5. What do you think about the perspective in this video? Give your reasons.

Activity 3

1. Make a timeline in your class.
2. Work together to add to the timeline the key events from the video in the progress to recognition of universal human rights.
3. Work together to research key events relating to human rights in your country or another country of your choice.
4. Add these events to the timeline.

Activity 4

> **Extract from the Universal Declaration of Human Rights**
> "Article 16.
>
> 1. Men and women of full age, without any limitation due to race, nationality or religion, have the right to marry and to found a family. They are entitled to equal rights as to marriage, during marriage and at its dissolution.
> 2. Marriage shall be entered into only with the free and full consent of the intending spouses.
> 3. The family is the natural and fundamental group unit of society and is entitled to protection by society and the State."

1. What human rights issues are raised in this document?
2. 'Parents should make decisions about who their children should marry because young people do not have enough experience to make such an important decision.' Discuss this view.
3. 'It is better to marry someone from a similar background because you will have more in common and have a stronger marriage.' Discuss this view.

Team project
Worksheet: 4 Language and communication

Activity 1

1. Why was the telephone such an important breakthrough for communication?

2. What do you think is the most important breakthrough for communication?

3. Write a short story or poem based in a world without telephones or computers for communication. You could come up with your own story or use this beginning:

   Kahendra watched the blood trickling from his leg. He looked at the steep valley sides and knew that he would need a miracle to survive.

Activity 2

1. Watch this video: https://www.youtube.com/watch?v=ZY4TT3VtR8o.

2. Can you understand the version of English (Geordie) in the video?

3. Research videos of three or four more variants of English. These might be English dialects or variants, such as Singlish.

4. How much affect does an accent have on your ability to understand someone?

5. How much affect does an accent have on your beliefs about someone's education and social status?

Activity 3

1. Watch this video: https://www.ted.com/talks/ajit_narayanan_a_word_game_to_communicate_in_any_ language?language=en.

2. Ajit Narayanan speaks one particular version of English. Do you find him easy to understand? Why or why not?

3. What is the speaker's main point?

4. 'Meaning is what comes after thought but before language.' Do you agree with this? Does it match your experience of trying to express yourself in a second language?

5. Daniel Webster said, "If all of my possessions were taken from me with one exception, I would choose to keep the power of communication, for with it, I would regain all the rest." Do you agree? Would you keep the power of communication, or would you keep something else?

6. Research the history of Helen Keller. What do you think is the most remarkable aspect of her story?

Team project
Worksheet: 5 Poverty and inequality

Activity 1

1. Watch this video: https://www.youtube.com/watch?v=GjJv7SQ9Wvg.

2. In this clip, which image or statistic do you find most moving, most disturbing, or most shocking? Give your reasons. Do you all agree? Why or why not?

Activity 2

1. Watch this video: https://www.ted.com/talks/mia_birdsong_the story_we_tell_about_poverty_isn_t_true/ transcript?language=en.

2. What is the main point of this video?

3. Do you agree with the speaker about the solution to poverty?

Activity 3

1. Watch this video: https://www.ted.com/talks/gary_haugen_the_hidden_reason_for poverty_the_world_needs_ to_address_now.

2. What is the main point of this video?

3. Do you agree with the speaker about the solution to poverty?

Team project
Worksheet: 6 Sport and recreation

Activity 1

Document 1

A Sporting Chance

If it's black you want then black you will get.
Each sunrise a ball kicked from one end of a blue field
Sails across to a black goal mouth and sinks into it and all
The lights in the stadium plunge out,
But the game never ends for another begins in a field
On the opposite side of this bigger ball we are all pinned to
Which responds to a giant kick as it spins around in an
Even bigger blue field, a ball wary of a hot foot, gearing up
So it seems, not for another kick, once and for all,
More for a death-dealing embrace,

As if a Euclidian dribble started eons ago
Is brought to an instantaneous stop,
A one-foot catch (not kick) and immediate burn up.

I cannot help but think this with the World Cup
When I hear about your lock up and the case
Made against you by the giant state,
I see this global football as you and the big foot
Of the Big Bang wielded at us all is like the boot
Swung at you that sends you into a black hole
For a portion of your life that adds up to an embrace
Of this oil-slicked planet by our sun in a starlit stadium;
Black for you means black for me for kingdom come.

Fred D'Aguiar

1. What is the main point of the poem 'A sporting chance?'
2. What do you think of the comparisons made in 'A sporting chance'?
3. Research the poet. What can you find out about him? What can you find out about his cultural perspectives?

Activity 2

1. Watch this video: http://www.bbc.co.uk/education/clips/zyhrkqt.
2. What tips are given for being the best? Note down as many as you can.
3. How important is it to be the best? Justify your answer, thinking about personal and national perspectives.

Activity 3

Find a video clip about a sporting event that means a lot to you, or about a hobby that is important to you. Show it to the class and explain why it is important to you.

Team project
Worksheet: 7 Tradition, culture and identity

Activity 1

1. Research living bridges.
   a) Who makes these bridges?
   b) Where are they made?
   c) What else can you find out about the culture of the people who make them?
   d) What customs and practices make your culture unique?
2. Find images of three extraordinary bridges and find out what makes the culturally important. Give a short presentation about your three bridges. Remember to discuss their cultural importance.

Activity 2

1. Watch this video: https://www.ted.com/talks/taiye selasi_don_t_ask where_i_m_from_ask_where_i_m_a local/transcript?language=en.
2. Do you agree with Taiye Selasi nations and being local Why or why not
3. How much does it matter where you are from? Justify your opinions.
4. How much does it matter where your parents are from? Justify your opinions.
5. Write a story about a child whose country no longer exists.

Team project
Worksheet: 8 Water, food and agriculture

Activity 1

Document 1

Document 2

1. Compare the two different types of agriculture you see in Documents 1 and 2.

   (a) How are they different?

   (b) How are they similar?

   (c) What are the advantages and disadvantages of each?

   (d) What are the consequences of large-scale farming?

2. Write a story based on one of the images. Make sure that you link your story to issues relating to food, water and agriculture.

Activity 2

1. Watch this video: https://www.ted.com/talks/josette_sheeran ending_hunger_now/transcript?language=en.

2. Does the speaker offer a realistic solution to the hunger problem? Justify your answer.

3. What other perspectives can you think of on this issue?

Activity 3

1. Watch this video: https://www.ted.com/talks/joe_madiath_better toilets_better_life/transcript?language=en.

2. Summarise the key points of the talk.

3. Do you agree with the speaker? Why or why not?

Activity 4

1. Watch this video: https://www.ted.com/talks/fahad_al_attiya_a country_with_no_water/transcript?language=en.

2. According to the speaker, what is Qatar's main problem?

3. How are they overcoming it?

4. What links can you see to other topic areas in this talk?

Individual report
Worksheet: 1 Belief systems

Activity 1

1. How strongly do you believe each of the claims in the table below? Add your scores to table.

2. Why? What evidence do you have for this? Complete the table.

   1 = I do not believe this at all

   2 = I doubt that this is the case

   3 = I am not sure whether this is the case or not

   4 = I believe this could be the case

   5 = I strongly believe this to be the case

	Claim	Score	Why?
1	The earth moves around the sun.		
2	Ghosts linger in some special places.		
3	Astronauts spend months at a time living in space.		
4	People have evolved gradually over millions of years from ape ancestors.		
5	Some people can communicate with the dead.		
6	Everything in this world can be explained by science.		
7	Some people have a sixth sense that allows them to predict the future.		
8	Your star sign and the alignment of the stars at your birth can predict your future and your personality.		

	Claim	Score	Why?
9	Smoking can cause cancer.		
10	Black cats are unlucky.		

Activity 2

1. In the table above, claims 1, 3, 4, 6 and 9 are related to science, while claims 2, 5, 7, 8 and 10 are related to the paranormal or superstition. Did you have higher scores for the scientific claims or the paranormal ones?

2. Categorise the reasons behind your beliefs, using the table below to help you.

	Someone told me	Science can't explain what happens	I have tested this and seen the evidence	I have read about this and thought about the evidence	Other
1					
2					
3					
4					
5					
6					
7					
8					
9					
10					

3. How many of your beliefs have you *really* thought about carefully?

4. How happy are you to simply accept what you are told without checking?

5. Science is a way of thinking that emphasises testing, checking evidence and being prepared to change what you believe if new evidence appears. How many of the scientific claims in Activity 1 do you believe simply because someone has told you they are true?

Activity 3

1. Watch this video: https://www.ted.com/talks/michael_shermer_on_believing_strange things?language=en

2. Think about how you could test one of your own beliefs scientifically.

Individual report
Worksheet: 2 Biodiversity and ecosystem loss

Activity 1

Document 1

Trophy hunting is a legal activity in more than twenty sub-Saharan countries in Africa. Estimates claim that sixty percent of these commercial hunters are Americans, with South Africa, Botswana, Zimbabwe, and Tanzania being the most popular hunting grounds.

Regulations around the activity vary from country to country, with some countries unable to effectively control the practice. Meanwhile debates rage over the morality of big-game hunting, with some claiming that hunters are in fact conservationists and that the commercial value placed on these animals provides a greater protection from extinction than they would otherwise have.

Document 2

Many animals that are popular in trophy hunting are kept in large, privately owned reserves across sub-Saharan Africa. In fact, because of the revenues that some of the larger males can generate, it is far more cost effective to maintain these large wildlife reserves rather than using the land for cattle grazing.

As a result of this financial incentive, the last century has seen huge reductions in cattle farming and a recovery of wildlife across Southern Africa.

Document 3

Hunting animals is the opposite of protecting them. These pro-hunting groups argue that the controlled amount of hunting on the continent is so small that it doesn't affect populations, but this is simply not the case.

According to National Geographic, each year approximately 600 lions are killed from hunting. The adult male lion is the most sought-after big game animal, and its death can cause destabilisation of the pride as other males compete to take over. Lion populations are already declining as a result of other factors, and hunting makes the problem much worse.

The economic argument that hunting is key to development in Africa is also misguided. The proportion of GDP that the revenue from hunting contributes is so small that it's negligible, and the money rarely reaches rural communities.

1. Skim read the documents.
2. Make lists of reasons for and against big game hunting.
3. Research more arguments for and against big game hunting.
4. Hold a class debate on whether big game hunting should be allowed or not.

Individual report
Worksheet: 3 Changing communities

Activity 1

Document 1

1. The image on the left shows the Hong Kong skyline as it is today. Research how the Hong Kong and Dubai skylines have changed since 1970. What differences can you see?

2. How do you think these changes have affected local communities?

3. Research how the local communities in Hong Kong and Dubai have changed, and what consequences these changes have had.

Activity 2

1. Find images of your home town and its inhabitants from these years:
   - 1930
   - 1970
   - 2010

2. Research changes in communities in your local area. You could interview older relatives as well as using the internet. You could also refer to books and television programmes about your area. Think about:
   - the places that people meet
   - the ways that people interact with each other
   - the ways that people depend on each other
   - the opportunities that people have.

3. Give a short presentation to the class summarising your research.

Activity 3

1. Watch one of the following films, or a similar film that shows a community struggling to come to terms with change:
   - *Billy Elliot* (2000)
   - *The Full Monty* (1997)
   - *The Help* (2011)
   - *The Lady* (2011)
   - *Black Butterflies* (2011)
   - *Hotel Rwanda* (2004)
   - *The Hundred-Foot Journey* (2014).

2. What are the major changes experienced by the community in the film?

3. How do the characters deal with the changes?

4. Do you think they deal with the changes well? Why or why not?

5. Research the historical background of the film and find out more about the real changes the communities went through. What solutions did the communities come up with?

6. Write a short report to summarise your findings.

Individual report
Worksheet: 4 Digital world

Activity 1

"When I was growing up, all that was available to me was the local record shop or the odd radio show," says Penny. "My son has just started university and his attitude to culture is completely different. He has grown up with access to any music he chooses and has an encyclopaedic knowledge. If he finds a band he likes, he will trace all their influences and listen to all those bands too. There is a library of culture that is readily available to young people, which my generation just didn't have."

1. Research how digital technology has changed the music industry.

2. In your groups, discuss whether you think these changes are mostly positive or mostly negative. Consider the perspectives of:

   (a) New bands trying to get known

   (b) people working in the music industry

   (c) People who want to listen to music.

3. Give a short presentation to the class explaining your group's view.

Activity 2

1. Complete the table below.

   1 = Not at all acceptable

   2 = Not really acceptable

   3 = Neither acceptable nor unacceptable

   4 = Quite acceptable

   5 = Very acceptable

Behaviour	How acceptable?	Why?
Checking your phone while someone is talking to you.		
Posting an embarrassing photo of your friend on social media.		
Writing unpleasant, anonymous comments online.		
Continuing to play online games when your parents have asked you to help them.		
Playing music loudly in a public place.		

2. Discuss your results in a group. Do you all agree? Why or why not?

Activity 3

1. Research the consequences of cyberbullying and possible strategies for reducing cyberbullying.

2. Write a short report summarising your research findings.

Individual report
Worksheet: 5 Family

Activity 1

Document 2

It remains common today for women to marry very young in some developing countries. Thirty nine countries have data showing that 20% of women married by age 18. In twenty countries, a full 10% of women married by age 15. In only 2 countries, however, are 10% of men married before the age of 18. Still, men and women are getting married later in every region of the world. The average age of marriage for women increased from 21.8 to 24.7 years from the seventies to the mid 2000s, with the average age for men rising a comparable amount.

Document 2

Child marriage is much less of an issue in the U.S. than it is in other countries with similar laws. By 2002, only about 2.1 percent of American girls between the ages of 15 and 17 were considered "in a union," and just one-tenth of 1 percent were married. Meanwhile, in Niger, 39 percent of girls are married by 18, and 22 percent are in Bolivia.

Most U.S. states set the age of consent at 18, but minors can get married younger if their parents approve or if a judge thinks it's in their "best interest."

Document 3

I focused on my career for so long, assuming that my love life would fall into place. When I was in my late 30s, I began to understand that having a successful love life required conscious effort and focus. This was the beginning of many firsts: focusing more on my love life than my professional life, understanding the unhealthy relationship patterns I was repeating, learning to love myself and accepting my self-worth.

I'm 46 and was married on June 8th, this past summer. One of the benefits of being an older bride is that with age comes a different perspective. I know if I had gotten married at a young age, I would have missed out on becoming my own person. Marrying at a later age has given me the benefit of knowing who I am and experiencing life as my own complete person.

1. Consider the information in Documents 1, 2 and 3.
   - **(a)** Research the names of five countries where 10% of women are married by the age of 18.
   - **(b)** Name five countries where you have to be at least 18 to get married.
   - **(c)** In your opinion, what should the minimum age be at which you can get married? Why? Discuss this in your group.
2. Research the advantages of getting married relatively young.
3. Research the advantages of getting married relatively old (late twenties or early thirties).
4. What do you think is the best age to get married? Why?

Activity 2

1. Make a list of the best five films you have seen that deal with family issues. Family issues must be at the centre of each film.
2. For each film, make brief notes on the key family issues.
3. Work in groups to compare your notes, and try to agree on the top five films.
4. Watch one of the films in your group, or as a class. Analyse the family issues and how they are dealt with.
5. Do some research on the family issues raised in your chosen film.
6. Write a short report summarising your findings.

Individual report
Worksheet: 6 Humans and other species

Activity 1

1. Watch this video: http://hereandnow.wbur.org/2015/08/05/big-game-hunting-cecil.

2. Do you think that 'ethical hunting' can exist? Why or why not?

3. 'Hunting is what pays for wildlife and wildlife management.' Can this claim be verified?

4. What do you think about the claim that people care more about lions in Africa than about people in Africa?

5. Is hunting for food better than hunting for trophies? Justify your view.

Activity 2

Document 1

Hunting major source of revenue for ZANU-PF elite

Hunting had long been a source of ill-gotten revenue for members of the Zimbabwe African National Union-Patriotic Front elite and they were developing new hunting schemes to earn more foreign currency.

Sally Bown, administrative officer for SOAZ, said that numerous photographic safari operators

in Hwange National Park were sending emails reporting commercial elephant hunting incidents within the park.

Bown and Save Valley Conservancy director Clive Stockil believed that this frantic last grab at hunting revenue was one more aspect of ZANU-PF insiders' efforts to strip assets and fill their pockets before losing power to the Movement for Democratic Change.

1. The hunter in the video in Activity 1 claims that the money made from hunting funds wildlife conservation. To what extent does Document 1 oppose that view?

2. How reliable do you think this article is?

Individual report
Worksheet: 7 Sustainable living

Activity 1

Document 1

Document 2

Asking questions about the rich has been portrayed since the dawn of wealth as envy; asking questions about the poor is considered practical and sympathetic, moral and problem-solving. But no problem can be solved while political institutions won't recognise that poverty has a cause.

Zoe Williams, journalist

1. What issues does the cartoon raise in Document 1?

2. In your opinion, what does the journalist Zoe Williams think is the cause of poverty in Documentv 2?

3. Do you agree? Why or why not?

4. What do you think would be the consequences of asking questions about the rich?

Activity 2

Document 3

1. What issues does the cartoon raise in Document 3?

2. What are the UN's Sustainable Development Goals?

3. Which of these goals do you think is most important? Why?

4. Which of these goals do you think is most realistic? Why?

5. Has your country signed up to the SDGs?

6. In your opinion, which measure does your country need to work hardest at? Why?

7. Is it possible to end poverty by increasing economic growth, while also reducing our use of resources and living sustainably?

Worksheet: 8 Trade and aid

Activity 1

1. Watch the video and read the information on this web page: http://www.bbc.co.uk/news/world-africa-33505312 How likely do you think it is that Ethiopia will soon be able to prosper without aid?

Activity 2

Watch these two TED talks:
https://www.ted.com/talks/andrew_mwenda_takes_a_new_look_at_africa?language=en
https://www.ted.com/talks/ngozi_okonjo_iweala_on_aid_versus_trade

1. Which perspective do you agree with more? Why?

2. Research the lives of Andrew Mwenda and Ngozi Okonjo-Iweala.

3. Research Nelson Mandela, Abdirashid Duale, anf Fatou Bensouda.

4. Choose one significant African. Give a short presentation on their key achievements. What roles did trade and aid play in these achievements?

Answers to worksheets

1.1 Searching for information

Activity 1

	Word	Definition
1	Definition	The exact meaning of a word.
2	Fact	Information or an idea that can be proved to be true (can be verified).
3	Opinion	A personal belief that may or may not be based on facts and knowledge.
4	Value judgement	An assessment or personal belief about how good or bad something is.
5	Prediction	A statement about what might happen in the future, or what the consequences of an act might be.

Activity 2

(a) Brazil

(b) Rabat

(c) Encourage student to discuss various options. Note that many of the sites that can appear on the first page of a search for this are somewhat sarcastic blogs or opinion pieces, and are not very helpful. Remind student not to take this kind of information at face value.

(d) In brief, as part of a series of measures put in place after the Second World War to avoid any possible recurrence of such a conflict.

(e) Encourage students to undertake research and compare notes. Depending on your country, answers may include: affects the weather; leads to flooding; leads to erosion; affects food security; affects the availability of medicines; doesn't have much real effect now, but will have in the future.

Activity 3

Encourage students to apply their skills thoughtfully. Encourage them to think about what precisely they want to know and to identify that the vague topics are not helpful.

2.1 Identifying information and trends

Activity 1

1. There was a general decline in tourism in Vietnam between June 2014 and March 2015. This was particularly steep in July and November 2014.

The decline is much stronger for Chinese tourists than for non-Chinese tourists; this is evident in the line showing tourism excluding Chinese tourists, which is less steep than the line for all nationalities.

2. Why did tourism in Vietnam decline during this period?

   (a) Encourage students to use their general knowledge and to predict what might cause tourism to decline. Suggested answers: acts of terrorism, civil unrest and violence, economic factors, poor tourist experience.

   (b) Factual information about events that have happened, statistical information about economic factors, opinions about the tourist experience in Vietnam.

   (c) to **(d)** Encourage students to apply their skills

   (e) Encourage students to discuss their findings.

Activity 2

The following are suggestions only. Accept any reasonable answer.

(a) We need to know: whether getting to Vietnam is cheap from where we are, what there is to see and do in Vietnam, whether we will enjoy the tourist experience in Vietnam, whether there is civil unrest or any terrorist threat, whether we can afford a holiday at all, how complicated the journey will be.

(b) We need to know: whether guns are already illegal, how easy it is to acquire guns illegally, whether the people who die in gun fights are killed by legal or illegal guns.

(c) We need to know: whether using less paper will be an effective way to save the rainforest (on the whole it won't, as paper generally comes from sustainably managed softwood forests), what value the rainforest has and whether it is worth saving, what would be practical and effective ways to prevent rainforest loss.

(d) We need to know: whether remote tribes want to develop economically or whether they prefer their traditional lifestyles, whether they would get a phone signal in their remote location or whether they would actually need to invest in much more technology, whether mobile phones are the best communications technology to start with.

(e) We need to know: the value of biodiversity, that the schemes we are campaigning for are likely to be useful, whether protecting wildlife is the best move (perhaps protecting habitats or focusing on how people benefit would be more effective).

2.2 Understanding key issues

Activity 1

1. When students have chosen names, ask them what their choices tell them about their cultural and national perspectives? Why have they assigned particular genders to each person? Do the names they have chosen reflect power politics in their culture? For example, has the migrant woman been given a name that reflects the migrant ethnicities in the students' country? Do those who say they are struggling for money have names that reflect a lower social status? The purpose of this exercise is to help students to understand their own cultural perspectives and the assumptions they make, which is one way of identifying key issues.

2. Encourage debate and discussion, keeping the focus on the key issues. Suggested answers:

    Person 1: How to overcome a traumatic past, how to be welcomed by a (fairly hostile) new community, how to achieve peace, how to ensure her children get a good education in a secure environment.

    Person 2: How to deal with the threat that gangs pose to children and to security, how to earn enough (in a low paying job) to live well, how to deal with the new, people arriving in the community, who seem to pose a threat.

    Person 3: How to help from a distance, how to deal with the fear and economic threats that accompany the arrival of new migrants.

    Person 4: How to minimise the impact on the environment.

    Person 5: How to use resources that are scarce.

    Person 6: Philosophical questions about what it means to be a nation and whether being born in a place should give you more right to its resources.

3. Encourage discussion and debate. Suggested answers:

    Person 1: Religion and education are important to this person, and the recent experience of losing their home, of abusive rule and migration will have affected their perspective. What does it mean to have a national perspective if the nation you were born in no longer exists?

    Person 2: Although this person comes from a (presumably) wealthy nation, they seem to be of low socio-economic status, and are economically rather vulnerable.

    Person 3: This person, too, is of fairly low socio-economic status and is strongly attached to the local area, as seen in the use of 'we', 'our' and 'local'.

    Person 4: This person is attached to the local area, but does not give much sign of other national and cultural influences. The fact that they have the leisure to think about the environment may suggest they are well educated and that they have fewer financial worries.

Person 5: This person has a very nationalistic perspective, which makes it likely that they see migration as a threat.

Person 6: This person appears to be well educated, and seems more strongly attached to their local area than to a sense of nationalism.

2.3 Identifying causes and consequences

Activity 1

1. Passage 1:

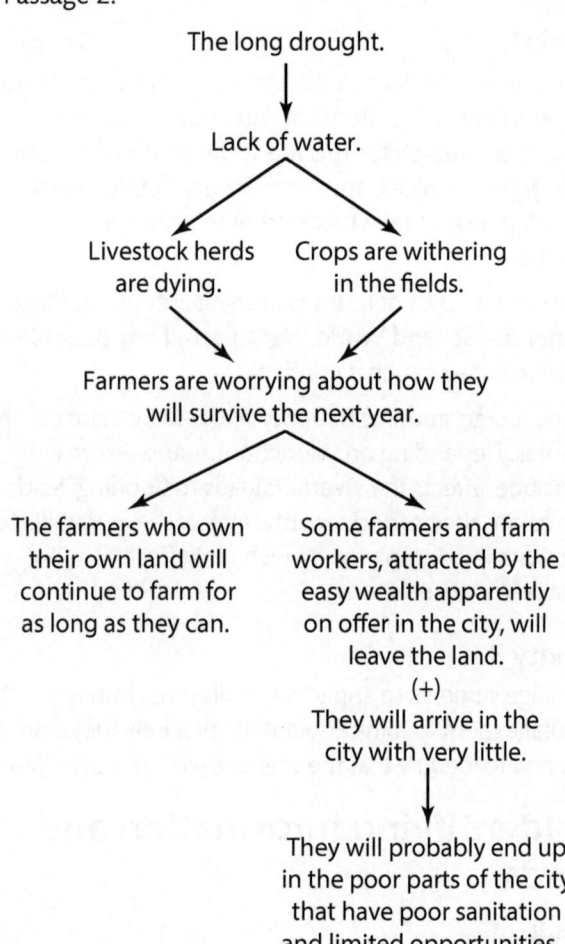

    People burn fossil fuels.

    ↓

    Greenhouse gases are produced.

    (+)

    These gases linger in the atmosphere.

    ↓

    The gases trap heat in the Earth's atmosphere.

    ↓

    Climate change occurs.

    ↓

    There are more extreme weather events.

    Passage 2:

    The long drought.

    ↓

    Lack of water.

    Livestock herds are dying.   Crops are withering in the fields.

    Farmers are worrying about how they will survive the next year.

    The farmers who own their own land will continue to farm for as long as they can.   Some farmers and farm workers, attracted by the easy wealth apparently on offer in the city, will leave the land.

    (+)

    They will arrive in the city with very little.

    ↓

    They will probably end up in the poor parts of the city that have poor sanitation and limited opportunities.

Activity 2

Encourage students to think carefully about causes and consequences, and especially the degree of certainty we can have. Encourage them to consider how we know about causes and consequences, and the roles of authority, working it out (reason) and evidence.

(a) This is a sequence of events. Both are caused by the rotation of the Earth, but neither causes the other. We know this because we have been told or because of our understanding of basic science.

(b) This is probably a sequence of events. The postman probably walks away because he has already delivered the letters to the house. However, in some circumstances, there may be a cause and consequence. The postman may walk away because he is scared of the dog. We know this because we can apply our general knowledge. So we would need to know more about this specific instance. Has this postman been badly bitten by a dog? Is the dog loose in the garden? Does the postman know this dog?

(c) This is almost certainly a case of cause and consequence. Although many people argue about it, the scientific consensus is that burning fossil fuels does cause climate change. Most of us know this because we have been told, or perhaps because we have seen some of the evidence.

(d) This is a clear case of cause and consequence. Crops need water, so if it doesn't rain for over two years, the crops will fail.

(e) It is tempting to think that Dinesh has caused Amir's serious gunshot wound. However, we cannot know this and we would need more information to be certain about cause and consequence. It may be that a third person caused Amir's wound, and that Dinesh, hearing the shot, has raced into the room and picked up the pistol. (This could be developed into an interesting exercise, in which students act the part of the police, thinking of the right questions to ask.)

(f) This is probably a case of cause and consequence. Earthquakes do cause buildings to collapse; we know this from past experience and from being told.

(g) This is a case of cause and consequence. We know this because of our understanding of basic physics: Newton's Laws of Motion, especially the third law.

(h) This is probably, but not certainly, a case of cause and consequence. We would need to establish whether the car was moving fast enough to break bones, and whether the broken bones are the typical result of being hit by a car. We can know this by working it out and by using our general understanding of what might break bones. In some cases like this, forensic scientists might become involved to establish what the actual causes and consequences are. We might also need to know whether the broken bones might have some other cause; for example, the child may already have had broken bones from a separate incident.

2.4 Identifying and evaluating possible courses of action

Activity 1

1. and **2.** Encourage students to think carefully and to apply their skills.

The situation described in the text is based real events. The following links give information on the these events; the first link includes a video clip about two astronauts' mission to spend a year in space.

http://time.com/3838851/russian-resupply-spaceship-difficulty/

http://www.theguardian.com/science/2014/oct/28/antares-rocket-explodes-nasa-launch-pad-orbital-science

http://www.slate.com/blogs/bad_astronomy/2014/06/08/back_to_earth_how_astronauts_get_back_from_the_space_station.html

https://www.nasa.gov/mission_pages/station/structure/elements/soyuz/landing.html

2.5 Identifying different perspectives

Activity 1

Document 1 has a Chinese journalistic perspective, reporting what a Chinese politician has said in a Chinese newspaper (for an English language audience). The belief expressed is that Chinese involvement in the Middle East is positive.

Document 2 is from CSIS, a, nonprofit organization with its headquarters in Washington, D.C. The 'About' page on their website says, 'Since 1962, CSIS has been dedicated to finding ways to sustain American prominence and prosperity as a force for good in the world'. This document clearly comes from an American national perspective and, while it tries to be objective and academic, it clearly sees China's growing role in the Middle East as a threat. The reference to China's economic development without political liberalization as 'not outright attractive' indicates that the authors have an underlying concern about China's role.

Document 3 comes from a British newspaper and expresses a Western perspective with no attempt at academic objectivity. The Telegraph is a serious, broadsheet newspaper, not a tabloid, but its views tend to be rather right wing and somewhat nationalistic. This specific perspective seems to be formed by fear of China's influence, with concerns expressed about China destabilising the Middle East and not having Western interests at heart.

3.1 Questioning knowledge claims

Activity 1

Document 1: 'They're stealing our water' is using emotion to persuade us; after all, what makes it 'our' water? Also, this is not a strong enough reason to explode ships. Perhaps negotiation would be a better alternative? There are many other things that we need to know – for example, about the planned dam, about agreements between the countries regarding the water, about the likely consequences if we explode their ships – so the reasoning here is not effective.

Document 2: First of all, this argument is not based on strong evidence. The claim that we are running out of oil might be unlikely and needs to be supported. Also, there is a gap between the claim about running out of oil and the proposal that the government should ban us from using cars. We need to know why this is the right action to take. This argument is weak and illogical, and the reasoning is poor.

Document 3: This passage uses emotive language and many opinions, unsupported by reasoning or evidence, to convey its point. It predicts consequences that might sometimes occur, but not for all children. For example, it immediately describes tiger parents as 'pushy' and producing 'intolerable children'. This use of language shows that the author is biased, unprepared to consider any possible benefits of tiger parenting, and mainly interested in expressing their negative opinion. There are many other examples of emotive language that students could pick up on here.

The passage consists of a string of assertions, or unsupported opinions, rather than reasoning or argument. The claim 'Tiger parenting is vanity parenting' is an opinion that is not supported at all, and is pretending to be a fact. Students could pick on any sentence in this passage and show that it is unsupported opinion.

The passage predicts consequences: for example, that tiger parenting will produce 'intolerable, precocious children and smug, arrogant adults'. This is, of course, possible, but it is not certain, and no evidence is produced to show that this is often or generally what happens. This claim is very strong, and needs to be supported.

In terms of values, students could talk about the values of excellence (here belittled), parental authority (here belittled), or free choice (made much of here), or discuss the value of hard work and believing you can succeed. It is not at all clear why the author objects to this value, or in what ways this can glorify the efforts of the parent rather than being useful to the child.

3.2 Questioning the reliability of information

Activity 1

This involves a slightly different application of the skill of judging reliability, and is based on personal testimony.

Encourage students to think through to what extent they can trust each statement, to compare the statements and to debate the different possible interpretations of the evidence.

(a) These claims are based on bias and prejudice because Sukie comes from a difficult family. Neither Miss Hiddlestone nor Eloise can provide any evidence to support their claim. Miss Hiddlestone's claim is based entirely on biased, prejudiced beliefs about Sukie and her family. Eloise's claim is based on second-hand, biased testimony: it is possible that Sukie might look at Amarantha's things for a number of reasons (because they are beautiful, because they are inappropriate in school, because they are flashy), but looking at something does not necessarily mean you are thinking of stealing it. We also don't know whether any of Amarantha's things were stolen.

(b) As she is a teacher, we might expect Miss Hiddlestone to be truthful and reliable (depending on the status of teachers in the community). However, she does not seem to be sure what she did with her phone ('I would have put it in my bag'), and Mrs Smith's testimony indicates that Miss Hiddlestone does tend to leave her phone lying around. Mrs Betteridge's testimony indicates that Miss Hiddlestone was either mistaken or lying about when she last saw her phone, which makes her rather less reliable.

(c) Sukie would have a reason to lie to protect herself if she had committed the thefts. However, her claims about what she was doing are supported by Mrs Smith, who does not have a reason to lie (as far as we know). Sukie could not have committed the thefts while in exams or revising. It seems unlikely that Sukie could have committed a number of thefts (and disposed of the items) in the five minutes when she went to the toilet. So her statement is, overall, reliable.

(d) It is impossible to say with certainty what happened to Miss Hiddlestone's phone. She may have left it near the school gates after using it, or indeed anywhere in the school, if Mrs Smith's testimony is accurate. Alternatively, it may have been taken, either deliberately stolen from her bag, or simply taken from where she absent-mindedly left it.

(e) It was probably not Sukie who took the items, as she was in exams and revising under the supervision of a teacher. Of course, we only have partial information, but from the information we have, there seem to be two options: Miss Hiddlestone or Eloise Charborough.

It was rather unprofessional of Miss Hiddlestone to accuse Sukie without proof, which could be a tactic to divert suspicion from herself. We also have Mrs Smith's comment to indicate that Miss Hiddlestone is sometimes in parts of the school that she shouldn't necessarily be in. So there are questions we might need to ask Miss Hiddlestone, but we have no direct evidence to support the theory that she is the thief.

Eloise Charborough also accuses Sukie without proof, which could similarly be a tactic to divert suspicion from herself. We could also question why Eloise had a diamond bracelet of such high and sentimental value in school. Most schools would have a policy against bringing such valuable items into school. We could speculate that Eloise was setting herself up as a target of the thefts to divert attention from herself as the thief, but this speculation would certainly need to be supported with evidence. The main reason to suspect Eloise is her argument with a boy through the school gates while she should have been in lessons. This would give her opportunity to dispose of the stolen items, and it makes it clear that Eloise was doing *something* she shouldn't have been doing. We would, however, need to ask more questions about this incident.

3.3 Evaluating causes and consequences

Activities 1 and 2
Encourage students to apply their skills.

3.4 Questioning underlying beliefs

Activities 1, 2 and 3
There are no specific answers. Encourage students to engage thoughtfully.

4 Developing a line of reasoning

Activity 1
1. **(a)** Use the most recent Cambridge mark schemes for this activity.

Answer A is a weak response to the question. It does state its conclusion, but it does not consider whether globalisation is making the world a better place; it only states advantages and disadvantages without relating them to the question. The response lists advantages and then lists disadvantages without development; it needs reasons, examples and an understanding of causes and consequences. Giving advantages and disadvantages is not the same as considering different perspectives. There is no logic in this argument, and no sense that the student has thought about the issues.

Answer B does not state its conclusion in answer to the question. There is some knowledge of globalisation, but it is impossible to tell whether this student thinks that globalisation makes the world a better place or not. The first section is mostly unlinked: a list of three different facts about globalisation. The second section has some sense of cause and effect, which the first section lacks. This feels like the work of a student who has learned something about the subject but is not really able to manipulate the information; for example, 'hegemony' does not really sound like natural language for this student. As this is not a knowledge-based assessment, this is not helpful. A charitable marker might say

that there is a paragraph of advantages and a paragraph of disadvantages, but this is not really clear.

Answer C is a reasonably strong response. There is an overall conclusion at the end, which shows understanding of both sides of the question. This conclusion does follow from what the student says. The student includes reasons and mini conclusions that are fairly logical, and considers different perspectives. However, they also need to consider causes and consequences; for example, they could explain how the poorest people might be worse off. The student could also improve the way they have structured their response.

(b) Encourage students to work with the criteria, and to make specific suggestions for improving the responses. They could also explain *how* their suggestions would improve the responses.

5.1 Reflecting on issues and perspectives

Activity 1
There are no right or wrong answers to these dilemmas. It is the essence of a dilemma that whatever choice you make, it will feel wrong. The ideas below are intended to support thinking.

1. Dilemma 1: If we make the decision about which action is right based only on the consequences, we might value five lives over one life. However, it would feel as though the doctor were actively killing the one patient by withholding medical care in order to save the five, which is not the same as saving five lives when someone happens to die. Does it make a difference who the people are? What if the five are criminals and the one is a brain surgeon, or if the one is a murderer and the five are scientists?

2. Dilemma 2: Torture is generally held to be wrong and is forbidden by international law. However, people are increasingly likely to agree that torturing a (or an alleged) bomber in these circumstances is the right thing to do. If most people agree that something is right, does that make it right?

3. Dilemma 3: This is a real incident from the Charlie Hebdo shootings of 2015. Corrine Rey did open the door for the shooters to protect her child, and twelve people died. What we do not know is how many people would have died if Corrine Rey had not opened the door. Whether it is right or wrong, most people would probably be powerless to resist a gunman who was threatening their child.

4. Dilemma 4: This example comes from Dostoyevsky's novel *The Brothers Karamazov*, although it has been rewritten here to simplify the language. This dilemma, too, involves the question of sacrificing one life for the greater good, or for the benefit of many, but the scale here is bigger. Could the result really be happiness and peace if it were based on the torture of a little girl?

5. Dilemma 5: This dilemma makes us think about the difference between action (deliberately killing) and omission (allowing to die).

5.2 Reflection on teamwork, outcomes and own performance

Activity 1

Student 1: This is not reflection. It describes what happened, and does not consider what the problem was or how to solve it. This student needs to consider that they may need to listen to Samara, to move away from who was right and who was wrong, and to find a compromise.

Student 2: This is reasonable reflection. This student identifies a specific problem for the team, talks about its causes, and proposes a solution. It would be useful to have more detail on the solution, as this is rather vague at the moment. The student also identifies a specific reason why their own performance is problematic, as well as a possible solution, which seems reasonable.

Student 3: There are some attempts at reflection here, but they are not fully successful. This student does identify some problems within the team, but does not seem to recognise their own role in these problems. It may be true that Zakia's comment was not made in a helpful way, but it may have been a comment that needed to be made in order to improve this student's performance. The student seems to be deflecting attention away from the weaknesses in their own performance rather than identifying ways to deal with them. The phrase 'Tomorrow we will do better' is a weak form of reflection; it is vague and unspecific, and does not relate to particular goals.

Student 4: This mostly narrates events, describing the crisis and how it came about. There is some reflection at the end, which appears realistic, providing the student's description is accurate. It does seem as though the team worked together to find a solution to a difficult situation, and as though the student whose reflection it is played a key role in this. So the reflection on teamwork and individual performance here seems realistic, even if it is not deep or developed.

5.3 Reflect on personal learning

Activity 1

1. Students tend to think of learning as 'remembering information'. They could also consider these definitions, amongst others:
   - Increasing understanding
   - Developing new concepts
   - Starting to see the world in different ways
   - Connecting ideas
   - Developing skills (including, but not limited to, all the Global Perspectives skills)
   - Analysing, interpreting, evaluating
   - Applying knowledge and understanding to new areas
   - Reflecting with more depth
   - Coming up with new ideas
   - Creative processes.

It may be useful to introduce students to (or remind them of) Bloom's Taxonomy of Thinking Skills and the SOLO Taxonomy of Learning Development (http://www.johnbiggs.com.au/academic/solo-taxonomy/).

Students might categorise learning in these ways:
- Learning how to do something
- Learning what to do
- Learning information
- Learning how to improve.

Activity 2

1. Encourage students to justify their thinking. Students may be surprised to discover that playing games, teamwork, etc. are good ways of learning many of the Global Perspectives skills. Studies indicate that *doing* and *teaching* are both effective methods of developing understanding, learning how to do things, and developing skills.

Activity 3

1. (a) Emmeline is starting to reflect on issues and on her own thinking. She has had an insight into how she thinks about migration, and has started to see other people's perspectives, realising that she normally only sees issues from her own perspective. She has some insight into her preferences for individual work, but she has not developed this into useful reflection.

   (b) Emmeline could improve her reflection by going deeper: she could ask why she likes class discussions, what skills she uses, and what she gets out of the discussions. Where she identifies a negative aspect, she could think about how to improve it in the future.

   (c) Emmeline could think of strategies to encourage other team members to have more input instead of feeling resentful and doing more work herself.

6.1 Planning a project

1. Encourage students to think through what needs to be done and when.

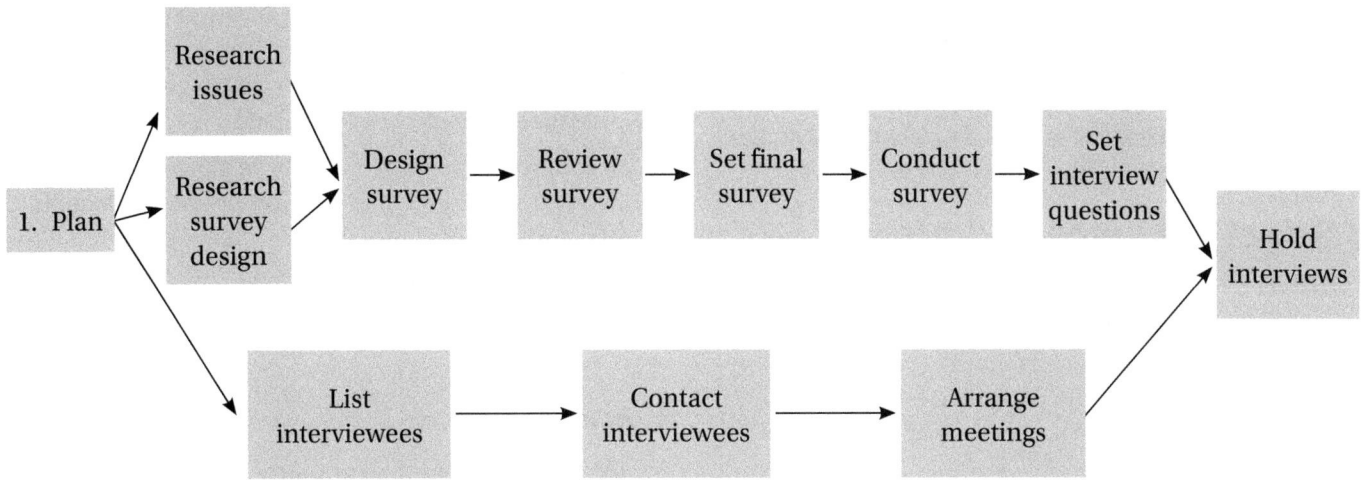

2. There are various possible ways of doing this. Ensure that students leave enough time at the end for assessment related paperwork. (In reality you would not have students still conducting interviews days before submission – this task may help them to see why!)

3. Students will need to plan for the interruption of the holiday.

4. This affects what happens when, because the person writing the survey will need to be finished before the holiday. If they expect to finish their tasks after the holiday, the project will probably fail, because it won't be possible to conduct the survey and use it to inform interview questions before the interviews are actually happening. If this person cannot finish their task before the holiday, another person will need to complete these tasks.

5. Students will need to get permission to interview people before they hold the interviews. They will need to allow time afterwards for video editing. This may mean bringing the interviews forward to an earlier date.

6.2 Teamwork and individual effort

Activity 1

1. **(a)** Characteristics of effective teams:

- There are different people who contribute in different ways.
- There are clear goals that everyone understands and has agreed on.
- The group can overcome differences in opinion.
- Everyone understands the tasks they have to do and helps one another.
- Team members are comfortable expressing their opinions.
- The group learns from experience. It reviews and improves performance.
- Group members listen to one another.
- Team members provide criticism in a positive way.

(b) Characteristics of ineffective teams:

- Some people talk all the time and some people don't say anything.
- Decisions are vague and unclear, and people aren't sure what they have to do.
- People talk more than they listen.
- Some people's ideas are ignored or even mocked.
- There are unpleasant arguments.
- One or two people make all the decisions.
- Some people complain about decisions but do not do anything about them.
- Team members do not keep to the point in discussions.
- Team members ignore deadlines.

2. Encourage students to be realistic about the characteristics of the teams they work in.

Activity 2

There are a number of useful team building games here, the first of which is particularly interesting:
http://nasasearch.nasa.gov/search?
utf8=%E2%9C%93&affiliate=nasa&query=
moon+survival+team+game.

Many other team building games would be just as effective for this activity.

The identification of individuals' skills should help groups to improve their teamwork. Observers should write down a name every time they notice a positive behaviour. If Jamal's name is written down five times under 'Original ideas', for example, this would be evidence that Jamal is strong in this area.

Choose observers depending on the particular needs of your class. For example, you may wish to take a dominant character out of the activity to let quieter students have the chance to demonstrate their skills; this would also be a way of demonstrating these strengths to the dominant character. Alternatively, a quieter student may thrive as observer.

7 Select evidence and present research

The Additional Worksheet concentrates on plagiarism because this is such an important issue. There are many university sites that explain what plagiarism is and why it is wrong. Some of these are accessible even to 14- to 16-year-olds.

Fundamentally, plagiarism is wrong: it is cheating and it is illegal. School students can be banned from taking examinations if they are found to be guilty of serious plagiarism.

The following link includes a video that demonstrates comedienne Amy Schumer apparently plagiarising other people's jokes: http://www.pastemagazine.com/articles/2016/01/an-exhaustive-primer-on-the-amy-schumer-scandal-ye.html. This may serve as an accessible and interesting introduction to the issue.

Activity 1

1. All of these count as plagiarism.

2. Encourage students to express their own opinions. Some students may be confused as to why plagiarism is wrong; some may even think that it is acceptable to plagiarise if it improves their grade.

3. Encourage students to do the research, referring to news and academic sites. It is important for students to understand that plagiarism is cheating and it is illegal. Furthermore, students who plagiarise do not learn or develop their own skills; this means that they will struggle when they reach the workplace.

Activity 2

1. **(a)** Theft of intellectual property (text, ideas), theft of credit, theft of opportunity.

   (b) Theft of opportunity. Encourage students to use their own language to express the ideas in the article.

   (c) Encourage students to discuss the issues.

Topic worksheets

Encourage students to apply their skills.